Social Rules

Social Rules

Social Rules

Origin; Character; Logic; Change

EDITED BY

David Braybrooke

WestviewPress

A Division of HarperCollinsPublishers

Transitions: Asia and Asian America

Published in 1998 in the United States of America by Westview Press, 5500 Central Avenue, Boulder, Colorado 80301-2877, and in the United Kingdom by Westview Press, 12 Hid's Copse Road, Cumnor Hill, Oxford OX2 9JJ

A CIP catalog record for this book is available from the Library of Congress.
ISBN 0-8133-9103-2

This book was typeset by Letra Libre, 1705 14th St., Suite 391, Boulder, Colorado 80302

10   9   8   7   6   5   4   3   2   1

Contents

EPILOGUE
SCHEMATIC SYNTHESIS

APPENDICES

Preface

Rules have never ceased to be a subject of interest in social science and philosophy. Lately, however, they have been getting especially vigorous attention in several quarters: For example, among political scientists James March and Johannes Olsen are leading the way in the "new institutionalism," which treats the state and other institutions as systems of rules.[1] Among historians some (like Christopher Lloyd) are calling for more attention to structures of rules as conceived by anthropologists like Clifford Geertz.[2] Though not committed to Geertz's perspective, the economic historian Douglass North has for some time been focusing upon social rules and changes in rules.[3] Along with their emphasis on rules, March and Olsen have, furthermore, proposed a distinction between "the logic of consequentiality," under which rational choice theory in its many forms falls, and "the logic of appropriateness," where people argue to actions from social rules.[4] They have urged more attention to the latter.

So far, however, for these purposes little has been made of philosophical studies in the logic of rules (deontic logic), though Elinor Ostrom is making a start among political scientists.[5] Little or nothing has been done to relate these studies, and the approach characteristic of them to defining and formulating rules, to the approaches that economists take to the study of rules, including the approach characteristic of game theory. A substantial number of philosophers have taken up game theory in studies of rules, but they have not been philosophers working in the perspective of deontic logic.[6] Nor have they been concerned with other things that economists have found to say about rules, treating them, for example, as straightforward least cost solutions to problems about transaction costs (North) or as devices for reducing uncertainty (Ronald Heiner, Norman Schofield[7]).

This book embodies a pioneer effort to bring philosophical developments in the logic of rules, and indeed the legal (and socio-anthropological) perspective in which the logic naturally arises, into an intelligible relation with the leading ideas of economists about rules. At this stage, the relation must be more one of mutual challenge than of easy harmonization, but the prospects of benefits from mutual learning are already striking.

To appreciate these prospects, different readers will probably do best to follow different paths through the book. Readers coming from economics could begin with Part Three; some readers coming from the law could begin with Part Two. Both these sets of readers might then read the Epilogue, which is the nearest thing in the book to a general synthesis, before deciding which chapters to read next. Before deciding, they might also read the running commentary to be found at the beginnings of the several chapters.

Readers coming from philosophy or anthropology or history, and some readers coming from the law, might find it most congenial to read the chapters in the order in which the chapters are presented. Even these readers might, except for the philosophers, find it best to reserve Chapters 2 and 3 for last. Reading them carefully and sympathetically is essential to getting the full benefits of the book. In topics and in sorts of questions, however, they operate (as does Chapter 1, to some extent) a disconcertingly great distance away, it seems, from the preoccupations of non-philosophers.

A convenient device for explaining the organization of the book consists in taking as a point of departure a simple distinction of three conceptions of "rules" set forth by Lewis Kornhauser in a contribution that on other grounds has been placed late in the book.

Kornhauser's three conceptions include

(1) social rule as a regularity of behavior;
(2) social rule as convention;
(3) social rule as a norm (or as a special type of authoritative reason for action).

This book is preoccupied throughout almost exclusively with the second and third of these conceptions. It begins in Part One with extensive treatment of the third conception, which may be identified with the sense of "rule" at work in the perspective that the logic of rules shares with anthropology, sociology, and legal scholarship. (There is, unfortunately, no anthropologist in our present company, but there is a sociologist, and a substantial delegation of legal scholars.) The second conception is given incidental attention in Part One, and there are a number of references there to game theory and the economists' perspective on rules. However, the game-theoretical approach to convention, taken as an approach belonging, with other ways of bringing in the costs of coordination, to economists, is left to Kornhauser himself and Part Three of the book, where further ideas about rules that economists have been working with also come up. Those ideas may be connected with game theory; but to connect them with Kornhauser's third conception and the logic of rules is equally inviting.

The picture of rules given in the logic of rules is taken in Part One first from G. H. von Wright's logic of rules, with an application to a thesis from Marxist theory. Then, treated much more amply, the logic of rules developed since von Wright by a team of philosophers working at Dalhousie University becomes the vehicle of illustration. Applications of the Dalhousie logic are drawn from the team's book *Logic on the Track of Social Change*.[8] They include rules for appropriating the social surplus, rules demanding the use in industry of up-to-date mechanization, and rules requiring peasants to submit to their own displacement from the land and yet forbidding them to remain idle. Besides this picture of rules and many illustrations of application, including those just mentioned, the Dalhousie team has arrived in their book at a non-circular definition of rules in terms of the blocking operations first used in teaching rules. This definition is set forth in the chapter; and the chapter ends with an argument for the use in history and the social sciences of the logic. The chapter leaves the deeper aspects of the logic that require attention in logical theory to the chapter following, where Peter Schotch, the logician on the Dalhousie team, takes up a number of these aspects.

Geoffrey Sayre-McCord comes next in Part One with an argument that highlights the explanatory uses first of rules in Kornhauser's third sense and then of what Sayre-McCord calls "transconventional" rules. A number of contributions from other hands follow, with real illustrations, some contemporary, some historical, of explanatory uses, and with (in one way or another) a special concern with changes in rules, that is to say, in settled social rules. The two contributions that come first among this number come from the Dalhousie team and illustrate the Dalhousie logic, at once in characterizing rules and in treating change in them. Bryson Brown's gives the logic application in the history and philosophy of science to changes early in this century in the rules that physicists followed during the early stages of coping with difficulties in quantum theory. Braybrooke's examines an application in politics, broadly conceived, to "issue-processing," sometimes deliberated, often not. Here the conception of rules offered in the Dalhousie logic joins a conception of issues (issues about policies, taking policies to be rules) that reflects the logic of questions developed by the Pittsburgh logician Nuel D. Belnap, Jr.[9]

The contributions that follow hard upon these raise various objections and questions about the room for a logic of rules like the Dalhousie logic in accounts of historical change. Lloyd Bonfield pictures the manorial courts of medieval England as reaching their decisions with little or no concern for rules that later law would make indispensable in such matters. Were the manorial courts following any rules at all? Richard Miller welcomes the Dalhousie project, but wonders whether it embraces too many different things under the heading of social rules and wonders besides whether rules play as much part in Marxist accounts of historical change as the Dalhousie team holds. Ronald Aminzade gives a comparative account of the legitimation of political parties in France and the United States after their respective Revolutions, and gives rules and changes of rules prominence in this account. He questions, however, whether quandaries, of the sort that the Dalhousie team specifies with its logic, play as important a part, compared with matters of interest and power, in changes of rules as the team suggests. Braybrooke brings Part One to a close by replying to the questions raised by these contributions, seeking to give them due weight, but not (he thinks) needing to concede anything essential to the Dalhousie project.

Part Two is transitional. It consists of a contribution by Charles Silver that has to do with changes of rules, and in particular with rules of law that may be conceived as Part One conceives them, but focuses less upon rules or changes in rules than on an economic analysis of the diffusion of information about such changes. In a comment on Silver's article, Kornhauser compares Silver's approach to rules with Bonfield's and points out that with its use of economic ideas, Silver is shifting away from the perspective adopted by Bonfield (and, I add, by the other contributors to Part One).

The stage is thus set for the final four contributions, coming in Part Three, which apply economic ideas not just to explaining diffusion of information about them, but to explaining the very origin of rules, their function, and what in the economists' view are the fundamental causes of changes in them. After a brief preface by Braybrooke—a larger than usual segment of the running commentary, but still brief—sketching the possibility of reconciling the economists' approach, however far carried, with the approach taken in the perspective of Part One, come contributions by Douglass North, Kornhauser again, Heiner, and Schofield.

North sets forth a general perspective on changes in social rules, in which some get treatment in economists' terms, though characteristically in terms emphasizing transaction costs rather than ideal market considerations, and some are assigned for treatment under the heading of "ideology." (Under that heading there would be a place for issue-processing in which rules are invoked, sometimes without any calculation of costs, to select less basic rules; and hence a place for matters suited to illumination by the logic of rules.) Kornhauser, Heiner, and Schofield, in the contributions that follow North's, push the question, "What difference to social phenomena does having rules make?," to successively greater theoretical depths. Kornhauser emphasizes how rules seize opportunities for game-theoretical solutions of coordination problems. Heiner shows how rules reduce the overall, long-run costs of acting on imperfect information in a succession of choice-situations; and hence produce regularities of behavior in the face of uncertainty (where conventional ideas would expect uncertainty to defeat such regularities utterly). Schofield understands rules, not just as the basis for dealing with uncertainty in one or another connection or for seizing opportunities here and there for social coordination, but as the basis of the common knowledge without which chaos would have its way instead of any social order at all, but he shows that coordination is still fragile, liable to break down rapidly in the case of rules for collective decision if certain trains of small events get underway. This, from a deep mathematical perspective in chaos theory, is perhaps the most dramatic observation about rules to be found among the contribution. The alarm that it might awaken is mitigated to some extent, Schofield contends, if the rules crucial to collective decision are understood as rules for aggregating beliefs rather than aggregating preferences.

The final chapter of the book is an epilogue—a tentative, schematic synthesis of the discussion—offered by Braybrooke as a further device for relating the points and points of views expressed in the book to one another.

David Braybrooke

Notes

1. March and Olsen, *Rediscovering Institutions* (New York: The Free Press, 1989).

2. See Lloyd's *The Structures of History* (Oxford: Blackwell, 1993), in which pp. 103–116 hold up Geertz's work as exemplary.

3. See, for example, his *Structure and Change in Economic History* (New York: W. W. Norton & Co., 1981), and North's contribution in Part Three to the present book.

4. *Rediscovering Institutions*, pp. 160–162.

5. Ostrom, *Governing the Commons* (Cambridge: Cambridge University Press, 1990) especially pp. 51–52, 139–142 (where, joining up on these points with March and Olsen, she insists that institutions are to be treated as systems of rules and changes in them as changes in the rules); and her paper (with Sue Crawford), "A Grammar of Institutions," forthcoming. Notably, Ostrom has read and benefited from G. H. von Wright's *Norm and Action* (London: Routledge, 1963), a great resource for the analysis of rules that, having been classified as logic or philosophy, has almost entirely escaped the attention of social scientists.

6. The journal *Ethics* a few years ago devoted a whole issue (Vol. 100, No. 4 [July 1990]) to the study of rules. Game theory got a great deal of play in the issue, and a variety of insights were achieved by this means and others, but the learned gathering completely missed the boat as regards the logic of rules. There was not, for example, a single citation of von Wright's landmark work.

7. See Heiner's and Schofield's contributions to Part Three of the present book.

8. Oxford: Clarendon Press [The Clarendon Library of Logic and Philosophy], 1995. (This will be referred to as *Track* in the body of the present book.)

9. In a monograph of 1968 that was subsequently incorporated in a book by Belnap and Thomas B. Steel, Jr., *The Logic of Questions* (New Haven: Yale University Press, 1976).

Acknowledgments

Professor Judith Schafer of the Murphy Institute for Political Economy at Tulane University and Carroll S. Zehner, the secretary at the Institute at the time, worked with Richard Teichgraeber, the director of the Institute, and me to organize the conference sponsored by the Institute from which this book derives. At later stages in its gestation, Judith Fox and Margaret Odell, secretaries in the Dalhousie philosophy department, Elizabeth Harper and Cynthia Botteron, my research assistants at the University of Texas, James Endersby, the computer whiz of the Department of Government there, Joanna Lee of the computer staff of the university, Allison Sole and Cindy Rinehart of Westview Press, and Jon Brooks and Andrew Davis of Letra Libre all put in substantial amounts of time and effort to advance the project. Cynthia Botteron's effort was especially committed and invaluable. I override Peter K. Schotch's attempt at self-effacement to mention long hours of word processing on his part. Nearer the time of production, James G. March supplied useful comments, which I have responded to in the Preface. I am very grateful to all of these memorably kind and helpful people.

D.B.

Contributors

Ronald Aminzade, professor of sociology, University of Minnesota–Twin Cities.

Nicholas Baigent, director of Institute of Public Economics, University of Graz, Austria.

Lloyd Bonfield, professor of law, Tulane University.

David Braybrooke, Centennial Commission Chair in the Liberal Arts [Government and Philosophy], The University of Texas at Austin.

Bryson Brown, associate professor of philosophy, The University of Lethbridge.

Ronald A. Heiner, professor of economics, George Mason University.

Lewis A. Kornhauser, professor of law, New York University.

Richard W. Miller, professor of philosophy, Cornell University.

Douglass C. North, Henry R. Luce Professor of Law and Liberty and Distinguished University Professor (Department of Economics), Washington University at Saint Louis.

Geoffrey Sayre-McCord, professor of philosophy, The University of North Carolina at Chapel Hill.

Norman Schofield, William Taussig Professor of Political Economy and director of the Center in Political Economy, Washington University at Saint Louis.

Peter K. Schotch, professor of philosophy, Dalhousie University.

Charles Silver, W. James Kronzer Chair in Trial and Appellate Advocacy, School of Law, The University of Texas at Austin.

PART ONE

The Logicians' and Philosophers' Approach to Rules

1

The Representation of Rules in Logic and Their Definition

David Braybrooke

We begin with a chapter outlining work that has been done in the logic of rules. From the work done specifically by the Dalhousie team the chapter draws a new definition of rules (in the third sense distinguished by Kornhauser), which avoids the circularity of definitions currently in circulation. The definition reduces to near a vanishing point the difference between rules in the third sense and conventions, though it enables us to do justice to the intentional features of both, and also to the tendency of rules to be accompanied by systematic provisions for sanctions. The chapter ends with an argument for giving a place in the work of historians to the logic of rules. (The argument extends to giving it a place in the work of social scientists as well.)

For the time being, in this chapter and in a number of chapters following, we shall be occupied with rules in Kornhauser's third sense—rules that have authority and give reasons for acting. These may or may not be settled social rules. They may be new proposals; or old counsels of perfection, honored more often in the breach than in the observance. If they are settled social rules, however, they do imply regularities of conformity and are often accompanied by regularities of enforcement in deviant cases (even if the regularities are not perfect in either case). Paying one's taxes or refraining from incest are not settled social rules if most people most of the time do neither.

Starting up closer to the concerns that ethnographers have with settled social rules than to the concerns of economists or decision-theorists, some philosophers have asked what distinguishes rules from other social phenomena, in particular, from other phenomena that involve expressions in language. Though this will not do in the end as an accurate picture of rules, we may go some distance toward the distinction demanded—most if not all the distance to a logic of rules—by thinking of a rule as standing to its linguistic expressions in a relation parallel to that in which a statement stands to the sentences that express it. We would thus make no more in either case of rule or statement than a device for talking about a variety of linguistic expressions and their instances. How do rules differ from statements (singular, existentially quantified, or universally quantified), value-judgments, optatives ("Would that x were the case !")?

Work on this question has been overshadowed lately by discussions of rules as solutions to game-theoretical problems of coordination, relating to rules in Kornhauser's second perspective. A recent issue of *Ethics* specially devoted to the discussion of rules (norms) is typical in having contributors preoccupied mainly by such considerations.[1] Work has also been deflected year after year by a preoccupation, inspired by Wittgenstein, with what following a rule amounts to, taken up as a problem in the philosophy of mind. How does the person following a rule know "how to go on"? How do we tell that he knows? There is perhaps some consensus on Wittgenstein's position that the problem cannot be resolved without invoking, for use in every case, public criteria for identifying any rule in question, even an idiosyncratic personal one.[2] But this still leaves open the questions about how rules differ from other phenomena in which language and behavior intersect.

More in keeping with the aim of answering these questions than Wittgenstein's preoccupation has been the general project of deontic logic, which consists in trying to specify the features of rules crucial to their directive aims and effects on the one hand and to making visible their logical relations on the other. The chief contributor to deontic logic—several times over, producing a variety of analyses and logical formulations—has been G. H. von Wright.[3] It is remarkable that in the special issue of *Ethics* mentioned earlier there is no reference to his work. That, however, is rather evidence of the shift of fashion in the direction of game-theoretical considerations than of the work's having been superseded in the line of thought to which it contributed. There it remains the richest contribution so far.

The Logic of Rules (Deontic Logic)

von Wright's Version (in Norm and Action*) of the Logic of Rules*

In his book *Norm and Action*,[4] von Wright arrives at a logic of norms through a three-tier construction on top of the propositional calculus (which concerns elementary relations between propositions taken as wholes). Each tier adds logical operators to help specify those forms of propositions which the logic of norms is especially concerned to identify among the possible substitutions available in the propositional calculus. The propositional calculus itself is so general as to accept propositions of any—i.e., wholly unspecified—forms as substitutions for the propositional variables, **p**, **q**, **r**, etc.; it considers those relations of such propositions to one another that are established by proposition-combining operators standing (approximately) for "if ... then," "and," "or," "if and only if." ((**p** ∨ **q** → **r** & **s**) & ~**r**) → ~(**p** ∨ **q**), for example, is a symbolic sentence belonging to the propositional calculus; it may be read, "If, if **p** or **q** then **r** and **s** yet **not r**, then **not** either **p** or **q**."

Consider a proposition **p**, which describes some state of affairs ("N holds office"); if the state of affairs does not obtain, then, of course, ~**p**. Let there be an operator, **T**, to be placed between propositional variables (or combinations of these) and to be read "changes into." Four basic forms of propositions in the logic of change can then be envisaged: **pT~p**—a world in which **p** changes into a world in which **not-p**; ~**pTp**—a world in which **not-p** changes into a world in which **p**; but also **pTp** and ~**pT~p**, in which, significantly, no change in the ordinary sense occurs, but to which the **T**-operator and the logic of change are conveniently extended by deliberate convention.

The logic of change constitutes the first tier above the propositional calculus. The logic of action, in von Wright's scheme, comes in the tier next above and relates change-propositions to human intervention by introducing **d** and **f** operators that indicate, respectively, acts and forbearances. These operators may be applied to any formula of the logic of change. While **d(pT~p)**, for example, might symbolize in an obvious way someone's acting to remove **N** from office, **f(pT~p)** would symbolize forbearing to do so. But **d(pTp)** and **f(pTp)** are also intelligible formulas; and symbolize, on the one hand, acting so as to maintain a state of affairs that would otherwise change; and, on the other hand, forbearing to do this, letting it change though it could be maintained. Thus **d(pTp)** might stand for keeping **N** in office (when otherwise he would be ejected); **f(pTp)**, for letting him be ejected (though he could be kept).

Finally, in the topmost tier of the construction, von Wright reveals his logic of norms, and with it two further operators: an **O**-operator (best thought of as standing for "must") and a **P**-operator (for permission). The **O**-operator, applied to **d** expressions of the logic of action, produces prescriptions—**Od(pT~p)** "N must be removed from office." Applied to **f** expressions, the **O**-operator produces prohibitions—**Of(pT~p)**, "N must not be removed from office." The **P**-operator produces permissions, either to do something—bring about some change—or to forbear. To these permissions, as well as to the prescriptions or prohibitions formulated with the **O**-operator, various conditions may attach; and von Wright provides for expressing them by associating further formulas of the logic of change with the formula representing the change to be brought about or forborne. **Pd(pT~p/qTq & rT~r)**, for example, is the formula of a permissive norm showing two conditions: It might be taken to symbolize the rule, "It is permitted to eject **N** from office if he owes his office to a patron and the patron has himself left office."

However complex an **O** or **P** expression may be, it can always be substituted for a propositional variable, **p** or **q** or **r**, in the propositional calculus.[5] Thus all the connections, oppositions, and inferences made available by that branch of ordinary logic are available also for formulas in the logic of norms. There are, besides, some connections and oppositions peculiar to the logic of norms. **Od(pTp)** is, for example, incompatible with **Of(pTp)** (though neither may hold, they cannot both hold together). It contradicts **Pf(pTp)**: If one must do something, then one is not permitted to forbear doing it; and vice versa. **Od(pTp)**, in fact, entails **not Pf(pTp)**; and **Pf(pTp)** entails **not Od(pTp)**.[6]

The application of von Wright's logic can be illustrated by taking up a contention of Engels's in *Socialism: Utopian & Scientific*. Engels maintains that so long as artisans owned their own tools, it made no difference whether the foundation of their claims to their products was the work that they put into making them or (then a secondary consideration) the fact that they owned the tools (the capital equipment) used in making them. But once it ceased to be the case that the people who did the work were the same people as the people who owned the tools, a conflict in rules appeared, between

$$Od(\sim rTr/\sim wTw),$$

under which people were enjoined to respect a right of ownership (by some specific person to some specific product) on the condition that the work of making it had been put in by the person in question, and

$$Od(\sim rTr/\sim tTt),$$

under which the right to same product was accorded to someone on the condition that tools belonging to him had been used in making the product. For suppose—as Engels supposes became generally the case—the person who did the work was not the same person as the person who supplied the tools. Which of the two claims was to be respected by other people? So long as those other people felt the force of both rules they were in a quandary that obstructed them from acting so as to respect fully either claim.[7]

The Logic of Rules Emerging from the Dalhousie Project[8]

The multi-tier picture of rules given by von Wright in *Norm and Action* remains the fullest logical characterization of rules available in the literature (von Wright's remarks on aspects of rules that he does not include in the "norm-kernels" expressed in his formulas are also rich in instruction). The philosophers in the Dalhousie project have kept the multi-tier picture in mind and intend in their own work to preserve its availability as much as the balance of considerations allows.

For example, von Wright asserts that in general we must expect to have added to basic rule-formulas a statement of the conditions under which the prescription or prohibition in question comes to bear upon the people to whom it is addressed. This point is carried forward in our logic.

We distinguish three features in our formulas for rules—**volk**, the demographic scope; **wenn**, the conditions under which the rule comes to bear upon conduct; **nono**, the routines (sequences of actions) that the rule forbids. For example, an example drawn from *Track*, under the feudal social order in France, the king and nobility enjoyed the benefit of a rule under which they appropriated the social surplus and did what they pleased with it:

> **volk** = FRENCH
> **wenn** = $\exists(a)(\exists x)[SURPLUS(x) \ \& \ OWNS(a, x)] \ \& \ aft \ r[DISPOSES(a,x)]$
> **nono** = BLOCKS (r',r).

The **wenn** component here says that x is a part of the social surplus and somebody a owns it and disposes of it. (r stands for any routine, i.e., any action or sequence of actions.) Given this condition, which notably leaves the way in which a has disposed of x completely unspecified, the **nono** component forbids any action or sequence of actions r' that BLOCKS r, the disposal of x by a.

Another example from *Track*, which like the one just given will relate to a discussion later in this book (in the comment by Miller, below), is a technical norm consolidating advances in mechanization:

> **volk** = WORKERS
> **wenn** = $(\exists r)(\exists w)[(TASK(t) \ \& \ WORKSHOP(w) \ \& \ \sim MECH(t,w) \ \&$
> $\qquad aft \ r[MECH(t,w)]$
> **nono** = $aft(r') \ (\exists a)[HASRUN(r,w) \ \& \ PERFORMS(a,t,w) \ \&$
> $\qquad \sim MECH(t,w)]$.

$aft(r)$ signifies that after a routine r has been run the proposition that follows is true. The rule in this case forbids workers to perform in a given workshop w an unmechanized task that has been mechanized there (by running an available routine for mechanizing it). It is a rule that prudent employers would adopt and enforce; if they did not, Marx for one would hold that they would be outdistanced by competitors who were more exacting about productivity.

Thus the Dalhousie logic makes of von Wright's conditions for a rule coming to bear one (the **wenn** component) of the three characteristic features that it ascribes to rules. We make the doing or forbearing component (the **nono** component in our case) more general, refraining from specifying that it must apply to actions with the form proposed for actions by von Wright. It embraces routines that may include series of actions and we do not insist on describing actions in truth-functional propositions—we allow for three values where von Wright has one, truth. An action for us is just starting or not; is running now or not running now; has already run or not. The routines to which our formulas apply may involve many different actions; and alternative routes to the same end. They may also belong to very different overall sequences; if we are forbidden to block some nobleman's disposal of his share of the social surplus, we are forbidden to do it in any way, and forbidden to do it in the course of bringing in the harvest as much as in plundering the granary afterwards.

Donald Davidson has complained that von Wright's formulas for action do not take into account the variety of ways in which somebody might get from the state of affairs in which she begins to the state of affairs in which she ends (from p to ~p in d(pT~p).[9] We are better prepared than von Wright to satisfy Davidson's complaints about the ambiguity of von Wright's action-propositions, though we think von Wright could do a good deal to meet those complaints by simply having the actions in question specified in greater detail, as, for example, not just going from San Francisco to New York, but going by plane; or specified by analyzing them more finely into sequences of actions. We are better prepared because our semantics brings in intermediate stages (INT) of a protracted action as well as the terminating stage (TERM). Thus, where for von Wright actions starting at A are differentiated solely in terms of what sentences they make true when they terminate, so that all actions starting at A and ending in B are (without further analysis) identical, the Dalhousie logic treats every action starting at a as characterized by two sets. One set, TERM(r, s) is a set of ordered pairs associating r turn by turn with the various states in which it would be said to terminate successfully; the other set, INT(r, s) is a set of ordered pairs associating r turn by turn with the sequences of intermediate states that occur on various routes on the way to termination. The actions do not always terminate; there may be no sentence B such that TERM(r, s) = B.

Our semantics also accommodates another complaint that Davidson makes about von Wright's logic. The set TERM(r, s) in which r terminates in Mary's being kicked viciously clearly relates to the set TERM(r, s') in which r terminates in Mary's being kicked. The first set is in fact a subset of the second, hence from Mary's being viciously kicked one may infer that she was kicked. Yet changing to our semantics does not mean a break with von Wright's—it is a special case of ours, in which the sets INT(r, s) are empty. We can accommodate in our routines all the forms of change that the actions and forbearances in von Wright's formulas involve; and all the actions and forbearances (which we treat as so many routines, simple or complex).

We do tighten up the logic in a way that von Wright did not anticipate, by following a fruitful lead by the Australian philosopher Hamblin[10] and treating conflicts of rules as quandaries, in which all actions are ruled out. To express such situations as clearly as possible in accordance with common sense understandings of them, we furthermore reduce all rules to prohibitions (hence the doing or forbearing component comes under the heading **nono**), where von Wright gives prescriptions an equal footing. (We make of his prescriptions prohibitions of failing to provide in the routines that are done for timely inclusion of the routine prescribed.) Our motivation in focusing on quandaries is to avoid the "explosions" to which von Wright's, and other "standard" deontic logics, are subject. Once a contradiction appears in any system of rules described within a standard deontic logic, the system explodes: One can infer that every action is permitted, indeed prescribed, which is tantamount to the system's being rendered useless for more guarded inferences. Is the lesson to be that one should refuse to recognize any contradictions? But conflicts between rules are common, especially when rules change, and to refuse to bring them within the ambit of a logic is to withdraw logic from use in expressing both stable systems, when they are imperfectly consistent, and from full use, too, in tracing changes in rules through stages in which conflicts between them exist. (It means, among other things, sacrificing the possibility, long mistakenly beclouded, of making good sense of the genuine insights involved in the notion of a dialectic in history.)

Another point of difference from von Wright—in this case, not so much a difference as a supplementation—is that whereas he treats goals as internal to the logic of change (thus, if one brings about the change pT~p deliberately, for von Wright this is done with the goal of realizing ~p), we (reserving the right to treat typically what von Wright also treats as goals) treat goals as external to rules. Rules themselves, we insist, typically come into being in order to serve external goals—peace, order, and good government, for example; and among these goals, as that phrase itself suggests, may be the institution of other rules. (Thus, in Hobbes, there are rules specifying the form of contract that makes the rules of justice with their enforcement feasible.[11])

The Dalhousie philosophers join with von Wright in treating provisions for punishment as external considerations. In this sense, our formulas for rules are, like von Wright's, formulas for "norm-kernels," and may serve as formulas for conventions and quasi-conventions as well. Under David Lewis's leading example of a convention (one that he says used to prevail in his hometown of Oberlin, Ohio) about resuming interrupted telephone calls, it is prescribed that the person who initiated the call make the connection again, while the other person waits.[12] This combines a prohibition imposed on the first party against doing any action or sequence of actions that precludes making the connection again in a timely way with a prohibition imposed on the second party of making the connection from her side.

The effect, with the reduction to prohibitions, of escaping contradictions of the standard sort and the associated paradoxes of material implication, is to substitute quandaries for contradictions. In quandaries, the rules accepted by the people affected combine to prohibit every action open to them, for example, the action of abolishing slavery and the action (forbearance) of respecting private property including property in slaves (where these are held to be the only means of making plantations profitable). Another example (which, again, will be discussed later by Miller) can be found in the prohibition, in force in England in the sixteenth century, against interfering with lords driving peasants off the land, conjoined with the prohibition, laid down by Parliament in the act against vagabondage:

On the one hand, there was a rule f_t,

$$\begin{aligned}
\textbf{volk}(f_t) &= \text{ENGLISH} \\
\textbf{wenn}(f_t) &= [\text{LAND}(x)\ \&\ \text{HASDOM}(a,x)\ \&\ \text{USEOWNS}(b,x)\ \& \\
&\quad \sim\!\text{HASDOM}(b,x)\ \&\ \textit{aft}(r)[\text{DRIVEOFF}(a,b,x)]] \\
\textbf{nono}(f_t) &= \text{BLOCKS}(r',r),
\end{aligned}$$

which forbade anyone to do anything that blocked some a who with dominion over a piece of land x drove off someone b who as a peasant merely had useownership of the land.

On the other hand, there was a rule f_v,

$$\begin{aligned}
\textbf{volk}(f_v) &= \text{ENGLISH} \\
\textbf{wenn}(f_v) &= \text{LANDLESS}(b) \\
\textbf{nono}(f_v) &= \textit{aft}(r)[\sim\!\text{WORKING}(b)].
\end{aligned}$$

which forbade b, once b had been driven from the land, from doing anything that included a routine or sequence of actions that left b wandering about the country without working. But very likely there was no work for b off the land; he and thousands like him were in a quandary, forbidden to resist being driven off the land where they had been working and forbidden at the same time to be idle.

A quandary is certainly an uncomfortable situation, crying out for some change in the rules, but it is one that is, logically, perfectly in order. The going set of rules continues (by paraconsistent implication) to sustain nothing but reasonable inferences, even inferences from the rules directly in conflict. Partitioning the going set into subsets each of which by itself makes at least one action available that can be done without violating the rules in the subset has the effect here that in the propositional case comes from partitioning an inconsistent set of propositions into subsets each of which by itself is consistent.

The Definition of Rules

Rules could be defined simply as whatever is expressed by the formulas of a logic of rules, like the formulas that we have inspected, either von Wright's formulas or those of the Dalhousie logic. This would at least be in one respect an advance over the most common definitions, which are circular—as "normative constraints"[13]—or seem to leave the root-idea unexpressed—as systems of imperatives (which prescribe or prohibit, too).[14]

It is, however, quite unsatisfactory to treat rules as linguistic entities. The forms of words in which they are expressed can hardly by themselves be supposed to compel obedience, or indeed to influence conduct in any way: We can read in Empedocles, "Keep your hands off beans!,"[15] understand the words as conveying a rule (he is not using the same form of words to express a one-occasion imperative). Yet we may be moved not in the least to heed the words. If we move back from the expressions of rules to what in analogy with propositions they express, we have done no more to capture the action-compelling or action-guiding aspects of rules. We understand that one and the same rule can be expressed in English by "Keep your hands off beans!," in French by "*Ne pas laisser les mains toucher de fèves,*" in Greek by "*kuamown apo cheiras,*" and not be moved by contemplating the shared meaning of these locutions.

What we need for a satisfactory definition is a definition that exhibits the place of rules in ordinary life and practice. Work on the Dalhousie project has led to just such a definition. We have found, in the course of formulating rules in one illustrative connection after another, that the notion of blocking was steadily playing an indispensable part in the ideas that we were working out of what the rules amounted to. This notion, in turn, has led us to an especially satisfactory definition of rules.

Rules, we say, are in origin physical blocking operations that prevent people from acting in ways prohibited; or, better, systems of such blocking operations, since unlike the imperatives issued for a moment, rules apply over and over again to many instances. Consider a child being blocked (by a successful blocking operation) from going into the street and from this blocking learning the rule against going there. When she comes to understand that she may expect to be blocked every time she tries, she understands the rule that she faces. In time, it will suffice for her mother to say,

"Don't go into the street!," as she sidles in that direction; and this form of words serves as a verbal substitute for a physical blocking operation, just as the mother's speaking those words substitutes for her using a physical means in the blocking operation. She performs a blocking operation, whether successful or not, in either case. Thus, in general, we can define rules as systems open-ended in time of blocking operations with means physical or verbal; and license under this definition speaking of physical imperatives as well as verbal ones.

The blocking operations here, even the physical ones, are not instances of punishment; and both sorts, physical and verbal, may actually occur very rarely, and only at the beginning of any person's rule-learning history. Their rarity, perhaps even more their transience, have no doubt contributed strongly to overlooking their importance for the definition of rules. They are rare not only because people internalize rules, so that rules learned from blockings physical or verbal are maintained without any need to repeat the blockings, since with internalization blocking operations are anticipated and forestalled. They are rare because, beginning early in childhood, people learn most rules by simply hearing them set forth; or even simply by observing examples of their application (as when a parent says "stju" rather than "stu" when stew appears on the table).

Yet the force of rules depends on the blocking operations that impend (or could be brought to bear). Rules are not linguistic entities, important as their linguistic expression is to identifying them in most cases and to understanding exactly what they involve. They are binding practices that involve people in structures of motivation for themselves and others and structures of social control. Nor (as I long thought myself, and as others in the Dalhousie project inclined to think until very late—later than the Murphy Institute conference) are rules distinguished from conventions and the like by having measures of punishment attached to them. The physical actions that figure, in elementary cases, as blocking operations may sometimes be actions of the same sort that are imposed as punishments; but they are not punishments when they serve as blockings—they are corrections, and as such belong alongside physical interventions of gentler, even caressing kinds, as well as verbal utterances that range from explicit imperatives to gentle hints. The mother may kiss and cuddle the child as she picks her up and takes her away from the street.

Conventions may originate as mutually advantageous solutions to coordination problems: in David Lewis's example, as a solution to the problem of who, the original caller or the original recipient, will start up a telephone call again after the connection has been broken. As such, they need not be taught by blockings or maintained either by blockings or by punishments. People may go on abiding by them, just as they started them up, simply from being aware of the mutual advantages. Yet, just as, once people have learned some rules, they can learn most others (along with settled conventions) simply by having them stated, so conventions, once established, can in some cases be taught by blockings, and as with rules there may be no occasion to go on to back them with sanctions. These observations reduce the distinction between rules and conventions to the vanishing point, even if one makes their being game-theoretical solutions a defining feature of conventions. Or rather they reduce the distinction to accepting conventions as falling into a subclass of rules all of which are in fact solutions to coordination problems, though some may not have originated because they were identified as such. (They may have been laid down by authorities with other things in mind.) Outside this subclass, there will be rules (maybe perverse ones) that do not constitute solutions to coordination problems and do not minimize costs.

There will be no need to go into this definition of rules in subsequent chapters. Yet it can be assumed throughout, and it can be usefully recalled whenever questions arise about how rules can have force as reasons or causes in human activity. It will even relate usefully to discussions in which regularities short of being rules are in question rather than rules proper. A child will learn what rules are by learning from others social rules. But a child who has perhaps not yet learned any rules may exhibit a regularity of avoiding touching stove tops after he has once been burned by touching one. He will come to the stage of making rules for himself only after he has advanced some distance in learning social rules and learning what rules are in the course of doing so.

A Place in the Work of Historians for the Logic of Rules

The definition of rules given makes it plain that there is more to rules— in their workings upon people—than there is to mere forms of words. Thus the definition helps forestall any inclination to believe that rules must be (as mere words) superficial phenomena. There are important questions about society and history still to be asked when rules have been identified. Some of those questions are questions about rules—where did they come from? who supports them and why? who benefits from general adherence to them? Rules may show up again, sometimes, in the answers to some of these questions; for example, some rules are inferred from others and get their support because people support those other rules.

Rules are not the whole story: power and interest (including class-interest) have to be considered. Some social scientists, and some historians, may be so much more interested in questions about power and interest that they hesitate to give the study of rules its due. I expect social scientists, however, will be easier to persuade than historians both that rules have some interest and importance and that a logic of rules is an aid to studying them. There has, after all, been resistance among historians to using any of the special techniques developed in the social sciences[16] (though they are used), while social scientists are used to having new techniques start up and used to trying them. We may expect there to be resistance among historians to the use of logic, too, especially since in this case its use—the use of a logic of rules—has not been established in the social sciences either. Indeed, our expectations are easily confirmed. They were confirmed by the reactions expressed at the conference from which this book originated by an historian who took part.[17] I shall, apologizing for the fact that he will have no opportunity for a rejoinder, take up one by one the concerns that he expressed.

We would ask, given the variety and ubiquity of rules, which we may expect historians not to deny, whether historians are already clear enough about them to have nothing substantial to learn from a logic of rules? They may nevertheless say they fail to see that translating the rules cited by historians makes any advance in clarification upon what Marx (in the examples given above) or other historians have done in expressing them in a natural language, German or English. Not only historians react in this way; as we have carried on the Dalhousie project from stage to stage we have encountered philosophers who (perhaps not distinguishing sufficiently between the importance of having a logic and the importance of having a convenient notation for the logic) react on first sight by claiming that everything that needs to be done in treating rules can be done in English without any explicit recourse to a logic. Yet these reactions misinterpret the care that we have taken—notably, in the initial applications of the logic set forth in *Track*—to demonstrate that the rules for which we have developed the logic are rules of sorts that historians are concerned with. To comment that we seem to be only saying the same things but expressing the rules in different terms or a different notation is not an objection but a measure of our success in the demonstration that we intend. It is true that—once we have got historians to acknowledge that we are talking about rules as they themselves already understand them—we have further claims to make for the logic. The first reactions fail to appreciate in this regard that those claims begin by citing only very modest possible advances on what historians are already doing, which we acknowledge that they could do, certainly without our notation and perhaps without any explicit attention to our logic or any other. They also fail (we think) to give due weight to the point that advances may be modest and nonetheless worth making.

Moreover, as a hypothesis in the psychology of scholarship, is it not probable that historians will actually make those advances in precision only if they make use of a logic of rules, even of a notation that continually reminds them of the components to look for? The use of a logic of rules is likely to alert investigators to logical issues that might otherwise go unnoticed and likely also to sharpen their appreciation of the variety of logical distinctions that issues call for once identified. This modest hypothesis falls well short of claiming (as we have been been mistaken to claim) that by applying the logic of norms to historical evidence scholars may experience a kind of "gestalt shift" wherein new patterns suddenly come into focus. I expect that the term "gestalt shift" reflects Thomas Kuhn's discussions of changes in scientific paradigms.[18] We do not want to disavow the possibility of gestalt shifts, from paradigm to paradigm, or within paradigms; but the idea that we are introducing a new paradigm for historical thinking lies outside our most ambitious aims. We are not so presumptuous. In any case, the hypothesis expresses only our claims at the beginning level of modest advances; and clearly falls far short of gestalt shifts, even within paradigms.

Some examples bearing out the hypothesis can be found in the discussion in *Track* of the abolition of the British slave trade and in the discussion also in *Track* of the rise of clinical medicine. Porter, one of the historians on whose account of the abolition of the slave trade we rely, omits to ask what happened to the rule of respecting the private property of the West Indian planters, which stood in the way of abolishing the trade in the 1790s (because cutting off their supply of fresh slaves would so far reduce their labor forces as to make their plantations unprofitable)?[19] Was the rule still in force when the slave trade was abolished in 1807? If it was not, how was it that the more general rule about respecting private property had ceased to give it force? It does not seem likely that the possibility of applying the general rule in this connection had simply been forgotten. Foucault, in his account of the rise of clinical medicine, identifies a rule forbidding giving diagnoses that did not relate external symptoms to internal pathologies correlated with them. However, he omits to consider that this rule, characteristic as it may be of clinical medicine once this has fully developed, could not be followed at the beginning of the development. He has thus failed to see precisely part of what has to be brought in (perhaps some rule under which the development could begin, which would also guide the development from stage to stage) to explain how clinical medicine came about.[20]

Here we are already advancing—modestly—beyond the modest claims of the hypothesis set forth above. Attention to rules, with the logic of rules, has brought to light an aspect of the history of clinical medicine that even its most brilliant investigator, emphatic as he was here as elsewhere about the importance of identifying social rules, had not come upon. We claim in *Track* to make further advances. We identify quandaries; and track social changes through the resolutions of the quandaries. We have found our illustrations in cases in which the resolutions came about by deliberations that cannot be made intelligible without identifying the rules at issue and their implications, including the implications that set some of the rules at odds with each other. But (as I shall claim, with some beginnings of illustrations, in a chapter below) the assistance that the logic of rules gives to tracing changes in rules (and social change in that sense) is not confined to deliberated change.

Historians may also be worried, we have found, that inherent in the logic of rules is some potential for "reifying" them. This is even farther from being anything that we claim. We do hope that the logic will lead to at least modest advances in historians' making more of rules than they have done, holding the rules that they identify longer in view as distinct objects of attention. Does this mean reifying them? It may give an exaggerated impression of the extent to which a rule holds in a given society to formulate it exactly and then suppose that it holds exactly for every subgroup and every member. But this impression can be checked, by consciously treating the rule as a sort of idealization familiar from accounts of language. (It is not everywhere in English the rule that the third-person negative form used for the verb "do" is "doesn't.") For some purposes, e.g., constructing a perspicuous, simplified model of the rules in a given society (for example, the rules of their kinship system), such an idealization is useful. It is useful, among other ways, as a benchmark for charting the variations on the rule found in different subgroups and with different persons.

One need not suppose that rules can be detached from the behavior that is evidence for them—the behavior of human beings doing things or avoiding things that we would expect them to do or avoid if they had invented and held to the rules in question. (I am using "invent" here to cover processes of arriving at rules that are not deliberative and may issue in rules that the people who abide by them are not aware of.)

Our hypothesis does not exclude—nor should it exclude—the possibility that some rules may persist while the people who invent them disappear, so long as in disappearing they give way to other people who in their own time accept the rules. All along—consistently with the existence of the rules, so long as deviation is subject to punishment—in a minority of cases (or maybe for less important rules, even in a majority) people, people of the first instance, maybe newcomers, people of the second instance, may choose to defy those same rules; and if defiance rather than conformity becomes paramount, the rules will disappear. Nothing in our conception of the logic of rules gainsays these points, or implies more in metaphysics than is needed to hold them.

Does ascribing causal efficacy to rules fail to take into account their dependence on the invention and support of the people who have adopted them as rules? This question may reflect a further ingredient in misgivings about reification. One might be led to imagine the rules, though arising from human invention, operating regardless of human efforts to shake loose from them. But causal efficacy does not imply anything so bizarre. The most that it implies is that it may not be easy to abandon a rule. Certainly it is not in many cases easy for individual persons living under the rule; for them, taken singly, the rule is an irreducible fact while it has general support from other people. It may not be easy to abandon the rule even when everybody wishes to abandon it; there may be no decision procedure for doing so in the society in question; and whether there is a decision procedure or not, other rules may go with the rule at issue, even rules not implied by it, but depending for continued support on powers and expectations that do depend upon the rule that invites abandonment. Think of the ramifications of abandoning the rule ascribing the power to dispose of the means of production to those who privately own the means.[21]

Changes in settled social rules is not a subject that embraces the whole of history; it nevertheless takes in a lot of historical phenomena, some very grand indeed. Changes of rules figure centrally in our conceptions of how feudalism came about and how it gave way to capitalism (which might in turn give way to another culture or social system defined by other rules). The rules for distributing the social surplus, for example, were very different under feudalism from what they have been under capitalism; and under socialism, in principle, they would be very different again. At its most ambitious, the subject of change of rules rises to the heights of the overall dialectic of history. Many people, not without reason, distrust such grand themes; changes of rules is an important subject for them as well. A great deal of the intimate tissue of social life under any culture comes from the social rules distinctive of the culture (for example, rules about the choice of spouses, which may or may not give children even a veto over the choices made for them by their parents); and changes in this tissue must be traced through changes in the rules.

To represent these changes, historians and social scientists must express the rules at stake in them. The importance of having some logic of rules rests upon the importance of specifying the rules that change (the *ex ante* and *ex post* rules), along with the rules that define the context of change, some of them perhaps in ways that prescribe the path which change takes. We must at least have a working idea of what sorts of content with what components to look for. Furthermore, if we agree that it is desirable to have a working idea that fits into a logic by giving clear views of harmony, connection, and conflict between rules, we have in effect agreed to welcome having a logic, because to define harmony, connection, and conflict is to define a logic.

Notes

1. *Ethics*, Vol. 100, No. 4, 1990.

2. Ludwig Wittgenstein, *Philosophical Investigations* (Oxford: Basil Blackwell, 1953). See, for instance, Part I, paragraphs 54, 154, 198–9, 202.

3. People can be found who think that Wittgenstein in his studies of rules put an end to all work on rules in formal logic. von Wright, whose main works on deontic logic came after Wittgenstein's death, was one of Wittgenstein's most intimate students.

4. London: Routledge, 1963.

5. von Wright holds that normative statements asserting that given norms hold, not norms proper, which to him do not have truth values, can figure as propositions in the propositional calculus. I am passing over this distinction, which I do not anyway give as much weight to as he.

6. The five paragraphs just set forth are taken by permission, with minor amendments, from David Braybrooke, "Refinements of Culture in Large-Scale History," *History and Theory*, Beiheft 9, "Studies in Quantitative History and the Logic of the Social Sciences," 1969.

7. The example just given is taken from David Braybrooke, "The Logic of the Succession of Cultures," in H. E. Kiefer and M. K. Munitz, eds., *Mind, Science, and History* (Albany: State University of New York Press, 1970), pp. 270–283.

8. The following passage comparing the Dalhousie logic of rules with von Wright's reproduces, except for some additional examples and formulas and minor variations in phrasing, a passage on the same subject in Chapter 3 of *Track*, from p. 63 (at the bottom) to p. 68 (at the top) along with footnotes.

9. Donald Davidson, "The Logical Form of Action Sentences," in Nicholas Rescher, ed., *The Logic of Decision and Action* (Pittsburgh: University of Pittsburgh Press, 1966), pp. 81–95.

10. C. Hamblin, "Quandaries and the Logic of Rules," *Journal of Philosophical Logic*, Vol. 1, No. 1, 1972, pp. 74–85.

11. *Leviathan*, Chapters 17 and 18.

12. David Lewis, *Convention* (Cambridge, Mass.: Harvard University Press, 1969).

13. See, for example, Philip Pettit, "The Reality of Rule Following," *Mind*, Vol. 99, No. 393, 1990, pp. 1–21.

14. David Braybrooke, in *Philosophy of Social Science* (Englewood Cliffs, N.J.: Prentice-Hall, 1987), pp. 48–50.

15. Brad Inwood, ed. & tr., *The Poem of Empedocles* (Toronto: University of Toronto Press, 1992) (Greek with English translation *en regard*), p. 261.

16. No doubt few historians would be quite so bold in their resistance as G. R. Elton, who in *The Practice of History* (New York, 1967), extolled the "instinctive rightness" with which a professional historian poses his questions and assesses his evidence, whether or not, we are to understand, he makes any systematic use of concepts from social sciences (pp. 17, 19, 73).

17. George K. Behlmer, an historian from the University of Washington.

18. Thomas S. Kuhn, *The Structure of Scientific Revolutions* (Chicago: University of Chicago Press, 1962).

19. Dale H. Porter, *The Abolition of the Slave Trade in England, 1784–1807* (Hamden, Conn.: Archon Books, 1970). See the discussion in *Track*, Chapter 10.

20. See the discussion in *Track*, Chapter 8, of Foucault's *La Naissance de la Clinique* (Paris: Presses Universitaires de France, 1963).

21. If Sayre-McCord is right in his chapter (below) about the rules of logic being transconventional, that distinguishes them from being conventions that vary from

culture to culture and even from being conventions that can be found in all cultures (which is a metaphysically less demanding way of looking upon them). Thus they would no longer arise from human invention and acceptance; but even so they need not be taken as more than conditions that human discourse and human actions in relation to human discourse must adhere to if confusion is to be avoided. (This is the way that Habermas treats them after toying with the idea of establishing them a priori by transcendental arguments.) As with humanly invented rules, people could conform to them aware only in various degrees of what they amounted to.

2

Hyperdeontic Logic: An Overview

Peter K. Schotch

Behind the three-component picture of rules offered by the Dalhousie project and the definition of rules offered in addition there lie some significant choices respecting issues of logic, and respecting the relation of logic to human intentions and actions. For example, there is a choice between more or less general forms for the representation of actions; and a related choice between leaving prescriptions unreduced alongside prohibitions, on the one hand, and reducing them, on the other hand, in a way that helps define rules more precisely, to prohibitions. Schotch's contribution, which runs deeper into logical theory than anything else in this collection, shows what these choices have been and what the justification was for making them.

The Roots of Hyperdeontic Logic

The idea that some, at least, of the terminology of moral philosophy can be treated by means of formal science is hardly new. No doubt it arises again and again to express a longing for reassurance that questions of morality can be adjudicated ultimately, in the same manner as questions of formal provability. The most recent programmatic exfoliation of the idea began in the 1930s with the work of Hofstader, Becker, and others who concentrated on formalising the concepts of imperative and obligation. This work drew upon the, then still fledgling, discipline of formal modal (propositional) logic, a dependency continuing through the work of G. H. von Wright and surviving to this very day. The body of lore which has resulted from this tradition has come to be called deontic logic. There is no concise description which will capture the whole of this subject but we may discern two central features:

(1) The proposed logic is taken to be an application of alethic modal logic at least in the limit.[1]
(2) The ontology of the formalisation is propositional.

These features evidently overlap to some degree. If one thinks of one-self as a consumer of modal logic, one will tend to focus on propositions as the objects to which the "moral" terms apply. This has resulted in a drift away from talk of obligations (which don't fit the model so well) toward talk of propositions which ought to be true. When one is forced to address questions concerning actions (virtually impossible to avoid in moral philosophy) these must receive a propositional treatment as well. Actions will be determined (i.e., individuated) solely in terms of what propositions they "bring about." Similar remarks apply to obligations, imperatives, and other notions of interest in the moral sphere.

From the perspective of the present day it would be fair to say that deontic logic has not achieved any notable success. Moral philosophers would seem to have "voted with their feet," leaving the area isolated from the main stream. When reminded of this humiliating fact, deontic logicians are often heard to mumble something about the unfortunate resistance of moral philosophers to formal methods. This may furnish part of the explanation, but it cannot sit comfortably with the fact that there are a significant number of philosophers who have embraced the methods of the formal social sciences (e.g., game theory) as an adjunct to their moral theorising. The time has come to entertain the hypothesis that deontic logic is simply inadequate to formalise its target area in a useful way. One is reminded of the beginning logic student who when asked to symbolize "To err is human, to forgive divine" gave as the solution "P."

It is not so much that we in the Dalhousie project wish to revitalise deontic logic, as that we wish to make a break with the tradition, thinking to secure a better "fit" with the phenomena of interest to us. Our resolve is strengthened in this enterprise by the fact that we are casting our net rather more widely than the deontic logicians. The centerpiece of our study is the notion of a *rule*, a notion of interest to students of morals to be sure, but of interest to many others besides. It is in order to signal that we have crossed a divide (in our own thinking about these matters at least) that we name our new formal science *hyperdeontic logic*. As a matter of fact, it will turn out that, though we put the pieces together in a new way, not very much of it *is* new, properly speaking. In this manner we maintain a certain continuity with the very tradition which we wish to transcend.

We first adopt an ontology which is somewhat wider than the traditional one. The essential difference is this: In addition to objects out of which propositions are cobbled (what most deontic logicians call *possible worlds* after their modal logical forebears), viz., what we call *states*, we recognize also the formal counterparts of *actions*; we shall call these *routines*. We must also recognize, as must the deontic logicians, the class of those who perform the actions, the *agents*. In singling out actions as a primitive type we explicitly eschew the view canvassed above that actions are to be described only in terms of their (propositional) consequences. On the basis of this ontology, hyperdeontic logic is built up in three layers which we call respectively *action theory, rule theory,* and *goal theory.*

Action Theory

Once upon a time there was a school which was called "ordinary language philosophy" (OLP). It had certain connections with what was called "analytic philosophy" (AP) except that it took no (or very little) thought of matters logical or with the philosophy of the exact sciences. OLP folk did think of themselves as analytical though; several of them even characterised their field as "conceptual analysis." Possibly this was an attempt to distinguish themselves from those whose interest in language was merely linguistic and from those of Continental inspiration whose interests (to this very day) defy any precise description.

While it is rather difficult to uncover any common research programme which is characteristic of OLP, a number of projects were undertaken during its brief heyday which had to do with the philosophy of the social sciences and correlatively with action theory. From this period spring book-length ponderings concerning the difference between raising one's arm and signaling the passage of wind, and conundra of the same sort. Anybody who expects to receive an infusion of this discipline in the sequel should take warning that their expectations will be largely forlorn. This is not to say that questions about how actions are to be individuated will be ignored but rather that we shall start from a different point and use a methodology which owes very little to OLP.

Our formalisation of action theory uses the methods and notation of recent work in the logic of computer programming, a logic which is often called *dynamic logic.* The first person to suggest that applying this sort of logic to actions might be a fruitful thing to do was K. Segerberg.[2] In what follows we adopt some useful suggestions made in Segerberg's seminal paper and leave others aside (because of even more useful counter-suggestions). The whole enterprise begins, on the semantic side, in the familiar modal logical way. There we find the objects with respect to which sentences take on truth values. We call the objects *states* rather than possible worlds since we wish to allow them to be relatively small (the states of a finite machine for example) and we refer to the set of them by S.

Let A be any sentence of our object language. In order not to clutter the exposition we do not give a complete account of our object language here. Further let s be any state (we shall by convention use lower case s, with or without subscripts to refer to states). Then A must receive a truth value relative to s. When A is true relative to s (or, as we shall say *at* s) we use the notation: $\mathfrak{S}(A,s)$, although this is elliptical for a more complex expression in which a more comprehensive structure than just the set of states is at issue.[3] We also use "corner braces" to depict the semantic value function so that expressions like <A> will refer to $\{s \in S \mid \mathfrak{I}(A,s)\}$, also known as the truth-set of A (i.e. the set of states in which A is true although the earlier remark concerning missing parameters applies here also).

At this point things get a bit more exotic. We admit a class of objects, distinct from states, to be called *routines*. Routines are the sorts of things that can be *run*: sequences of actions, in the limiting case, single actions. In the standard account, one associates a pair of objects with the running of a routine: a state (the *starting* state) and a set of states (the *termination set*). The idea here is that if we initiate the running of a certain routine in a starting state it will finish running (if ever) in one of the termination states. The account we require has a little more detail: in addition to providing a termination set for each starting state, we provide also a set of *intermediate* states. To elaborate on the previous motivation: a routine starts in a given starting state, ends (if it does) somewhere in its termination set and on the way, traverses some of the intermediate states. Lower case r's (with or without subscripts) will be used (in our object language) to denote routines and R denotes the set of them (in the metalanguage of course).

We shall require that <r> (the semantic value of r—which cannot be a truth set, since r is not a sentence)—be, for every r, a set-valued function defined over S. More precisely, it a function defined over S the values of which are pairs of sets. Where <r>(s) represents the value of the function at the state s, we refer to the first of the pair as INTMED(<r>(s)) and interpret it as the set of intermediate states. The second of the pair is interpreted as the termination set and referred to by TERM(<r>(s)). A difficulty is that <r> can be only a partial function since it seems more realistic to allow that some routines are not runnable in certain states. We cannot settle on <r>(s) = <∅,∅> to indicate that r is not runnable in s, since we wish to use this expression for a routine which does not terminate.[4] In view of this problem we will introduce an extra element I which serves as the value of <r> at those states s for which r is not runnable.[5]

As we know very well from dynamic logic, a lot can be done with routines. We might choose to characterise R in great detail, but we give ourselves some slack in this respect. We conceive of R as having been constructed out of basic or elementary routines (which we are tempted to call *instructions*, on the machine analogy) by means of operations. But we shall not be concerned to give full details of the construction. We single out initially: *concatenation*—where r_1 and r_2 are two routines, r_1r_2 is the routine which consists of running r_1 followed immediately by running r_2, and *combination*—if r_1 and r_2 are two routines $r_1 \wedge r_2$ is the routine which consists of running both r_1 and r_2 (i.e. of starting both in the same state).

Of these two, the first is familiar from dynamic logic and has a non-problematic semantics. $<r_1 r_2>$ will simply be the composition of $<r_1>$ and $<r_2>$.[6] The second is both unfamiliar (except of course in ordinary life) and difficult for the compositionality of our semantics. The naive approach would be to say that $< r_1 \wedge r_2 >$ is just the intersection of $<r_1>$ with $<r_2>$, but this will not do. For one thing intersection is idempotent (i.e., any set intersected with itself is itself) and it is not clear that the combination operation is. For this reason and several others which would appear on even a cursory examination of the matter, we must equip our semantics with a special function (which we call " $\wedge$ ") such that $< r_1 \wedge r_2 >$ will be the function $\wedge \left(<r_1>, <r_2> \right)$.

This much is not really unfamiliar, even though it might be a bit more fine-grained than usual. But we intend to go farther, into what is virtually *terra incognita*. We said earlier that our ontology recognizes both states and routines, which is to say that we take both types as primitive. We shall not regard routines as being derivable (if only in some hand-waving and arcane way) from propositions (i.e., sets of states). What all this fine rhetoric comes down to is that we must be prepared to admit semantic predicates other than the truth-predicate.[7] Just as we define truth at a state for sentences, so we shall define the "corresponding" predicate for routines. Of course there really isn't any single predicate that stands to routines as truth stands to sentences. Instead there are three predicates: STARTS(r,s), RUNS(r,s), and HASRUN(r,s).

There is a noticeable analogy between the definitions of this trinity and the definition of truth,[8] but there are important disanalogies too. The most important one is that every sentence must receive a truth-value at every state, but not every routine must fall within the ambit of one of the three predicates at every state. Intuitively this makes the most sense for it is easy to think of state, action pairs such that the action is neither starting, nor continuing there, nor did the state arise through the prior performance of that action.

Before pursuing this further we had better say something about agents. After all, an account of agency is the better part of action theory and indeed of moral philosophy. From an intuitive viewpoint, agents are the folk who run the routines (or in more common parlance, who perform the actions). It is tempting to regard the agents as simply sets of routines, but this would raise at least as many problems as it would solve.[9] So instead we will help ourselves to some set of agents A. We shall use lower case a, possibly with subscript, to range over this set, with boldface a as a constant. Even though we do not identify an agent with a set of routines, we will have as part of our semantic structure, a function taking us from $<a>$ to an associated set of routines (at a given state) which represents a's powers in that state.

We now return to propositions. It is important not to let talk of the distinctness of routines from the "bringing about" of propositions blind us to the fact that routines do (at least sometimes) change the truth-values of propositions. The major part of the business of dynamic logic deals with just this phenomenon. For each routine r and sentence A, dynamic logic allows as well-formed the expression: [r]A, read "when r terminates, A is true."

We shall arrange matters semantically so that:

$$\Im\big([r]A, s\big) \Leftrightarrow \text{TERM}\big(\langle r\rangle(s)\big) \subseteq \langle A\rangle$$

In words: "r terminates in an A-state" is true at the state s if and only if the termination set for r, given starting state s, is included in the set of states where A is true. We must take a bit of care here since the form of words we have just used has (at least conversationally) the implication that r has a non-empty termination set given starting state s. Such an implication we now cancel explicitly for the duration of this essay. Strictly speaking we ought to render our modal locution: "r terminates (if at all) in an A-state," but we shall hardly ever speak as strictly as that.

Most frequently, the operator which corresponds to this locution appears in the embedded form:

$$A \rightarrow [r]B$$

Such a conditional, read "when started in an A-state, r terminates in a B-state," is called a *partial correctness assertion* in dynamic logic. In the context of computing, a fundamental problem is one of designing programs which are provably correct. Folk who work on this problem want to be able to produce routines which take us from A-states to B-states in such a way that a conditional like the one above is provable.[10] For the most part this ambition remains unrealized but it does not take the wisdom of Solomon to see the practical consequences of the project.

We shall not be concerned with proving partial correctness assertions but we shall certainly be interested in describing (at least some) routines in terms of their converting A-states into B-states. In addition, we require some predicates of routines which do not customarily arise in dynamic logic. We shall be invoking the notions of one routine interfering with another, and of one routine being compatible with another.

There are several senses in which two routines can conflict, many of which are lumped together in the following. r_1 and r_2 are said to be *incompatible* at s iff $< r_1 \wedge r_2 > (s) = \varnothing$, which is to say that the two cannot be started together at s, or neither can be started if the other is running, or neither will terminate if the other is running. This is a bundle of commutative notions. We also use a non-commutative mode as well. r_1 *prevents* r_2 (at s) iff for every r_1 termination state (at s) s_1, either $<r_2>(s_1) = ($ or $TERM(<r_2>(s_1)) = \emptyset$. With sufficient dexterity and physical presence I can run a routine which is incompatible with you tying your shoes. I untie the shoelaces of whatever shoe you have just done up. On the other hand lacking the dexterity or the presence, I simply make away with your shoes while you sleep thus preventing the tying.

When, as sometimes happens, we wish to ignore nice distinctions, we use a "top-level" predicate $BLOCKS(r_1,r_2)$ which is true of a pair of routines subject to any of the infelicities just mentioned.[11]

Rule Theory

For us all rules are rules of *forbidding*. What they forbid are routines and those to whom the routines are forbidden are agents. We also adopt the convention that rules do their forbidding under conditions. In the real world, prescriptions are at least as common as prohibitions but the formalism is simplified by taking our approach and we lose no generality. A moment's thought will convince us that a rule which *enjoins* some agent a, to run a routine r, under condition C, is simply a rule which forbids the running of anything else in those circumstances.

We use variables of the form f to represent rules (a set of which will be called a *book*) and given what we have just said each rule has three components which will be written: **volk(f)**, **wenn(f)**, and **nono(f)**. The first of these is a predicate of agents, the second of states, and the last of routines. The components of a rule are called respectively: its *demographic scope, condition*, and *burden*.

To say that something is a rule is to say just that it has (at least) the three components mentioned. In ordinary speech we sometimes distinguish between a rule which is *in force* and one which is not. This is a vague matter, and one which might be thought to be represented in our scheme by the distinction between an empty versus a non-empty demographic scope. We would rather use empty demographic scopes to do other work and, for that reason, we provide a predicate of rules: INFORCE to do the job of the ordinary distinction.[12]

On this construal of rules, there is such a thing as a *logic of rules*. Conjunction and implication among rules have a natural definition and thus, as we might expect, so does the notion of a book "entailing" a rule (so natural in fact that we shall not, in the sequel, trouble ourselves to insert quotes around the word).[13] Even that traditional bugbear *negation* need not, in the context of rules, be the occasion of terror. This is because there is a straightforward notion of contradiction or absurdity upon which to ground negation (as straightforward as the one we put to use for the same purpose in the classical logic of sentences).

A book (which might contain just a single rule) is said to be *quandary free* just in case there is no state, which meets the condition of the book,[14] and no agent within the demographic scope of the book, such that every routine falls within the burden of the book for that agent in that state (and hence is forbidden to her).[15]

At this point we can ape the classical account of negation by saying that the negation of a rule is another rule having the same demographic scope and condition as the original and a complementary burden.[16] It follows from this that the book composed of any rule and its negation cannot be quandary free.

Negation is, frankly, not a particularly interesting notion to somebody constructing a logic of rules. This is because the natural history of quandaries is somewhat less rigid than that of contradictions. Every contradiction can be analysed as involving some sentence(s) and its(their) negation(s). Put more broadly, every absurdity (i.e., every sentence which "implies everything") can be so analysed. The same, or rather the analogous thing, is not true of quandaries. We certainly get a quandary when we bind a rule together with its negation but we get quandaries in plenty of other books as well. Finally, negation is a *natural* construction in the domain of sentences; certain things that we want to say come out most naturally as negations. For rules, negation is unnatural; nothing we want to say would normally be parsed into talk of negations of rules. Far more interesting and correspondingly more important is the notion of *triviality*. We can distinguish three senses in which a rule can be trivial, which parallel the tripartite nature of rules. We shall say that a rule f is trivial (written *triv*(f)) iff either <volk(f)> = ∅ or <wenn(f)> = ∅ or <nono(f)> = ∅. In words, a rule is trivial if nobody is bound by the rule, if the condition is impossible, or if the rule forbids nothing. Evidently, given what we have already said about our semantics, triviality is something that can be true or false of a rule *at a state*.

Goal Theory

Goal theory is a place where we can bring together several different lines of inquiry. Intuitively a goal is a set of states or, in the parlance of philosophical logic, a *proposition*. We might take this proposition to be descriptive of the sort of state that we want to achieve, for us an ideal sort of state. This is a way of talking which has captivated much of standard deontic logic since the 1960s but it is beset by difficulties on every side.

On one hand, our most common account of ideals requires a collateral notion of *respects* in which something is said to be ideal.[17] Thus when we call a state ideal we shall want to have ready a list of the respects in virtue of which this judgment is made and perhaps a theory of how just those respects came to be selected. On the other hand, judgments of this sort are often indexical. Just which respects come to the fore and perhaps how these are brought to bear on the question of ideal states depends upon the state in which such judgments are being made.

Goal theory is formal science's answer to policy analysis and a way of relating its various components. When we speak of respects we are not far removed from the study of that which Braybrooke calls *issue processing* where issue-circumscription questions ("What shall we do to accomplish x and y?") specify goal-respects, and issue questions proper deal with routines proposed as policies for realising the respects.

Once we descend from the rarefied Olympian heights of foundational considerations, what we have is a question which overlaps that of choice theory. How shall we apply the goal-respects to actually select ideal states? This question will typically be answered in terms of ordering relations defined on the state space (betterness orderings or preference orderings, etc.) and is the central concern of choice theory. It may come as a surprise to practitioners in the mainstream of choice theory that it also the central concern of that branch of (standard) deontic logic sometimes called formal axiology.[18]

But what has all this to do with rules? The answer is that goals and rules connect in two main ways. The first is quite obvious and relates to the adequacy of systems of rules, while the second is a bit more subtle and relates to the characterisation of goals.

A goal is a region of the state space, a region that we have reason to think is preferable, or desirable. Rules govern the movement of agents through the state space, so these two notions inevitably come together in the idea of a book being *adequate for a goal*. A book B will be said to be adequate for a goal G provided the book has a sort of ergodic property; provided that is, following the rules in the book leads from the states outside the goal to one inside, and following the rules inside the goal keeps us there. In other words, by following the rules, movement is assured from any state outside the goal, to a state inside the goal (at least eventually) and following the rules never leads from inside the goal out of it.

Proper formalisation of this idea will require us to introduce temporal indices as well as all the other ones to which we are committed, but we could never realistically have hoped to avoid this. One always hopes to keep the formalisation as simple as possible but we must also take care not to keep it any simpler than that (to echo a sentiment expressed in my introduction). The concepts which we have begun to study have the sort of richness which cannot be confined within the bounds of a logic of the usual sort.

There is a gain in going beyond these bounds however. This framework suggests new ways of looking at questions about "rational behavior." An objection which is often heard to the standard accounts is that they impose too heavy a computational burden on the agents. The costs of all the computing an agent must go through in order to select the "rational" alternative makes rationality too expensive a policy! In our account of goals there is still a lot of computing to do but we only do it once, so to speak. Once the goals[19] have been computed and an adequate book constructed, all the agents have to do from that point on is follow the rules. Moreover, following the rules of what one believes to be an adequate book is just what rational behavior comes to under this picture. Of course there will be computing to do in determining which actions are permitted but this, we venture to suggest, is a simpler task than computing a new set of goals at each round.[20]

The other way that rules bear on goals is that in the selection of goals we might well want to say that a goal state is one in which certain rules have specified properties. In particular we might require that the rules in question be non-trivial. We might also require that certain rules which are required under present (suboptimal) conditions wither away in the goal states in the sense that they become trivial there.

There is another consideration which ought to be raised here. There is a sense in which goals, as we conceive them, form constraints on systems of rules. Having goals we require of systems of rules that they conduce to those goals, but in the ordinary way of doing these things, other constraints are brought to bear. It is not normally sufficient that rules guide us toward our goals. They must also do this in a manner which *avoids* certain kinds of states. A rule which required of us that we kill half the present population to bring about a new order of plenty for all, would offend against a principle of this sort.

It seems then that a full account would mention anti-goals as well as goals. This is an area much more at home in moral philosophy than choice theory. There is not some body of existing theory that will tell us how to compute anti-goals in the same way that we compute goals,[21] but they are no less compelling for all that. At this stage in our infant theory the only provision we make for anti-goals is to recognise their existence and allow our definition of adequacy to be expanded to require that an adequate book be one in which following the rules never leads from a non-anti-goal state to an anti-goal state (even if we are "on the way" to a goal state) and that following the rules inside an anti-goal leads (eventually) outside.

So Where's the Deontic Logic?

Deontic logic is supposed to be the logic of "ought" (or sometimes of "obligation"). In this essay we have not concerned ourselves with proving theorems and have had nothing to say about ought, so the decision to call what we do "hyperdeontic logic" might be called into question. We shall attempt now to mend some fences and shore up some defenses.

In the matter of "ought" we actually have a keen interest in both the "ought to be the case" sense and the "ought to do" sense. We clearly require some account of ought in the first sense since it is precisely what goal selection is all about. We have left the door open in our discussion of goal theory just so that we can attract theorists from other areas including standard deontic logic. When a standard deontic logician gives a bunch of axioms for "ought (to be the case)" what she is doing is telling us exactly which sentences are true in the goals (namely all those theorems of her system which are prefixed by "ought").

We also have something to say about the "ought to do" sense of ought though it is less likely to be well received by the practitioners of SDL. For us the question of what an agent ought to do in a given state is just the question of what routine the agent ought to run in that state. The answer is given by which rules are in force in that state. What the agent ought to do is run (any of) the routines permitted by the book which is in force. This is in opposition to the view that what an agent ought to do is "bring about" what ought to be the case. Apart from problems of supererogation, we feel this view is of a piece with the "compute a set of goals at every turn" account of rationality.

What ought *ultimately* to be brought about are the goals and we are on our way there when we follow the rules. There will, and must be, certain propositions that we traverse along the way (although, if our book is adequate none will be included in an anti-goal) and the ones that we cannot avoid we might say "ought" to be true. But that would be to make a virtue out of a necessity.

Notes

1. By "in the limit" here is meant that when one does whatever is necessary to make the logic one of the "usual" sort, one of the "standard" modal logics results. This is vague, and it is supposed to be. To amplify slightly, consider von Wright's system which is based upon a conditional obligation operator. To make this into a logic of the usual alethic sort (one based upon a unary operator) one passes to a notion of absolute obligation by conditionalising on an arbitrary tautology. The logic of this absolute notion is (and is required to be) the standard modal logic sometimes known as **KD**.

2. At least in detail. However see Goldblatt's review article on dynamic logic. *The Journal of Symbolic Logic*, Vol. 51. No. 1, 1986, pp. 225–227.

3. In particular, the full story might make reference to relations defined on the set of states together with assignments to elementary kinds of sentences (of which we have several distinct sorts).

4. It is better to say that non-runnable routines do not *start* rather than saying that they do not terminate. Also, we might wish to require that no intermediate state be a termination state for the same routine, which would be another reason to avoid this expression.

5. Routines are many and various but we single out two for special mention from a logical point of view, called *skip* and *crash*. In intuitive terms, *skip* is that routine which always terminates and leaves everything unchanged while *crash* is that routine which never terminates.

In the throes of this semantics, we explain the two routines and give content to the implied definite descriptions as follows:

$$("s)(<skip>(s) = <\varnothing,\{s\}>)$$
$$("s)(<crash>(s) = <S,\varnothing>)$$

skip has no intermediate states and it always terminates in the state in which it is started. In contrast, no state is a termination state for *crash* though every state is an intermediate state. To inject a note of whimsy, *skip* is never running though it has always run, while *crash* has never run though it is always running.

6. Except of course that composition for set valued functions needs a little explaining. We compute such a composition as follows:

$$INT(<r_1 r_2>(s)) = INT(<r_1>(s)) \cup \{\cup INT(<r_2>(s')) \mid s' \in TERM(<r_1>(s)\}$$
$$TERM(<r_1 r_2>(s)) = \cup TERM(<r_2>(s')), s' \in TERM(<r_1>(s))$$

7. In a sense, this is the opposite position to that of Montague who held that the truth definition was the central and only goal of semantics, and even of pragmatics.

8. Most prominently: we typically define truth (at a state) recursively on a prior account of truth (or something sufficiently like it) of atomic sentences at a state. That is, we begin with the gadget V (normally taken to part of the model) which assigns to every atomic sentence-state pair exactly one of two values (say 0,1). This is used in the basis clause of our truth definition, the clause governing atomic sentences, in the obvious way: for every atomic sentence A, and state s, A is true at s iff $V(A,s) = 1$. We then extend this (uniquely) to cover all sentences with a series of recursive clauses, the so-called truth-conditions for the various compounding operations we recognize.

In a similar way we start with "assignments" S, R, and H mapping basic or elementary routine, state pairs to $\{0,1\}$, and anchor our recursive definitions of STARTS, RUNS, and HASRUN. These we can also extend recursively by clauses which tell us that an arbitrary routine starts at s iff its "first" subroutine starts at s, is running at s if some subroutine is running at s, and has run at s if its "last" subroutine has run at s. The major difference is that V is required to be a total function (the law of excluded middle) but none of S, R, or H is subject to that requirement. We do not rule out the case that the functions in question are total, but neither do we rule out the case that they are nowhere defined. Both cases represent models for our "logic of action."

9. For one (major) thing it would require that there be enough routines to separate distinct agents, which might well require in its turn that the routines turn out to be analogous to actions rather than action types. On this account you cannot do *anything* that I can do (let alone do it better). My scratching of my head is different from your scratching of yours or even your scratching of mine (even if you use my hand to do the scratching). (This note, like the two preceding, and the brief passage to which they attach, literally reproduce assertions about the same topics in Chapter 4 of *Track*, p. 74 (in part), and p. 76 (at the bottom) to p. 77 (at the top).)

10. When a software engineer writes a program, she has in mind a certain task the program is supposed to perform: when started in an A-state the program terminates in a B-state (A and B might be ferociously complex but the assumption of correctness theory is that every task can be given in this form). How does the engineer proceed? Using all or some of the skills at her command, she writes the program and tests it. Testing consists of a number of trials or runs in which she initiates the program in an A-state and sees whether it produces a B-state. After a time the program passes all these tests but does she know that it will invariably convert an A-state into a B-state? No she doesn't, since she has only tested a few cases (out of infinitely many). Software design is still an empirical science and nobody can guarantee that a given program will always perform the task for which it was designed. It is this deficiency which correctness theory aims to eliminate.

11. There is obviously a lot of subtlety which is missed in this hydroplane tour of these notions. Our focus here is on BLOCKS, in the sense of preventing the termination of routines or preventing their starting. In actual practice, BLOCK-ing in this sense is often infeasible. Instead we make do with a somewhat less thoroughgoing approach which is best explicated in terms of goals.

You wish to run the routine r in order to bring about an A-state but I dissuade you by running a routine which ensures that your A-state, will also be a B-state. In this case, I do not ensure that when you run r it fails to terminate, strictly speaking, merely that your running of r will have, for you, consequences other than those you intend, and that the unpleasantness of these consequences makes your running of r much less attractive to you. There is no routine I can run which will BLOCK you from embezzling my money, but I can and do run a routine which makes it very likely that if you do embezzle my money you will go to jail.

We see BLOCKS lurking behind the notion just canvassed (SPOILS perhaps) when we notice that there is indeed a routine that is BLOCK-ed here, viz., that routine which produces an A-state which is not a B-state (for example a state in which you have embezzled my money and are enjoying it on the Dalmatian Coast).

12. INFORCE will be another "semantic" predicate, i.e. one of those provided by a model, like HASRUN, etc.

13. The details of these "natural" constructions are only moderately gory. Let f_1 and f_2 be two rules, their parts being **volk(f_1) volk(f_2)** etc. Then **volk$\left(f_1 \wedge f_2\right)$** will be just **volk($f_1$) & volk($f_2$)** and similarly for the condition of the conjunction of the two while:

$$\mathbf{nono}\left(f_1 \wedge f_2\right) \text{ must be } \mathbf{nono}\left(f_1\right) \vee \mathbf{nono}\left(f_2\right)$$

Or to put the matter set-theoretically and semantically: the semantic value of the demographic scope and the condition for the conjunction of two rules is just the intersection of the corresponding semantic values of the conjuncts. The semantic value of the burden of the conjunction is the union of the semantic values of the burdens of the conjuncts. Since all these semantic values are the values of predicates they will be sets.

In the same vein we would say that one rule "implies" another when the demographic scope and condition of the first are included in those of the second and the burden of the first includes that of the second (speaking semantically).

Finally we say that a book entails a rule when the conjunction of the rules in the book implies the rule. This is the strict analogue of the classical notion of semantic entailment, and shares with it the "feature" that inconsistent sets (i.e., quandary bound books) entail everything. There is also scope for a paraconsistent construal of entailment which eliminates many of these inferential "explosions."

14. By such terms as "the condition of the book" we mean the condition of the rule which results from the conjunction of the rules which make up the book. Similarly for the terms demographic scope and burden used in connection with books.

15. This terminology is due to Charles Hamblin, "Quandaries and the Logic of Rules," *Journal of Philosophical Logic*, Vol. I, No. 1, 1972, pp. 74–85. In his paper on the logic of rules he distinguishes between several senses of quandary freeness. In this brief introduction we need not avail ourselves of this sophistication.

16. Once again this is a bit too brisk. We can happily define a negation of f by saying that f's negations have the property that when bound to f result in a quandary. Said this way, it is not true that negation is an operation in the usual sense because a rule might have many negations of this sort. There is no requirement that a negation in this sense share demographic scope with the rule negated; just that the two demographic scopes have a non-empty intersection. Similarly there is no requirement that every agent in the demographic scope be in a quandary in every state. Given the definition of quandary, even one state with this property would suffice. So there are ways to weaken the definition and still satisfy the requirement that a rule and its negation be "contradictory." On that account we ought presumably to refer to our notion as "strong" rule negation.

17. It is not clear what sense is to be made of the claim that something is ideal in *every* respect, beyond treating the word "every" as an ellipsis for "every one so far considered." In this, "ideal" and "similar" would seem to be in the same boat, both tacitly indexed by a set of (sets of) respects, and neither supporting a *global* or *overall* version in any real sense.

18. This remark is meant to titillate. I amplify on the question of what deontic logic can (and sometimes does) contribute to choice theory in another note.

19. We speak of goals here and in the sequel, recognizing that the process for goal selection is likely to be fragmented, that something will be a goal *given* certain aims. Thus, in the normal course of events the process will produce several propositions all of which are goals. What we mean then by the singular term goal is just the intersection of these. Of course this raises problems. What if such an intersection is empty (i.e., what if the goals are incompatible)? What indeed.

20. In taking this view we are converging on the opinions of certain economists, in particular Ronald Heiner (see below, Chapter 14).

21. It would be a mistake, for example, to think that an anti-goal is just the (set-theoretic) complement of a goal. To say this would be to say that *every* state is either a goal state or an anti-goal state. Of course somebody might say such a thing, but not without offending common sense.

3

Normative Explanations

Geoffrey Sayre-McCord

With Sayre-McCord's contribution, we move on from the logical theory of rules to a general survey of issues about how—taking them in Kornhauser's third sense, which Sayre-McCord calls "normative rules"—rules enter into the explanation of human actions. Sayre-McCord deals first with rules originating somehow in human conventions; and then with the more problematic cases of rules—of rationality or morality—that may be " transconventional."

Introduction

There is a great wind of moral force moving through the world and every man who opposes that wind will go down in disgrace.

So wrote a widely respected historian, political scientist, and United States President—Thomas Woodrow Wilson.[1] Nowadays, Wilson's confidence in morality, his conviction that justice will out, that the righteous will rule, that morality can and does have an impact on what happens in the world, seems anachronistic, outrageously optimistic, and metaphysically peculiar. That it is anachronistic and outrageously optimistic, I don't deny. But I do hope to show that it is not nearly so metaphysically peculiar as many think. In particular, I hope to make sense of the idea that morality operates, if not as an over-powering wind, then at least as a gentle breeze in the course of history.

Less metaphorically, I want to explore the view that morality, and specifically moral rules, might help to explain social change.[2] I should emphasize, though, that my aim is to *make sense of the idea*, it is not to show that in fact morality actually does explain social change; I am after a plausibility argument, not an existence proof. Providing the first is hard enough.

Before moving directly to *moral* rules, and their potential role in explanations of social change, I will concentrate first on the more general issue of how rules (whether moral, legal, or social) figure in explanations. In

35

what follows, I will be moving back and forth frequently between moral rules and other (metaphysically less presupposing) rules. Throughout, though, I shall be concentrating on normative rules—rules that forbid courses of action, impose obligations, or grant permissions—not on descriptive rules that simply report empirical regularities. The contrast, I think, is intuitively clear, even if it doesn't lend itself to a rigorous definition: it is one thing to say that, in the U.S., there's a rule (in this case a law) forbidding speeds in excess of 65 mph; it is quite another to say that, as a rule, people in the U.S. don't drive over 65 mph. Likewise, it is one thing to say that one ought to make rational choices; it is another to say that people do, as a rule, make such choices. And again, it is one thing to say that in baseball one is permitted by the rules of the game to steal second base; it is another to say that, as a rule, people do steal second base.[3] Mere regularities do not constitute normative rules, even though recognized and enforced normative rules may be expected to give rise to regularities. The connection between regularities, on the one hand, and normative rules that are unrecognized, or unenforced, or both, on the other hand, is much less straightforward. That there is, or at least might be, such a connection is nonetheless something I argue for later in the paper.[4]

Normative rules are, of course, ubiquitous; they structure our interactions, inform our plans, define our options, and play a central role in our understanding of our own activities.[5] Yet the importance of normative rules, when it comes to explanation, as opposed to exhortation, remains dubious, at best. What in the world (we're inclined to ask) might rules explain?

In answer one could reasonably say: normative rules might explain why some action, say, counts as illegal, some utterance as ungrammatical, some proposal as rational, some institution as moral. Left lingering by this answer (right as it might be) is the suspicion that the facts explained by the relevant rules are just restatements of the rules. To say an act is illegal is, one worries, simply to say it violates a law; to say an utterance is ungrammatical is simply to say it violates a rule of grammar, and so on. Much more satisfying would be an answer that showed that the normative rules and corresponding normative facts they 'explain' themselves explain—*really* explain—some event, process, or situation, that is conceptually independent of the rules in question.[6] The nagging suspicion is that normative rules explain no such thing.

Doubts about the explanatory importance of normative rules come from many directions. Perhaps the most influential has its source in the conviction that there is a fundamental difference between fact and value, a conviction bolstered by the observation that what ought to be isn't always so, and that even when it is so, it apparently isn't so *because* it ought to be. The inclination is to argue that only facts *as distinct from values* explain people's behavior. Notoriously, though, the distinction between facts and values is extremely difficult to articulate. Moreover, even those convinced of its existence are usually willing to count many normative social rules (such as those governing language, constituting legal systems, and defining games) as firmly on the side of facts—even if they put moral rules on the other side of the divide.

Another source of these doubts is found in the observation that, whatever rules are, they are not the sort of thing you can bump into. No one has ever bruised her shin tripping over a normative rule. Yet the relevant question is not so much whether the rules themselves can be bumped into but whether they can help to explain why and how we bump into the things we do.

Two Ways to Figure in Explanations of Social Change

If normative rules do figure in explanations it will be in either of two roles: as part of what is *being explained* or as part of what *does the explaining*. In the first case, when it comes to explaining rules, we would be interested in explaining the origin and stability of the rules in question and in explaining the various changes they might undergo. In the second case, when it comes to explaining by appeal to rules, we would be interested in using rules to help explain other rules, to explain particular actions, or to explain general trends and patterns. Either role, that of explainer or that of explained, will give normative rules a place in explanations.

Still, the two roles are not of equal significance. Normative rules only become interesting objects of explanation to the extent they are also themselves explainers—to the extent the rules being what they are makes some difference to what happens in the world. If rules never make such a difference, and so never help to explain what happens, we would have much less reason to bother explaining them. In fact, it is hard to imagine what grounds one might have for believing the rules exist if they make no difference.[7] Rules as explained non-explainers seem just epiphenomena by another name with all the attendant problems. Even so, before turning to how normative rules might explain, I would like first to mention briefly a couple of the ways they might be explained. (I do this in part because some of our best explanations of rules themselves appeal to normative rules.)

Normative rules fall fairly neatly into two groups. The majority owe their existence and their force to various social practices and conventions; the rules of chess, the requirements of etiquette, the standards of grammar, and the laws of the land (to take a few examples) all come into being, and lay a claim on us, only because of things people do or have done. Such rules wouldn't be, and wouldn't matter, save for the particular local practices of people. These rules are conventional. Other rules apparently transcend convention; the demands of morality, the rules of logic, and the standards of practical rationality, all appear not to depend (at least in any straight-forward way) on what people do or have done. The former are unmistakably human products, while the latter hover above, and seemingly free from the influence of, human practices and conventions. Whether this distinction between conventional and trans-conventional rules marks a real difference in kind, or just a difference in the degree to which the rules depend on more or less local practices and conventions, is both unclear and controversial. One might, and people do, argue that the apparently trans-conventional rules of morality, logic, and rationality, are, despite appearances, conventional rules that find their origin and force in very widely shared, and perhaps socially necessary, practices or conventions.[8]

Regardless, to the extent the normative rules in question are dependent for their existence and force on what people do or choose, or on practices and conventions, they lend themselves to psychological and social explanation. Among the most elegant of such explanations are those that, by making use of decision and game theory, explain the rules as products of rational behavior.

Some rules, for instance laws handed down from 'on-high' by a dictator, are plausibly explained as rational solutions to problems of parametric choice (that is, as rational solutions to problems where the agent chooses from among what is viewed as a fixed set of options). Thus we might explain Noriega's imposition of a curfew as his least-cost solution to the problem of containing insurgency; given his preferences, situation, and nearly un-checked power, passing laws that constrain the liberty of others might be the rational thing for him to do.

Other rules we might explain on the grounds that they are rational solutions, not to problems of parametric choice, but to problems of strategic choice (that is, as rational solutions to problems where the agents choose from among options that are viewed as depending in part on the choices of others).[9] Plainly, social rules do frequently solve problems of strategic choice; they solve problems of coordination and problems of competition, and most often problems that mix elements of competition with the need for coordination. Moreover, that they solve such problems is plausibly taken to be the reason they exist. Traffic laws, to use a popular example, seem largely to have come about in order to coordinate behavior in a context where it doesn't much matter to people what exactly the laws are, just so long as there are some. Criminal laws serve primarily (although not exclusively) as a way of resolving predictable conflicts among the interests of people within a society. And anti-pollution laws have been introduced explicitly to militate against the tragedy of the commons, which is due to people exploiting unmercifully what is held in common and protected by no one.

Recognized, respected, and enforced social rules time and again shift expectations, circumstances, and motivations, so as to ensure that people won't act in ways that make all (or at least most) worse off. Without them social life would be unbearable. Game theoretic explanations recommend themselves as well, though, for social rules of a less salutary cast. In South Africa, for instance, the laws of Apartheid were quite clearly the instruments of class interest, explainable in part as an immoral solution to a problem of collective choice faced by those in power.[10] In the same vein, a more benign example can be found in casino gambling rules, which are calculated to give the 'house' a distinct advantage.

Still other rules may not themselves be consciously introduced solutions to choice problems at all, but are instead by-products of social practices and conditions. Rules of etiquette, for instance, appear often to impose capricious constraints that are not rational solutions to choice problems, despite their being predictable consequences of social conditions. Even in these cases, invisible foot explanations (that account for the rules as the unintended and detrimental consequences of rational behavior) and invisible hand explanations (that account for the rules as the unintended but beneficial consequences of rational behavior)[11] will sometimes be available. If they are available, such explanations will make use of decision and game theory to explain the behavior, practices, and social conditions, that produce the social rules as by-products.

Of course, the fact that some rule would be a rational solution to a problem that would exist if there weren't such a rule, can't explain the rule's existence unless the relevant people acted *because* the rule offered a rational solution. Importantly, though, this is not to say that the people must have acted because they *recognized* the rule offers such a solution; they may acknowledge and even enforce a rule *because* the rule offers such a solution without knowing that is why they act as they do. In any case, explanations that rely on decision and game theory will go through as *explanations,* and not simply as justifications or just-so stories, only if the people involved are suitably rational, only if their behavior is sensitive to what is rational under the circumstances. That people do live up to the demands of rationality is a crucial presupposition of decision and game theoretic explanations.

Just exactly what the demands of rationality are, needless to say, is a matter of extensive debate even among those who take advantage of the formal apparatus of decision and game theory, along with the essentially maximizing conception of rationality that underlies it. Neoclassical economists, for instance, embrace an unabashedly narrow, even cynical, view that ties rationality to self-interest; while others hold that the preferences of rational agents may range over the welfare of others. And some hold that rationality is simply a matter of maximizing expected satisfaction of (brute) subjective preferences; others impose restrictions (usually having to do with reflection or information) on the subjective preferences that are to count; while still others replace subjective preferences in the account with objective interests.[12] Despite these differences, the common framework provided by decision and game theory provides a strikingly powerful explanatory tool.

Such explanations are often among the best we have of why many familiar rules and sets of rules have been imposed or adopted. Indeed, a valuable, even if not always successful, strategy for figuring out why certain social rules have come into existence lies in discovering whose interests are served by the rules; where interests are served we are likely to find rational agents active. Of course this works only as a heuristic strategy. It would be a mistake to claim that the mere fact that interests are served can itself explain the existence of rules; there must be some reason to think either that the people were aware of the benefits to come or that some feedback loop would have adjusted the rules had the interests not been served.[13] When the strategy fails, when the rules in question are not plausibly explained as rational solutions to choice problems, either it will be because the rules simply are not rational solutions or, if they are, it will be because their being rational solutions doesn't (under the circumstances) explain their coming into existence—say because the people don't recognize their interests, or because they haven't for some other reason lived up to the standards of rationality.

What is interesting, here, about decision and game theoretic explanations of conventional rules (whether of the rules directly or of the social practices that generate the rules as by-products) is not that they exhaust the sort of explanations we have for social rules—they certainly don't— but that they evidently explain social rules by appeal to the rationality of agents and thus to normative rules of rationality. Of course, the explanations will count as *normative* explanations only among those who accept the underlying theory of rationality as at least in the running as a normative theory of rationality. But this is a very large group. So let's turn from explaining rules to using rules to explain.

Explaining by Conventional Rules

To the extent we try to use normative rules to explain suitably independent events, processes, or situations, there are three ways the rules might enter into an explanation. In setting these ways out, I will concentrate initially on conventional normative rules, only afterwards turning to the more problematic case of trans-conventional rules.

Most obviously, and least controversially, normative rules can figure in explanations as the *content* of agents' beliefs. People quite clearly often do things (say, drive under 65 mph or avoid splitting infinitives) because they believe doing so is required by certain rules (e.g., of law or grammar). Less often, perhaps, but no less clearly, people do things—out of perversity, indignation, or independence—because they believe doing so violates certain rules.[14]

It is tempting to stop here, saying that all the explanatory work done supposedly by rules is really done by appeal to beliefs, not rules. The beliefs do, of course, have rules as their content, but that hardly gives the rules themselves a robust role in explanations. After all, some people do things because they believe in Santa Claus, but we can explain their actions without sharing their conviction. Santa Claus himself, as opposed to beliefs about Santa Claus, figures nowhere in our explanations of things that happen in the world. In the same way, people may do things because they believe there are normative rules, but we might still be able to explain their actions without sharing their conviction. Normative rules themselves, as opposed to beliefs about such rules, might figure nowhere in our explanations of things that happen in the world. No doubter of the explanatory importance of rules need feel any discomfort allowing rules this role.

Nevertheless, the temptation to view the explanatory role of normative rules so narrowly should dissipate once attention is turned to explaining those beliefs that have rules as their content. For in many cases at least part of the explanation of why people believe the rules require them to act in certain ways is that the rules do—part of the explanation will involve there actually being the rules about which the people in question have beliefs. Often enough, if the rules were different, people's beliefs (and so their behavior) would have been different as well. For example, for several years, and until recently, the national speed limit in the United States was 55 mph. When the limit changed to 65 mph people's beliefs about the limit changed too, as did their driving habits. Were the limit to change again it is reasonable to think people's beliefs and behavior would change once more. In short, people's beliefs about the speed limit are explained (at least in part) by the speed limit itself, by the normative rule that forbids speeds in excess of 65 mph. Of course people's beliefs are not always sensitive to what the rules actually are; sometimes people believe rules require something of them when the rules don't. Clearly, in these cases something other than the rule will have to explain their belief. Even so, rules will often explain the beliefs people have about rules and so they will explain indirectly the behavior caused by those beliefs. In these cases, at least, normative rules will figure in explanations not just as the content of beliefs but also as causes of belief. Presumably, when it comes to explaining our own beliefs about rules we are committed to thinking the rules being what we take them to be is part of why we hold the beliefs we do.

Normative rules can figure as well, though, in explanations where their effects on a person's behavior are unmediated by her beliefs about the rules. Sticking with the example of traffic laws, we might explain why a particular person is driving within the speed limit by noting that she is disposed to drive at roughly the same speed as those around her, and that those around her have slowed to 55 mph because they noticed what she did not—a new speed limit sign. Ignorant though she is of the speed limit on the new stretch of road, the fact that it is the limit helps to explain her behavior because it helps to explain the behavior of those around her (whose behavior in turn explains hers).

Switching from rule-following to rule-breaking behavior, it's clear as well that rules that are unrecognized, yet violated, by a person can contribute to an explanation of what happens (just as rules that are unrecognized but followed can contribute to explanations). We might, for example, explain someone's being pulled to the side of the road by the police by appeal to the fact that he broke the speed limit (i.e., disobeyed some relevant law) and this explanation might go through even though the driver is ignorant of the law. His pulling to the side of the road will be explained partly by his having broken a rule about which he has no belief.

Of course, this particular explanation may initially seem plausible only to the extent we appeal to someone else's belief, in particular a police officer's belief, that the speed limit was broken. But there are two points to keep in mind. First, the fact that the driver broke a normative rule—and the fact's explanatory relevance—is completely independent of the *driver's* recognizing that he was breaking the law. Second, the fact that the driver broke the speed limit might figure in the explanation *even if neither the officer nor the driver believe the speed limit was broken.*

Consider this case: imagine the officer has been ticketing people all day for speeding and has as a result become especially sensitive to those going faster than the limit allows. It is not that she thinks of them as speeders (she usually doesn't, unless and until she clocks them on the radar); it is just that she is disposed to notice them.[15] Suppose that, her awareness of speeders heightened, she notices our wayward driver and the fact that his car fits the description of a car recently stolen. Suppose too that because the officer thinks the car suspect, she takes chase without even thinking about whether the driver was speeding. In this case, the officer will have pulled the driver over because she believed he was driving a stolen car and not because she believed he was speeding (she didn't). Nonetheless, part of the explanation for why the driver was pulled over will be that he was speeding—had he not been, the officer wouldn't have taken notice of the car.

So rules might play any of the following three roles in explanations: (i) they might be the content of beliefs that in turn explain actions, (ii) they might themselves explain the beliefs (about rules) that explain actions, and (iii) they might explain actions, events, processes, or situations unmediated by beliefs about rules. Unlike the first role, which leaves actual rules completely out of the explanatory picture, both the second and third roles have the rules themselves doing real explanatory work. The rules, and not merely people's beliefs about the rules, are accounting for events in the world.

It might seem as if the three roles are presented in successive order, from that allowing rules the least explanatory involvement to that allowing them the most. But there is no appreciable difference, in that respect, between the second and third roles. Once it is granted that rules can explain behavior when mediated by beliefs about rules, on the grounds that they explain the beliefs, it is no extra step at all to saying they can explain things without the mediation of belief. *For the role a given rule will play in explaining a person's beliefs about that rule will of necessity be one itself unmediated by that person's belief about that rule.* While you can explain my belief concerning some law by appeal to that law, you can't explain my belief by appeal to the belief being explained. Still, it is important to recognize that rules (unmediated by belief) can explain things other than beliefs about those rules, not least of all because in this capacity rules frequently have their subtlest effects.

Although related, the second and third roles do differ—most significantly in that only when people have beliefs about what a rule requires can they *intentionally* obey or violate the rule. One can, of course, conform to or violate a rule without realizing it; but one can intentionally respect or flaunt a rule only if one is aware of the rule. Unrecognized rules, although they may sometimes help to explain what happens to people and what people do, cannot explain people consciously obeying or breaking the rules.

This difference suggests a stronger claim: that explanations giving a rule the third role can account only for behavior that conforms to the rule, not behavior that violates it; while explanations that give rules the second role (that is, that invoke rules whose effects are mediated by beliefs about those rules) can explain behavior that violates the rule in question as well as behavior that conforms to the rule. One can of course break the speed limit, say, without having any beliefs about the speed limit, but it may look as if the fact that there is a rule setting the limit won't be relevant to explaining one's violation (even if it is relevant to the explanation of what happens once the rule has been broken). A rule that is neither recognized nor followed by a person may seem beside the point when it comes to explaining her breaking the rule.

But this stronger claim is too strong. There are at least a few (perhaps peculiar) cases where such a rule might still play an explanatory role, as when, for instance, a person wishing to stand-out from a crowd takes the necessary steps, only to discover (to her regret) that the crowd was simply obeying a strictly enforced rule. Here, the rule explains the crowd's behavior, and the crowd's behavior (along with the person's desire to stand-out) helps to explain her behavior (and her subsequent woes).[16]

To press the point further, even a rule that is unrecognized by everyone (who falls under it) and followed by no one, might explain events in the world if, consistently, those who followed the rule (if ever there were any) would be better off than those who violate it. In such cases, at least part of the explanation of why the people are not better off is that they violate the rule.

More generally, but along the same lines, a rule will be part of a legitimate explanation if the actions the rule enjoins, or forbids, constitute causally significant categories; and it will be an especially informative explanation if the set of relevant actions are otherwise heterogeneous. Explanations of this sort are made most plausible, of course, when there is some prospect of accounting for the causal feedback loop that renders reliable the effects of conforming to or violating the rule. However, even without a clear picture of how the feedback loop might work, if the effects are sufficiently reliable, and the pattern sufficiently evident, the rule will play a role in reasonable explanations.[17]

Explaining by Transconventional Rules

That conventional rules might explain what happens in the world is not, I take it, really all that controversial. In contrast, there are some apparently significant differences between conventional rules (of law, grammar, or games) and trans-conventional rules (of logic, rationality, or morality) that make much less palatable the suggestion that trans-conventional rules might explain.

The first difference has to do with what has become a standard test for explanatory import—the counterfactual test, which asks "what if the rules had been different?" and counts the rules as explanatorily important only if their being different would make a difference.[18] When we subject conventional rules to the counterfactual test, the test is conceptually unproblematic (we can make sense of the rules being different than they in fact are). More impressively, it is quite clear that conventional rules can in principle pass the test; often, if the rules had been different, people's beliefs (and their resulting behavior) would have been different as well.

The second difference turns on the fact that both the metaphysical status and actual character of particular conventional rules is fairly uncontroversial. People generally agree as to what the rules are and they share a sense of how to investigate and resolve differences of opinion when they arise.

On both counts, when it comes to trans-conventional rules things get messy quickly. First, in many cases it is hard even to make sense of the counterfactual test since it is hard to make sense of the trans-conventional rules being different than we take them to be. This is largely because the rules don't seem to be contingent in a way that allows us to imagine easily and with any confidence what things would be like if they were in any significant way different. Suppose it were morally permissible for people in our situation to torture young children simply for amusement ... what would people believe under the circumstances?[19] This seems like asking one to suppose that two plus two didn't equal four and then asking what people would believe under the circumstances. One is inclined to say these questions don't have answers because their suppositions are necessarily false, perhaps even inconceivable—a fact that makes it difficult, to say the least, to apply the counter-factual test.

Second, both the metaphysical status and the actual character of particular trans-conventional rules—especially those of morality, but also those of rationality—are very controversial. People frequently disagree as to what the rules are and also as to how one should investigate and resolve the differences of opinion that inevitably arise.

Despite these striking differences, sense can be made of trans-conventional normative rules (if there are any) contributing to our explanations of non-normative events, processes, and situations. To a great extent, the very real differences mentioned above, while they plague any attempt to defend one particular trans-conventional normative theory as over against another, leave largely untouched any particular conception's claim to explanatory import.

Recall that we already have on-hand a couple of plausible explanations that appeal to trans-conventional rules of rationality: the explanations of conventional rules mentioned early-on that made use of decision and game theory. There is room clearly to accept the decision and game theoretic explanations of conventional rules while at the same time rejecting as an inadequate normative theory the maximizing conception of rationality. Conversely, one might accept as right-headed the normative theory while doubting the success of the decision and game theoretic explanations. Yet for those who do accept both the normative view and the explanations (as many do), the decision and game theoretic explanations provide a nice example of normative explanations. The understandable controversy that will surround, say, the maximizing conception of rationality should warn devotees away from confident dogmatism; but to the extent they have reasonable (even if not conclusive) grounds for their view, there is no reason for them to refrain from using their normative theory in explanations. And, assuming the explanations are successful, there is no reason for them to refrain from seeing the normative theory they embrace as having explanatory credentials.

When it comes to trans-conventional normative rules, any attempt to develop a normative theory that will hold some promise of contributing to explanations will involve two steps. The first is to get some defensible account of what the relevant rules (of logic, rationality, or morality) are. This is the job of justificatory theory. Only if this first step is taken will the theory have any claim to normative force. (Taking it, obviously, involves defending one more or less controversial account among many.) The second step is to show that—on that understanding of the normative rules—the fact that some inference, choice, or action, violates or accords with those rules (so understood) explains something outside the inner circle of the normative theory in question—i.e., explains why the inferences, choices, actions, were made or taken, or explains some other non-normative facts. Only if this second step is taken will the theory have any claim to explanatory force. Neither step is trivial. Moreover, they may not be independent; one might hold that we are justified in believing only what might help to explain our experiences, so that being able to take the second step is a necessary condition for taking the first.

Even so, if the two steps can be taken successfully, one will be in a position both to justify one's account of the norms as the appropriate norms and to explain things that happen in the world by appeal to those norms.

It is worth noting that, as long as we are concentrating on trans-conventional rules, taking the second step involves making plausible the view that there is some nonconventional causal feedback loop that is responsive to the difference between what violates the rules and what accords with them. In the absence of some such nonconventional feedback loop the rules will have no role in explaining events independent of their recognition within convention. Significantly, though, when the explanation by rules is backed by such a feedback mechanism, the problem involved in applying the counterfactual test to non-contingent rules doesn't arise; for the relevant counterfactual doesn't have to do with what would have happened *had the rule been different*, but with what would have happened *had the behavior being explained been different* in such a way as to make it conform with the rule rather than not (or vice versa).

Not only is it plausible to think defensible normative rules (even trans-conventional ones) might figure as the contents of people's beliefs; it is reasonable as well to suppose that (with a suitable conception in hand) one might have reason to think, first, that people's beliefs are sometimes responsive to the rules (no doubt that will be the view one takes of one's own beliefs), and even, second, that people's prospects may vary, other things equal, according to whether they live up to the demands or not. The maximizing conception of rationality is a clear case in point; for it flows naturally from that conception that those who fail to maximize expected utility will, on average, do worse than they otherwise would have. One doesn't have to look far, though, to discover plausible conceptions of morality that fit the bill as well.[20]

I will close by describing (all too briefly) two sorts of moral theories, in particular; both of which—despite their deep and dramatic differences—hold the promise of giving morality not just a justificatory role but an explanatory role. One is a broadly utilitarian theory, the other broadly contractarian.

The utilitarian theory I have in mind begins with a conception of objective human good (a sort of naturalized view of human flourishing) that is grounded in the satisfaction of informed preferences. It then construes moral requirements as reflections of the demand that human good be maximized, without regard to whose good it is that is being advanced. On this view, actions, practices, and institutions, as well as particular moral claims, are seen as morally justified to the extent they contribute to the maximization of human good.

Within this view, so sketched, there is obviously a great deal of room for different specific views of morality, since a wide variety of accounts might be used to fill in more precisely the notion of objective human good. And there is room as well to embrace just the broader consequentialist outlines and, for instance, replace the appeal to objective human good with a purely subjectivist account that identifies human good with the satisfaction of human preferences whatever they happen to be (regardless of whether they are fully informed or reflectively held).[21]

The contractarian theory, in contrast, begins not with a conception of objective human good, but with a theory of rationality and, specifically, rational agreement. It then construes moral requirements as the products of rational agreement; the moral rules are those to which rational people would rationally agree, and with which they would then rationally comply, under appropriately specified conditions.

Within the contractarian view, too, there is a great deal of room for different specific views of morality, in this case because a wide variety of accounts might be used to fill in more precisely the notions of rationality and rational agreement. And there is room as well to embrace only the broadest contractarian outlines and, for instance, replace the appeal to appropriately specified, presumably hypothetical, conditions with simply the actual conditions real people happen to find themselves in.[22]

Despite the truly fundamental differences, both utilitarianism and contractarianism (of the sorts described[23]) maintain an over-all structure that makes the theories suitable candidates for use in explanations. For in each case, the demands of morality would be specified in a way that would make plausible the contention that there is a causal feedback mechanism that, by and large and in standard conditions, rewards compliance and penalizes non-compliance with (what each theory identifies as) the demands of morality—and does so regardless of whether the demands of morality are recognized.

Thus, for instance, on both the utilitarian and the contractarian accounts one might expect resentment, as well as dissatisfaction with the *status quo*, to grow roughly in proportion to injustice. Within societies (and also perhaps among societies) one could predict also that the social and political pressures would rise and fall in reaction to morally relevant changes in social institutions, consistently applying an impetus for moral improvement, if only with partial success. At the very least, unjustifiable institutions and practices likely suffer instability due to people's inability, on reflection, to endorse the norms to which they are subjected. Of course, because the social pressures will vary as well with factors other than the moral credentials of the institutions in place, the sanctions immorality suffers may be buffered, deflected, or simply neutralized. Yet, that forces will have no easily *predictable* effects in an exceedingly complex environment is no reason to deny their presence or their effect. And, to the extent morality is viewed in either a utilitarian or a contractarian way, there are even some grounds for thinking the effects of immorality are actually quite visible and predictable.

Needless to say, although the two approaches to moral theory each have the resources to make sense of how morality and immorality might be relevant to explaining both large scale and more local events and patterns of interaction, their differences will ensure that their various resources will be deployed in drastically different and fundamentally incompatible ways. They can't both be right about the nature of morality and so can't both be right about the ways and extent to which morality helps to explain social change. The important point for our purposes, though, is that either sort of moral theory—as long as it can be defended as a reasonable normative theory—will hook-up with our experiences, prospects, and fortunes, in such a way as to give morality itself, and not just beliefs about morality, a role in explaining what happens in the world. Either will give sense and substance to the notion that morality operates at least as a gentle breeze through the course of history.

⁂

Having spent all this time trying to defend the suggestion that morality might actually contribute to empirical explanations, a confession is in order. Much as I believe morality (at least on some plausible conceptions) does indeed have some explanatory force, I suspect as largely, perhaps even dangerously, misguided the view that moral theory's respectability depends on its having such force. The legitimacy of moral theory rests, I believe, not on its explanatory, but on its justificatory, force. But that is an argument for another time.[24]

Notes

"Normative Explanations," by Geoffrey Sayre-McCord, appeared in *Philosophical Perspectives*, Vol. 6, *Ethics*, 1992, edited by James E. Tomberlin (copyright by Ridgeview Publishing Co., Atascadero, CA). Reprinted by permission of Ridgeview Publishing Company. Since the time of the Murphy Institute conference I've given versions of this chapter at the United States Air Force Academy, at West Virginia University, the University of Kansas, and at the University of St. Andrews, Scotland. Thanks are due to all five audiences. They are due also to Simon Blackburn, Walter Sinnott-Armstrong, Michael Resnik, David Resnik, Christopher Morris, and, especially, to David Braybrooke, for detailed comments on earlier drafts.

1. Quoted in John Morton Blum, *Woodrow Wilson* (Boston: Little, Brown, & Co., 1956), p. 159.

2. Of course moral rules constitute neither the whole nor even the major part of morality. I concentrate on rules for two reasons. The first is that moral rules appear to be disembodied in a way that makes them especially problematic. Thinking that the rules of justice might explain social change is, initially at least, much less plausible than thinking, for instance, that someone's being courageous might explain why she does what she does is. The second reason is occasion specific: the conference for which this paper was written revolved around the proposal that a logic of rules might contribute to explanations of social change. Two convictions guided the proposal: (i) that the social rules the logic could be used to represent themselves play a role in social change and (ii) that the rules of the logic could in turn help to explain why the social rules play the role they do. Both convictions presuppose that normative rules (whether normative social rules or normative rules of logic) can explain things that happen in the world.

3. Many of the normative rules I have in mind contrast as well with the sort of 'ought' judgments that resolve neatly and easily into empirical 'if-then' claims. For instance, unlike "the gasoline ought to have an octane rating of at least 92," which might well be cashed-out as "if the gasoline has a rating of less than 92, then the engine won't run without pinging," claims like, "You ought (legally) to drive under 65 mph" are less plausibly translated into non-normative 'if-then' substitutes. Others, though, for instance the requirements of practical rationality, seem at least to be candidates for such a reduction.

4. Even if, as I believe, there are some unrecognized and unenforced normative rules that apply to people and societies, it seems one could have no reason to ascribe a rule to a society as a rule of that society unless it was at least implicitly recognized and enforced. For a discussion of this point, see David Braybrooke, *Philosophy of Social Science* (Englewood Cliffs: Prentice-Hall, 1987), pp. 47–57.

5. See Geoffrey Brennan and James Buchanan, *The Reason of Rules* (Cambridge: Cambridge University Press, 1985).

6. It might be satisfying enough if normative rules could be shown to explain normative facts that are conceptually independent of the rules doing the explaining. Many, though, would hold that normative rules are doing real explanatory work only if they contribute to explanations of non-normative facts, for instance only if they helped to explain some of our perceptual experiences. Behind this more rigorous requirement is the conviction that an adequate epistemology must ground justification in sensation. See my "Moral Theory and Explanatory Impotence,"

Midwest Studies in Philosophy XII (Minneapolis: University of Minnesota Press, 1988), pp. 433–457, and Gilbert Harman, *Thought* (Princeton: Princeton University Press, 1973).

7. The underlying assumption here is that we have reason to believe only in those entities, properties, laws, and rules, that contribute to our best explanation of our experiences. See my "Moral Theory and Explanatory Impotence."

8. I sketch a version of (what might be called) 'conventional moral realism' in "Coherence and Models for Moral Theorizing," *Pacific Philosophical Quarterly*, Vol. 6, 1985, pp. 170–190.

9. See Jon Elster, *Ulysses and the Sirens* (Cambridge: Cambridge University Press, 1979) for a discussion of the difference between parametric and strategic choice.

10. I've concentrated in the examples on laws, but decision and game theoretic explanations seem to work too for many other normative rules, for instance those governing membership in trade unions, and the authority of umpires in baseball, as well as less institutionally enshrined rules of social organization. David K. Lewis, *Convention* (Cambridge, MA: Harvard University Press, 1969) sets out elegantly the general structure of game theoretic explanations for social conventions (among which are all sorts of conventionally established normative rules). See also Russell Hardin, *Collective Action* (Baltimore: Johns Hopkins University Press, 1982).

11. Each person "intends only his own gain, and he is in this, as in many other cases, led by an invisible hand to promote an end which was no part of his intention. Nor is it always the worse for the society that it was no part of it. By pursuing his own interest he frequently promotes that of society more effectually than when he really intends to promote it." Adam Smith, *The Wealth of Nations* (New York: P. F. Collier & Son, 1905), Book 4, Chapter 2, pp. 160–161.

12. See R. D. Luce and Howard Raiffa, *Games and Decisions* (New York: John Wiley & Sons, 1957); Alan Hamlin, *Ethics, Economics and the State* (New York: St. Martin's Press, 1986); David Gauthier, *Morals By Agreement* (Oxford: Oxford University Press, 1986); Richard Brandt, *A Theory of the Good and the Right* (Oxford: Oxford University Press, 1979); R. B. Perry, *General Theory of Value* (New York: Longmans, Green, and Co., 1926); Stephen Darwall, *Impartial Reason* (Ithaca: Cornell University Press, 1983); and Peter Railton, "Moral Realism," *Philosophical Review*, Vol. 95, 1986, pp. 163–207.

13. See Elster's *Making Sense of Marx* (Cambridge: Cambridge University Press, 1985), as well as his *Ulysses and the Sirens*, and Richard Miller, *Fact and Method* (Princeton: Princeton University Press, 1987).

14. While these claims are, I take it, quite uncontroversial, they have (not surprisingly) been controverted, standardly on the grounds that talk of beliefs (not just beliefs about rules) is a relic of an outmoded conceptual framework ill-suited to explanation. In what follows, though, I will take for granted that at least sometimes beliefs may legitimately explain.

15. Such a disposition might, sometimes, reasonably be thought of as a (perhaps subconscious) belief, but not always. We may legitimately suppose, of the case at hand, that the disposition of the officer finds its expression unmediated by her cognitive states (even though she would not have acquired the disposition in the first place had she not had various beliefs).

16. Something like this apparently underlies the refrain, 'No wonder you are hurting, what you did was stupid!,' the idea being that, even if you didn't know

that what you were doing was irrational, its having been irrational explains your pain.

17. This importance of a patterned history, when it comes to explaining by appeal to rules when the rules are not recognized by anyone involved, does mean that in these situations the rules cannot provide a single-shot explanation of particular events—they can explain a single event only by relying on a pattern of events that the rule explains. See Alan Garfinkel, *Forms of Explanation* (New Haven: Yale University Press, 1981); Miller, *Fact and Method;* and for a slightly less lenient view, Elster, *Ulysses and the Sirens.*

18. This counterfactual test goes hand-in-hand with the counterfactual analysis of causation. See David Lewis, "Causation," *Journal of Philosophy,* Vol. 70, 1973, pp. 556–567; and "Counterfactual Dependence and Time's Arrow," *Nous,* Vol. 13, 1979, pp. 455–476. See too my "Moral Theory and Explanatory Impotence"; and Nicholas Sturgeon, "Moral Explanations," in *Morality, Reason and Truth,* edited by David Copp and David Zimmerman (Totowa: Rowman and Allanheld, 1985), pp. 49–78.

19. Notice that the relevant counterfactual does not ask us to suppose merely that people believe it morally permissible to torture for amusement, but instead to suppose such a belief true.

20. Although what follows is limited to a discussion of moral theories and their potential explanatory force, the problems faced by moral theory are exactly paralleled by problems faced by any attempt to defend the explanatory force of a normative system of deontic logic.

21. This sort of view goes back at least to Jeremy Bentham, *Introduction to the Principles of Morals and Legislation,* (New York: Hafner, 1948). For variations on this general theory, along with defense of its explanatory value see Railton, "Moral Realism"; Richard Boyd, "How To Be A Moral Realist," in Geoffrey Sayre-McCord, ed., *Essays on Moral Realism* (Ithaca: Cornell University Press, 1988), pp. 181–228; David Brink, *Moral Realism and the Foundations of Ethics* (Cambridge: Cambridge University Press, 1989); and Brandt, *A Theory of the Good and the Right.*

22. This sort of view has its own obvious roots, most clearly in Thomas Hobbes, *Leviathan* (New York: Penguin Books, 1968). For variations on the general contractarian theme, see Gauthier, *Morals By Agreement,* and "Why Contractarianism?" (in Peter Vallentyne, ed. *Rational Choice and Moral Contractarianism,* Cambridge: Cambridge University Press, 1990); James Buchanan, *Limits of Liberty* (Chicago: The University of Chicago Press, 1975); and Gilbert Harman, "Justice and Moral Bargaining," *Social Philosophy and Policy,* Vol. 1, 1983, pp. 114–131.

23. There is plenty of conceptual space within the paradigms of utilitarianism and contractarianism to allow for other versions that eschew the sort of contact with the world that these theories maintain. The non-natural moral ontology advanced by Moore and Ross, for example, leaves completely mysterious the impact morality is supposed to have on the world. Retreating to the claim that it does so by affecting our moral beliefs via (a special sort of) intuition hardly dissipates the mystery. See G. E. Moore, *Principia Ethica* (Cambridge: Cambridge University Press, 1903) and W. D. Ross, *The Right and the Good* (Oxford: Oxford University Press, 1930).

24. It is an argument I have begun in "Moral Theory and Explanatory Impotence."

4

Rules and the Rationality of Scientific Cultures

Bryson Brown

Brown's paper makes the most straightforward sustained application in this collection of the Dalhousie logic of rules, and makes the application to a subject not illustrated in Track. There, among other things, rules about marriage, and changes in such rules, are treated. Track also treats rules and changes of rules about landed property; rules and changes of rules about the appropriation of the social surplus; rules and changes of rules relating the United States Constitution to the organization of political parties; rules and changes of rules arising in the development of clinical medicine; and rules and changes of rules at issue in the abolition of the British slave trade. Only the subject of clinical medicine (as another episode in the history of science) comes close to Brown's topic, which is the history of quantum physics in the first part of this century; and that is not very close, so Brown would in any case be making a significant extension in the range of applications for the logic. But he is also on the way to showing how the logic can help resolve some continually vexing questions in the history and philosophy of science.

In *Logic on the Track of Social Change* (hereafter called *Track*), David Braybrooke, Peter K. Schotch, and I have developed a view of social rules and applied it to some interesting examples drawn from social history.[1] In this paper I will sketch some ways in which this view of social rules may be applied to questions in the philosophy of science. These include questions about the relation between this rules-oriented approach and other approaches to the philosophy and sociology of science, questions about how issues such as the role of rationality in science look from this perspective, and challenging questions about methodology. I will address each of these in what follows. Though I cannot hope to settle them, I hope to do enough to make my own interest in this approach to philosophy of science understandable.

I'll begin by distinguishing two types of rule-systems in science, the first representing the commitments scientists make to ways of acquiring data, and the second representing their commitments to ways of interpreting and explaining that data. Then I turn to questions about goals, which play a central role in the concept of a rational rule system. This discussion will raise methodological questions, and questions about relations between my views and the views of some other philosophers and sociologists of science.

We have already described, in broad terms, how we may justify attributions of rules and systems of rules to social groups. In practice we rely principally on behavioral regularities: behavior that generally fits the rule, together with special patterns of behavior surrounding failures to obey the rule. There are also patterns in the training of new members of the social system: the rules imparted to scientists-in-training are sometimes explicitly written down, and sometimes subtly conveyed by the role-models they encounter in the course of training.

Though I won't address skeptical worries about rules here, our position is that skepticism about rules is entirely of a piece with skepticism about explanatory hypotheses in general. There are always alternative "regularities" which fit the observed phenomena and whose holding as rules would explain the phenomena. How we choose from amongst these the regularities we are prepared to project is a difficult question, but it is not in principle a harder question for those concerned with rules governing the behavior of agents than for someone studying gravity or electromagnetism.[2]

We regard the use of rules in explaining behavior as modeled on an ideal case of rule following, in which an agent does not perform any action of a type violating a rule because she consciously recognizes that the rule applies and that such actions would violate it. Of course there are uses of rules in explaining behavior which don't met this ideal standard, but we regard them as defensible only if they meet conditions strongly analogous to these: For instance the agent may not be consciously applying the rule (native speakers of a language are rarely conscious of the grammatical rules they follow in constructing sentences); or she may not take conscious note of the fact that the rules applies in her circumstances, but follow the rule anyway.

I'll consider the question of how we go about attributing rules (and goals) to a social system in more detail later in the paper. There I'll discuss how rules and goals may interact, and how goals may be distinguished from side effects of following rules.

Rules of Evidence

There are rules governing the use of apparatus, the recording of data, and the proper reporting of measurements. The rules I have in mind here are social norms guiding the acquisition of bodies of information which D.

Shapere has called "domains." For Shapere, a domain is a body of information about some believed-to-be related phenomena. Domains form the subject matter of scientific investigations. The scientists engaged in investigating a particular domain make epistemic commitments to the rules for acquiring data, accepting claims established in accord with them as additions to the domain of investigation.

Shapere's work on domains focuses on how scientists decide what phenomena are related to what, and what problems there are for our understanding of them. He provides a sort of taxonomy of domains turning on the structure of the body of information in question.[3] The system of rules which are norms for the practice of atomic spectroscopy include practical rules governing the use of the spectroscope, the optical theory which guides interpretation of the resulting spectroscopic lines as related to characteristic frequencies, and the chemical methods needed to prepare and identify samples. Atomic spectroscopy is a good example for my purposes, since it was well established as a body of highly precise, repeatable phenomena long before any theory explaining its remarkable features was available. As a result, the independence of the domain from the theory which accounts for it is particularly striking in this case.

The data we acquire by following these rules are, of course, not certain or infallible. When we state the results of our use of different apparatus and measuring techniques, we adopt a vocabulary which may reflect a substantial scientific theory, or a simple set of common-sense background assumptions. But in either case, the upshot of data acquisition is not a conceptually pure empirical "given." Nevertheless, such data function as a starting point for the processes of interpretation and explanation in science. The rules I will cite, from *Recommended Practices in Spectrophotometry*, are only a brief selection of the rich variety of rules governing the practice of acquiring data on atomic spectra. They are intended simply as illustrations, since they are recent rather than historical. And the rules we find in such manuals are, of course, incomplete: The process of being trained to use the apparatus includes skills that are difficult or impossible to convey except through hands-on teaching.[4] However, all I want to show here is that we can reasonably regard such rules as a central part of the scientific enterprise; for this purpose, they'll do fine.

Some Rules Governing the Proper Use of an Instrument

(a) One of the most important parameters the analyst must select is the spectral slit width. Many factors in instrument design influence the selection so that it is necessary for an analyst to determine the optimum slit width for a particular analysis and instrument.

(b) The optimum slit width will be determined by the spectral characteristics of the sample and the dispersion of the instrument used (ignoring variation among detectors). The narrowest slit width should be used that will yield an acceptable signal-to-noise ratio. Where instrument resolution is more than adequate, the signal-to-noise ratio is maximized.

(c) The analyst must evaluate the effect that slit width has upon resolution. The preferred manner of expressing resolution is in terms of spectral band width, but methods of measuring this quantity in all spectral regions are not presently available. Until such tests are developed, spectral slit width provides an expedient means of expressing resolution.[5]

There are four rules explicitly before us here. In section (a) above, we find that the analyst is required to select the slit width. In section (b), we find two rules governing that selection: "The narrowest slit width should be used that will yield an acceptable signal-to-noise ratio," and "Where instrument resolution is more than adequate, the signal-to-noise ratio is maximized." And in section (c) the analyst is told to express resolution in terms of spectral slit width, though it's recognized that if the means become available it would be preferable to express resolution in terms of spectral band width. These explicit rules are aimed at two main ends: correct setting of slit width, and correct reporting of the resulting resolution. But in fact a very rich group of related rules is involved here. The rules before us appeal in their formulation to other rules needed to settle what is an "acceptable" signal to noise ratio, and what constitutes "adequate" resolution. The "rule density" in this area—the number of interacting rules all bearing, directly or indirectly, on the agents in question—is very high indeed. What the rules require is that a routine be carried out by the analyst, setting the slit width in a way which satisfies the criteria laid down. This is the fourteenth of twenty-two such groups of rules and commentary, including rules governing terminology, the recording of relevant data, the form of a report, appropriate reference wavelengths, and many other procedural details.

The purposes of such standardization are several: To ensure mutual comprehension by specifying how terms are to be used and results reported, to ensure the reproducibility of results by establishing conventional procedures governing the details of an experiment, and to ensure maximal precision and accuracy of the data by carefully giving procedures which prevent, minimize, or allow compensation for typical types of errors (miscalibration, use of incorrect settings on the instrument, and misreadings, for example). But purposes or goals and their role in these scientific rule systems will be taken up in greater detail later on.

The rules of evidence specify the procedures and circumstances which warrant certain types of assertions. When a social group has adopted such a system of rules its members can communicate much more effectively than when each individual has her own standards, even if some alternative standards might be better (more efficient or more reliable). But a full discussion of these rules and their uses will have to wait; we will now turn to another family of rules, which govern the interpretation and explanation of data acquired by following the rules of evidence. This second sort of rules guides the application of theory(ies) to the problems posed by a particular domain. We'll consider, in particular, the rules developed by Niels Bohr to guide the use of his atomic theory. Rules are particularly salient in this case because Bohr's theory was internally inconsistent. As a result, Bohr had to specify rules showing how to apply the theory without falling into absurdity.

Rules for Interpretation and Explanation

In the early development of his theory Bohr clearly had most in mind evidence from dispersion experiments, and from studies of molecules. The role of the hydrogen spectrum, so central to both the first paper of his trilogy and to the wide acceptance of his theory, emerged very late in his thinking. Nevertheless the potential for this application of his theory was there, and once he had recognized it Bohr moved very swiftly to incorporate it into the series of papers he was preparing for the *Philosophical Magazine*. The main thrust of Bohr's thinking was to prevent the classical collapse of the Rutherford atom by restricting its states to some set of stationary states in a way analogous to the restrictions Planck's quantum hypothesis placed on the energy emitted by oscillating charged particles:

> The essential point in Planck's theory of radiation is that the energy radiation from an atomic system does not take place in the continuous way assumed in the ordinary electrodynamics, but that it, on the contrary, takes place in distinctly separated emissions, the amount of energy radiated out from an atomic vibrator of frequency v in a single emission being equal to nhv, where n is an entire number, and h is a universal constant.[6]

Bohr applied this to the Rutherford atom by means of the following hypotheses:

1) The dynamical equilibrium of the systems in the stationary states can be discussed by the help of the ordinary mechanics, while the passing of the systems between different stationary states cannot be treated on that basis.

2) That the latter process is followed by the emission of a homogeneous radiation, for which the relation between the frequency and the amount of energy emitted is the one given by Planck's theory.

Bohr postulates that atoms radiate only during transitions between stationary states. The classical description of the stationary states allows straightforward calculation of the energy each involves, based on the assumptions that the atom is formed from a nucleus and an electron originally unbound and not moving relative to each other, and that the quantization rule for the energy states can be arrived at by insisting that at the limit of large values for n the frequency of the radiation emitted corresponds to the frequency of revolution of the electron.[7]

This view provides a clear and simple account of the lines of the ordinary hydrogen spectrum, a promising start at one of the greatest ambitions of atomic theorists. Much to Bohr's disappointment, his theory was never successfully extended to atoms with more than one electron. Nevertheless, together with the rest of "Old Quantum Theory" (OQT), it played an important role in the eventual development of modern quantum mechanics.

Bohr's attempt to extend the Rutherford model turned on finding some way to get useful results out of a theory that clearly could not be treated conventionally. The standard tools of classical physics could not be freely employed because classical electrodynamics requires any electron orbiting a nucleus to radiate a (huge) amount of energy and finally collide with the nucleus itself. Bohr's great success was to specify rules determining when one could apply classical techniques, and which ones could be applied. When combined with quantization of the allowed stationary states, and hence of emitted and absorbed radiation, these rules produced, among other things, accurate predictions of the frequencies of light that would be emitted (or absorbed) when different transitions between energy levels occurred.

Bohr regarded his approach as a significant improvement over Planck, since he was able to give general rules restricting the application of classical principles and quantum constraints so that incompatible principles were never jointly applied. This made it possible to see how one might go about applying Bohr's theory more widely. By contrast, it was difficult at best to decide how Planck's approach worked (to say nothing of how it might be extended) once it was found that inconsistent principles had been used in the course of his derivation of the black-body radiation law.

Formal Versions of the Rules

The rules we have been considering can be straightforwardly expressed with the logical apparatus developed in *Track*. The rule requiring use of the narrowest slit width providing adequate signal-to-noise ratio, for instance, demands that in the course of preparing to acquire spectral data on a sample, the experimenter perform a routine which results in the slit width being correctly set. We could express this as follows:

F_e: **volk**(F_e)   = Exp(a)
    wenn(F_e) = ˜SlitSet & (∃r)**aft**(r)SlitSet
    nono(F_e)   = **aft**(r')˜SlitSet & [(∀r)**aft**(r)SlitSet → **Blocks** (r',r)]

Where Exp(a) is true iff a is an experimenter and SlitSet is true iff the slit width is properly set. A full account of the logic would lead us too far astray here; I'll merely explain the bits and pieces I apply as we go along. Here we use the **aft** operator to say that when an action of type r has been performed, the slit width is set. And we use **Blocks** to express an incompatibility between two action types, thus **Blocks**(r',r) is true iff once an action of type r' has been performed, an action of type r cannot be successfully completed. So this attempt to express the rule treats it as forbidding all routines incompatible with the experimenter's setting the slit width properly (when it can be so set in the first place)—in fact this is our standard treatment in *Track:* We treat all rules as forbidding; rules which we would intuitively describe as requiring some action type we regard as forbidding all action types incompatible with an action of the required type being performed. Note that I take setting the slit width properly to include not only setting it to the minimum width providing an adequate signal-to-noise ratio, but doing so before beginning to gather data. On this reading, beginning to gather data before having set the slit width in this way will be forbidden by this version of the rule; of course, a more explicit version of the rule could capture this directly. Perhaps more significantly for the purpose of studying the relation between this rule and others, we could make the conditions involved in Slit Set much more explicit.

Bohr's rule forbidding the use of classical mechanics in the description of transition states of the atom could be expressed in this way:

FB_1:   **volk**(FB_1) = a=a
    wenn(FB_1) = Trans(A)
    nono(FB_1) = AppClassMech(A,r)

Where Trans(A) iff A, an atom, is in a transition state, and AppClassMech iff r is an application of classical mechanics to the state of A. And the closely related rule blocking the application of classical electrodynamics (CED) to the atom's stationary states could be expressed this way:

FB_2:   **volk**(FB_2) = a=a
    wenn(FB_2) = Sta(A)
    nono(FB_2) = AppAccelCharge(A,r)

Where Sta(A) iff A is in a stationary state and AppAccelCharge (A,r) iff r is an application to A of the CED principle that accelerated charges radiate. A third rule links energy transitions to the emission of a quantum of light energy at a certain frequency:

FB_3:   **volk**(FB_3) $= a=a$
       wenn(FB_3) $= DescTrans(r,A)$
       nono(FB_3) $= IncludesRadChang(r') \rightarrow$ **Blocks**(r,r')

Where $DescTrans(r,A)$ iff r is a description of A making a transition between allowed quantum states, and $IncludesRadChange(r)$ iff r includes the required change in the classical radiation field around a, either adding energy E at frequency E/h if A has moved from a higher to lower energy state, or subtracting it if A has moved from a lower to a higher energy state, where E represents the potential energy difference between the two states, itself calculated using the classical mechanical description of the stationary states.

Expressing these rules formally has several advantages; to begin with, it raises questions of detail that might otherwise be missed. For example, it is really right to regard these rules as applying to everyone as we do when we set **volk** $= a = a$? And does FB_3 really capture the right requirement, or should it simply forbid any r such that $DesTrans(r)$ and $\sim$Includes RadChang(r)? Reformulated in this way, we would have FB_3':

FB_3': **volk**(FB_3') $= a = a$
       wenn(FB_3') $= DescTrans(r,A)$
       nono(FB_3') $= \sim IncludesRadChang(r)$

However, it seems that a description might fail to include the change (at least explicitly) simply by virtue of describing only the change of state of the atom without regard to the radiation field. This is the reason I've chosen the **Blocks** formulation for FB_3 here. Perhaps in this context contradicts would be nearer the mark: No DescTrans routine should express a description *logically* incompatible with the required changes in the classical radiation field. But consistency is a touchy subject in OQT; it's not clear that any description of a transition is strictly consistent with any description of a surrounding field of classical radiation, and **Blocks** seems otherwise close to the mark. We can reasonably hope that a (plain and direct) inconsistency between two descriptions will (at least often) lead giving one to block giving the other.

A further, and more important advantage of formalizing these rules is the way in which it invites refinement. These versions of the rules are clearly only rough outlines. Careful attention to the details of how these changes in the radiation field are to be made, of what (not much, in Bohr's theory) is involved in describing a transition, and so on would lead to much more sophisticated formulations. Moreover, the relations between these rules and the rest of the rules involved in old quantum theory deserve careful expression. It's in the context of a rich and intricate system of rules that these rules do their job, and a fuller understanding of these rules will require both greater detail in our account of them and a full exposition of the system of rules they work together with.

FB_1, FB_2, and FB_3 are rules for applying certain theoretical principles to the interpretation and explanation of atomic spectra (and other phenomena, as the growth of old quantum theory illustrates). They guided subsequent research in very useful directions: The link FB_3 makes between frequency of radiation and the potential energy difference between stationary states of the atom (or molecule) is a central insight into spectra which has been retained, and in fact widely extended, since. And the program of seeking conservation principles and harmonic relations between different states to explain "missing" transitions and the relative brightness of different spectral lines has also proved fruitful. The need for such rules is particularly apparent in the case of old quantum theory, since the theoretical principles involved were inconsistent with each other. Some systematic way had to be found to prevent these incompatible principles from being jointly applied to get absurd results.[8]

However, such rules are in fact always of importance in science, as T. S. Kuhn has emphasized. A theory conceived simply as a set of propositions closed under deduction is of little use to scientists without rules guiding its application to some domain. Kuhn has made much of this in his remarks on the role of paradigmatic applications of theories in scientific communities.[9] Though Kuhn has insisted that much of what is learned when these applications are studied is at best difficult to express, thinking in terms of social rules is at least a useful approach to capturing what can be expressed.

Kuhn's pessimism about the possibility of identifying a shared set of rules governing the practice of a scientific community is a major part of his argument for the central role of "paradigms." But much of what he has to say against a rules-oriented approach stems from his failure to find shared rules governing front-line research. This should hardly be surprising; front line research involves the extension of a theory's application to new phenomena and ranges of parameters. New rules will often be needed, and different researchers will no doubt pursue different extensions of the practices accepted for known terrain. None of this should raise doubts about the importance of shared applications of the rules in already established areas.

Perhaps another important source of Kuhn's pessimism is the difficulty of seeing clearly the ways in which rules can resemble and differ. Our formalism makes a helpful contribution to this enterprise, by providing a standard form in which to express the contents of rules. The idea of cultural universals, in particular of rules held in common between different groups or cultures has been much disputed, in part, we suggest, just because the vague understanding of rules and their contents has made it hard to see unambiguously the various ways in which a rule might be held in common despite variations in its details. In turn, hidden ambiguities in accounts of what rules or aspects of rules are held in common can give the impression that no coherent account of shared rules is possible—especially in the context of the problem we consider next. For example we can distinguish straightforwardly between a **core rule**, which is the minimal set of prohibitions held in common amongst rules identified in various cultures i.e., the rule as normally expressed together with every exception to it observed in any of the cultures, and a **shared exceptions rule**, which is the rule as normally expressed together with the minimal set of exceptions (if any) shared amongst all the cultures in question.

Conceptual incommensurability is a separate problem: If we accept a strong form of holism, and regard the very terms in which rules may be described as inseparable from the entire theoretical context in which the rules appear, at most purely formal similarities can exist between rules belonging to different theoretical contexts. However, such an extreme view is unattractive: rules get part of their content from the system of rules in which they play their roles, but only part. Another source of content is the circumstances in which the rules apply, and the actions and agents they constrain. A modern chemist could use the same laboratory procedure to produce oxygen as a phlogiston chemist would use to produce "dephlogisticated air." Though the two would describe what they were doing in different terms, each could recognize the other's actual laboratory practice as adequate to produce the substance whose nature they disagreed about. To at least this extent, we can borrow a term from computer science and say that the rules involved in science are *modular*, that is, they have enough independence to be recognizably preserved through changes in other, related rules.

Kuhn's account of how a paradigm guides research in the absence of a universally shared set of rules appeals to the Wittgensteinian notion of a "family resemblance." This notion gives up the aim of reducing concepts like "chair" to a set of necessary and sufficient conditions expressed in terms of simpler properties. Instead, it proposes that the application of such concepts is decided by something like a "weighted most" of the properties had by a central group of standard cases. But the analogy to this in our case would involve extensive sharing of (at least extensively similar) rules even between workers at the front lines.[10]

An interesting historical example here is the development of quantization rules in old quantum theory. At first separate quantization rules were developed for distinct applications, but in the end (with the aid of Ehrenfest's adiabatic principle) a general quantization rule covering all periodic systems was developed. Moreover, the rule emerged from the application of thermodynamics to quantum systems, which turned out to require that allowed states of quantum systems be adiabatically invariant, i.e. that an adiabatic transformation of a system in an allowed quantum state should result in the transformed system also being in an allowed state.

Kuhn's other major objection to a rules-oriented approach is that the rules often remain unarticulated, especially during periods of "normal science." But this is hardly grounds for believing that rules are unimportant in normal science. Quite the contrary. That rules are more in the air when a crisis arises is hardly surprising; when the accepted rules are no longer working, explicit discussion of the rules and how they might be changed becomes central to the immediate practice of scientists. But so long as the rules need little modification for scientists to pursue their careers, they may be left largely unarticulated: they are part of the background, not of the debate. One place to look for such rules would be in referee's comments on journal submissions: this is one context where articulating and applying the rules governing good research is central even when the rules are not in wide dispute.

Finally, I should mention that Kuhn's aim here, to a large extent, is to argue that much of what a scientist knows about how to go about doing science is known only implicitly. This I am quite happy to accept; much of her knowledge, explicit or implicit, may nevertheless be expressed in terms of rules.

Questions

There is a wide range of questions which arise in connection with this attempt to represent science, in part, by rules for acquiring, interpreting and explaining evidence. I plan to briefly address two of these: first, the question of what account of the rationality of science can be given in terms of this picture. And second, the question of how this picture of science relates to positions which have been held by others in the philosophy of science.

On Rules and Rationality in Science

Our account of the rationality of rule-systems turns on a certain match-up between the rules of the system and the social goals it is intended to serve. The question is, do the rules constrain the agents' actions in a way which leads the actions to contribute appropriately to achieving the goals? Showing that they do may involve appeal to circumstance: the rules may be such that they contribute to achieving the goal only conditionally. If the conditions for their doing so are in fact fulfilled, for the most part, this may be enough.

I should point out here that the relation between goals and the rationality of rule systems is not as straightforward as we might at first think. The simplest picture of this relationship would be to suppose that the goals are settled prior to the rules, and that the rationality of the rule-system is established by showing that it contributes to the achievement of the goals. However, once we allow that we may change our goals, adding new ones, or discarding former goals as unimportant in new circumstances, the possibility of much richer interactions between rule-systems and their goals arises.

A more general picture of how goals and rules interact in the development and justification of rule-systems could begin both with some goals and with some rules. The rules would be rules initially regarded as reasonable constraints on the sorts of actions in question; the goals, likewise, would be an initially plausible set of purposes for such actions. The evaluation of the rules and goals would then proceed. New goals may be adopted on various grounds: perhaps they are recognized as consequences of following certain rules, and taken to be desirable on that basis alone; more usually, as we identify the consequences of following rules, we may find that some of these not considered initially as goals are nevertheless clearly desirable. We may come to realize that goals we initially thought must be pursued in other, very different ways can be achieved by following the rules, or by following a slight modification of the rules. Further, some goals may be dropped, whether because we find them incompatible with other goals, or perhaps because we find they cannot be successfully pursued in the sort of rule system we are working with. Similarly, new rules may be adopted on the grounds that they will contribute (in the context of the other rules) to some established or proposed goals. And rules may be dropped because they are interfering either with other rules, or with achievement of some goals. Finally, shifts in the goals can in turn lead us to discard or modify some of the initial rules.

I doubt very much if this is an exhaustive list of the possible interactions between rules, goals, and changes in both which could motivate changes in either. But the richness of the possible interactions, and reactions to them, is clear. Some of these sorts of interactions may be discerned if we consider the development of the rules we've been discussing. Rules like F_e, and the system of rules it belongs to, develop through a rich interaction between the enterprise of gathering data and the goals of making that data as rich, detailed, accurate and repeatable as possible. F_e reflects a compromise between two ways in which spectral data can be improved: the higher the resolution, the more precisely spectral bands can be located, and distinguished one from another. But the narrower the slit width, the lower the signal-to-noise ratio, and the more difficult it will be to find the signal in the noise. So the rule is intended to balance these two, with an eye to obtaining the best possible data. Our theoretical rules, on the other hand, reflect first of all Bohr's need, in extending Rutherford's theory of the atom, to retain its crucial features, including especially a central, positively charged nucleus, while preventing the application of classical electrodynamics to the orbiting electron(s). Bohr aimed to provide a systematic basis for this, rather than simply avoid applications which gave rise to trouble.

As we have already noted above, at first Bohr did not consider applying his theory to spectral data. It was a late addition to his work on the series of papers which introduced his theory to the world. But once Bohr recognized that the stationary states he had introduced could be used to capture the extant empirical formulae for the hydrogen spectra via FB_3 he quickly made it a central part of the first paper. Thus here we see a goal not originally contemplated become a central goal for a rule system, which played a large role in guiding further development and application of the system and its successors.

The upshot of this approach is a rather more sophisticated understanding the rationality of rule systems. Instead of straightforwardly demanding that following the rules contribute to the achievement of antecedently specified goals, it seems we must speak of a kind of equilibrium between our commitments to goals and our commitments to rules.

The rules we have been considering can be regarded, as I have already assumed in our discussion of them, as aimed at certain goals. So far, I've mentioned the acquisition of detailed, accurate, repeatable data, and the interpretation and explanation of that data. These are recognizably *epistemic* goals. So if my attribution of these goals to the system is defensible, science will turn out to be not simply rational in an "ends-means" sense, but epistemically rational in the sense that the goals of the enterprise are epistemic (rather than practical, aesthetic, or moral). On this account, we could say that what makes science considered in terms of the sorts of rules we have been discussing epistemically rational is that the *function* of the rules is to serve the scientist's epistemic goals. And we have tentatively, and very broadly, characterized these goals as the acquisition, interpretation, and explanation of a certain body of information.

"Function" here is meant in the sense used by L. Wright:[11] The function of something is both an effect of it (having these rules brings it about that the scientists achieve certain epistemic goals), and a cause of it (scientists commit themselves to these rules because of the contribution they make to achieving their epistemic goals). This notion of function works for machines: The function of a push rod is to transmit power from the piston to the crankshaft because the presence of the push rod causes the power to be transmitted, and its transmitting that power is the reason for its presence. But it also works for biological adaptations: The function of a chameleon's color-changing ability is camouflage because camouflage is an effect of that ability and this effect is the reason chameleons as a species have the ability. In the scientific cases we have been considering, the rules do have functions in this sense: They have effects (the reliable gathering of repeatable, accurate data, for example) which are responsible for scientists' continued adherence to the rules.

Difficulties

There are some difficult methodological questions which come up at this point. On our account, the rationality of a system of rules may be evaluated with respect to some goals. Thus if we characterize the enterprise of science in terms of some goals—empirical strength and adequacy,[12] problem solving power,[13] or explanatory coherence[14]—we could evaluate the rationality of rules like those we have been examining by determining whether they helped scientists accomplish such goals, in the historical contexts in which they were accepted. This is of course the sort of approach to capturing the rationality of science that is typical in philosophy of science.

However, there is a prominent program—the self-styled "strong program"—in sociology of science which denies that science is rational in any special sense suitable for philosophical as opposed to sociological investigation. They argue their case on many grounds, and I haven't space to consider them all here. But one view which some among them have expressed cannot be put aside. This is the claim that the goals of scientists are not really epistemic at all, but social: thus Barry Barnes remarks that the scientist acts in pursuit of the social interests of his group,[15] and Paul Forman, in presenting his historical account of attitudes towards causation among German physicists during the Weimar Republic, also treats the goal of bringing science into line with social attitudes as important, if not paramount, among the motives leading German scientists to reject classical mechanics in favor of the development of quantum mechanics.[16]

Even if we can show that science is rational in the sense that the rules which scientists adopt (or the claims they accept) contribute to achieving certain epistemic goals, however characterized, there remains a serious difficulty. The advocates of the strong program in sociology of science agree that science may well be rational in something like this sense.[17] But they seem to regard this as more or less accidental. Suppose we can show that the rules we've been considering, and their like in other fields of science, really do contribute to achieving such goals. The question remains, is this the reason scientists adopt the rules they do? Or is this a matter of circumstance, or possibly even (in some cases) coincidence? If it's the latter, then the epistemic rationality of science as an enterprise is, in a sense, accidental. In certain circumstances, the rules which are adopted will contribute to achieving certain epistemic goals. But if the rules are not chosen because they contribute to achieving these goals, in other possible circumstances we would expect scientists to select rules that don't make any such contribution. Science isn't intrinsically epistemically rational on such an account; it is only occasionally, circumstantially rational.

To decide if epistemic rationality plays a really important role in science, we need to know whether scientists adopt the rules they do because they contribute to their epistemic goals, or because they have some other property (for example, contributing to the interests of a social group). How can we settle this sort of question? In general there will be many effects of following a set of rules. Some of these may be goals of the rule system, but others may just be circumstantial side effects of following the rules. How can we distinguish between goals and what we might call "pseudo-goals"?

One way to approach this question is by considering certain counterfactual claims. If we wish to decide what the real goals of an enterprise are, we might ask what rules would be adopted in different circumstances. In particular, we can inquire what rules would be adopted when these different proposed goals are in conflict. This very point is a weak link in many of the strong program's favorite historical examples. To mention one, the study of physics in the Weimar Republic is a case in which the rule "Pursue the interests of your social group!" and the rule "Pursue the best explanation of the phenomena you can develop!" turn out to agree on their recommendations. As a result this study's value to the strong program is limited. Without supplementary evidence of some kind, it cannot help to show that scientists typically pursue their social interests *rather than* epistemic goals.

Consider a situation which might have arisen around 1925: in it, the same broad social rejection of physics and especially of the causal principle that Forman speaks of is present. But quantum physics turns out to be perfectly tractable from a traditional mechanistic viewpoint. Do we have any reason to suppose that the goals of physicists would be affected by such a change in circumstances? It seems not: No new doctrine separating physics from the experimental evidence is suggested by the description of the situation thus far. Nor is any sort of incompatibility within the epistemic goals of physicists forced by the situation. If physicists were really following the fashion rather than pursuing the epistemic goals philosophers have regarded as central to science, it seems they would have adopted (or at least pursued) non-mechanistic theories despite this change in circumstances.

This suggests that what we have here is just the sort of situation that we need to consider when we ask if the goals of the scientists are the pursuit of their social interests (which, with Forman,[18] we will assume can be achieved by "blowing with the social wind"), or whether their goals are the epistemic goals of acquiring, interpreting, and explaining data about certain physical processes or phenomena.[19]

To decide what these scientists would have done in such a situation, we must examine several sorts of evidence. We must inquire into what scientists have done in other, actual cases where the socially expedient and the epistemically justified have been in conflict. We must inquire carefully into the circumstances in German physics around 1925, to see whether (and to what extent) they resemble circumstances in which scientists have made the socially expedient choice, or circumstances in which scientists have made the epistemically justified one. And we must do our best to gain some psychological insight into the motives and choices of the individual scientists. My reading of Bohr, to choose one prominent example, convinces me that despite his strong commitment to the peculiarities of the quantum theory, he would have quickly embraced a straightforward mechanical theory of atoms and spectra, had one been possible. In both his letters and his papers he seems exclusively concerned with the interpretation and explanation of the phenomena. And, though this (of course) can't prove conclusively that these were his only, or even his chief, aims, it constitutes at least prima-facie evidence about the goals he was actually pursuing while working on his theory. I have found no evidence that the social expediency of a rejection of causation had any weight in Bohr's thinking.

The situation is, I would predict, parallel with that of other principal figures involved in the development of quantum theory. It is well known that Einstein strongly resisted the surrender of a deterministic model of quantum phenomena. The continuing ferment over the interpretation of quantum mechanics suggests that the theory, with all its peculiarities, has been accepted *faute de mieux*, and not because of any desire on the part of scientists to fit their theory to some social imperative. Even the attempts to understand QM in terms of various forms of eastern mysticism emerged after its status as the only serious contender in its domain was established; their point seems to lie not in defending or justifying QM so much as trying to find some way to understand how (as Richard Feynman put it) "things can be like that."

Furthermore, of course, even if one scientist (or many) looked on quantum mechanics with favor because she saw it as politically or socially advantageous, this shows very little if anything about why quantum mechanics actually became the dominant approach to its subject matter. A real *investigation* of the way German science worked would be needed to show whether the success of quantum mechanics derived chiefly from its successes in systematizing the evidence of atomic spectra and other interesting phenomena, or from some social imperative linked to a broad cultural rejection of classical causation.

This provides us with a straightforward reply to the strong program's rejection of any special rationality in science. If scientists adopt the instruments and theories they do in order to further clearly epistemic goals, then science is rational in a special sense. This is perfectly compatible with a naturalistic conception of science, a chief concern of proponents of the strong program. And it does not prevent sociologists from studying any part of science. There may well be sociological reasons why scientists pursue the epistemic goals they do, and sociological constraints on the kinds of circumstances in which the rational investigation of the world characteristic of science is possible. Both are compatible with the assertion that the function of the rules adopted in science is to serve certain epistemic goals.

There is the alternative, for defenders of the strong program, that the reason why some commitment has certain "epistemic" properties has to do with its contribution to the social interests of scientists. But this is putting the cart before the horse. The social interests of a scientist, or a group of scientists, may often be advanced by their accepting rules or claims which are epistemically justified. But the reason this is so is not that "epistemically justified" mean "in our social interests"; it is because science as a social institution is deliberately set up to reward certain sorts of epistemic accomplishment. We can find historical situations in which the social interests of scientists would not be served by their adopting epistemically rational rules. It would be very odd at best to claim that in these circumstances it really was epistemically rational for scientists not to adopt the rules. Even if this claim were tempered with the remark that, "Of course, it was not epistemically rational relative to *our* standards of epistemic rationality," to do so would be to *assume* the very relativism which in fact needs to be justified here.

Philosophy of Science

There are many accounts in the philosophical literature of what the epistemic goals of science are: van Fraassen speaks of empirical strength and adequacy, Laudan of problem solving, Lakatos of progressive and degenerative research programs. The major novelty we are proposing is the notion that the practice of science is, in a very detailed way, replete with rules guiding the activities of scientists. The rules articulated by these and other philosophers as the "rules of the scientific game" operate at a different level: the level of distinguishing science (or for Laudan any rational cognitive enterprise) from other social systems.

I prefer to characterize science at that level in terms of its goals, rather than in terms of rules of the game, since the goals may be constant even while circumstances lead the rules by which they are sought to vary considerably. (Consider the evolution of thought on scientific method within science—it is clear that the rules by which scientists work are subject to change, but it seems possible nevertheless to regard the contribution the changing rules make to achieving certain broad, highly stable goals as their *raison d'être*.) There are rules at many different levels, and goals as well. In science there are low-level rules governing very concrete and specific procedures for the use of apparatus and the recording of data, which have as their goal the acquisition of precise and accurately repeatable data. F_e above and manuals for laboratory procedure in general are cases in point. And other rules like FB_3, aimed at the interpretation and explanation of that data, persist through significant shifts in theory. Yet the focus of philosophers of science has been on broader epistemic goals, and on methodological rules which are aimed at those broader goals.

Consider the difficulties raised by Kuhn, and others, about scientific progress through large scale theoretical change. The rationality of such change was brought into question by the surrender of the observational-theoretical distinction as it had been drawn by logical empiricists. Without that distinction, comparison of competing theories became difficult at best, since a shared basis of observations against which theories could be tested was no longer available. Worse, it was also argued that the relative importance of dealing with some phenomena could vary with one's theoretical commitments. But the rationality of scientific activity remains quite visible on the small scale we have focused on: high standards for accuracy and repeatability of experiments remain, backed by detailed rules for making and reporting observations—rules which made a Rowland grating a good instrument by the standards of all involved. And though the theoretical rules are in flux, the detailed evaluation of proposed theoretical innovations continues to appeal to successful predictions, formal elegance, and explanatory scope. There is considerable continuity here, especially as regards the rules of evidence. This does not solve the problem of large-scale progress in science. But it enriches our understanding of the basis of scientific rationality, and it may ultimately contribute to a more satisfactory view of how (and in what sense) science does manage to progress.

Rules like FB_3 are often very stable indeed. The link between the difference of energy levels involved in transition between two states and the frequency of light emitted or absorbed in the process has survived vast changes in theory since the early days of old quantum theory. This particular link is particularly important given the existence of reliable methods of spectroscopy, since it allows theories with different implications for energy levels and transitions to be tested against a stable source of evidence.

If I am right, these two perspectives are complementary. But we call for a shift of focus: Our account aims at reconstructing very concrete and specific rules of science as directed towards epistemic goals. From this point of view the search for general methodological principles of the sort "falsificationists" and "hypothetico-deductivists" have sought seems less important; the rationality of science need not depend on any such general scientific method. The important thing may be that the quotidian, detailed rules of a science contribute to its epistemic goals in the right way. The large scale, long term rationality of science may be the result of this sort of small scale rationality, combined with the modularity of rule systems, which helps us to repair the ship while still at sea. On this smaller scale the apparent discontinuities of large scale "revolutions" seem to resolve into a much more continuous process. The problem of incommensurability may turn out to have more to do with the scale at which philosophers have attempted to describe science than with any fundamental discontinuities in the practice of scientists. Only time and further work will reveal how small scale rationality and large scale rationality are related, and what contribution the examination of the sort of rules we have been discussing may make to long-standing problems in the philosophy of science.

Another view held by many philosophers of science I reject: this is the claim that the sociologist's subject matter in science is to be restricted to irrational episodes in the history of science. Laudan and Lakatos are two who have been very clear about this. Both regard science as the territory of philosophers first, who explain rational episodes in the history of science by appeal to epistemic criteria of rationality. Only what is left over when this enterprise has been carried out falls to the sociologist's lot to explain. In fact, on Lakatos' view the philosopher's job has been done best when the least possible remnant is left for the sociologist.

On my view this is simply a mistake. Though identifying and carefully describing epistemic goals is primarily a philosophical concern, the social system which pursues these goals is perfectly open to sociological investigation. There may, as we've already remarked, be conditions under which these goals would be given over for others, conditions necessary for the development of a social institution which pursues such goals, and conditions under which an individual will come to view such goals as important and worth pursuing, all of which are material for sociological investigation. But the epistemic rationality of science is not threatened by any of this. So long as the rules for acquiring data and interpreting and explaining it have epistemic goals as their primary function, such sociological explanations will only deepen our understanding of how we have come to have, in our own society, such a fascinating institution.

Conclusion

This approach to social rule systems offers a middle-way between two extreme positions on the roles of sociology and normative epistemology in our understanding of science. The "strong program" represents one of these

extremes; its devotees deny the relevance of epistemology to a proper understanding of science, and claim philosophers of science should turn over
the study of science to sociologists. The other extreme is represented by
those philosophers of science who have held that proper sociology of science is limited to explaining events in the history of science which cannot
be accounted for by appeal to the norms of a sound epistemology. On this
view, "sociology of science" is a misnomer, since real, sound scientific work
is beyond the purview of sociology. From our point of view sociology and
philosophy of science are complementary enterprises. Both play a role in
explaining what goes on in science because, on my view, a commitment to
the importance of rationality in understanding the scientific enterprise is
perfectly compatible with a thorough-going naturalism.

I propose a view of science in which rich and detailed systems of rules
take center stage: Rules guide the use of instruments, the presentation of
data, and the interpretation and explanation of the data. From this perspective, the epistemic rationality of science consists in the fact that the
function of these rules is to serve epistemic goals. The characterization of
epistemic goals, their relations, and so on is a part of the province of philosophy. So philosophy has a special contribution to make to our understanding of science—a contribution assisted by philosophical work such
as ours on a logic for specifying the contents of rules and accurately tracing
changes in them. But this does not conflict with sociologists' attempts to
describe science as a social institution in the same way sociologists would
describe any other social institution. A sophisticated understanding of epistemology is an important component in any satisfactory account of a social
system aimed at epistemic goals. But this does not imply either that normal sociological investigation of such a system is impossible or that it's
pointless.

Notes

1. David Braybrooke, Bryson Brown, and Peter K. Schotch, *Logic on the Track of
Social Change* (Oxford: Oxford University Press, 1995).

2. Our position here follows Hume's view on freedom and the predictability of
human behavior. See L. A. Selby-Bigge, ed., David Hume, *A Treatise on Human Nature* (Oxford, 1888), pp. 399–407.

3. D. Shapere, "Scientific Theories and their Domains," in Frederick Suppe, ed.
The Structure of Scientific Theories (Urbana: University of Illinois Press, 1977), pp.
518-565. This works reasonably well for relatively limited domains, such as the
systematic relations between different chemical elements reflected in Mendeleev's
periodic table. But in other cases, as in geology during the early and mid-nineteenth century, things are somewhat more difficult. What we find there is a gradual
process leading to a wide range of related criteria for interpreting formations, including well-settled methods of rock-taxonomy, identification of fossil assemblages

and their role in the development of a world-wide stratigraphy, the gradual development of chemical and other methods for determining under what conditions a particular sedimentary formation was laid down, and so on. When so many different sorts of information are involved in a domain (which today includes the results of several methods of radioactive dating, the use of microfossils, and paleomagnetic data, to name just a few), the sort of taxonomy which Shapere attempts becomes difficult, and less illuminating.

Shapere links his taxonomy of domains to a structural taxonomy of theories aimed at the different types of domain he distinguishes. But the hodgepodge of data and types of data we find in the historical sciences requires explanation by a historical narrative whose events (with help from a variety of very different theories) account for the wide range of very differently structured data we have acquired. The shapelessness of the domain can only be accommodated by giving the narrative with its multiple theories the central role.

Rules of evidence are associated with different experimental techniques and instruments. In a given domain, as Shapere says, the claims warranted by the rules of evidence are taken to be related to each other in at least the sense that we expect one theory to handle the puzzles and problems which the domain gives rise to.

One example of such a system of evidence is the study of atomic spectra. Investigators in the nineteenth century generally held that they should be explained in terms of some properties of atoms or molecules; however, though the evidence was acquired by well-settled laboratory techniques, and a great wealth of such evidence was available, there was (until the development of Bohr's atomic theory) no theoretical apparatus which could actually be applied to the interpretation and explanation of any of this spectral data. A. Schuster wrote of these difficulties, remarking "it would baffle the most skillful mathematician to solve the inverse problem and to find out the shape of a bell by means of the sounds which it is capable of sending out" (Cited in William McGucken, *Nineteenth Century Spectroscopy* (Baltimore: The Johns Hopkins University Press, 1969), pp. 125–6).

4. See Norman Mailer, *Of a Fire on the Moon* (New York: Little, Brown and Co., 1970) for a nice discussion of the related gap between the engineer's practical knowledge of the equipment she has worked on and what can be found in even the most complete technical manuals.

5. *Manual on Recommended Practices in Spectrophotometry* (Philadelphia: American Society for Testing and Materials, 1966), p. 23.

6. Bohr, "On the Constitution of Atoms and Molecules," *Philosophical Magazine,* Vol. 26 (6th Series), 1913, pp. 1–25, 476–502, 857–875, at p. 4.

7. Bohr, p. 7. Different attempts were made, during the development of old quantum theory:

a. to expand the rules (Sommerfeld and relativistic orbits)
b. to apply the rules as new phenomena emerge (spectroscopic studies)
c. to extend the rules (attempts at He)
d. to clarify/specify the rules (Bohr's attempts at clarifying the quantum restrictions, the central principles of the theory.)

So the system of rules is, of course, far from a static thing. Note also here how the extension of the rules is driven by the aim of bringing new experimental results under the interpretive/explanatory power of the theory.

8. Bohr's approach can be represented using the resources of non-adjunctive paraconsistent logics developed by P. K. Schotch and R. E. Jennings. Thus there is reason to believe that a real consequence relation is involved when such contextual restrictions on inference are imposed.

9. Thomas S. Kuhn, *The Structure of Scientific Revolutions*, 2nd ed. (Chicago: University of Chicago Press, 1972), pp. 43–51.

10. See the discussion of cultural universals in *Track* for a more extensive exploration of how rules in different cultures may resemble each other without being identical.

11. Larry Wright, "Functions," *Philosophical Review*, Vol. 82, 1973, pp. 139–168.

12. Bas van Fraassen, *The Scientific Image* (Oxford: Clarendon Press, 1980).

13. Larry Laudan, *Progress and its Problems* (Berkeley: University of California Press, 1977).

14. See, for example, Gilbert Harman, *Thought* (Princeton: Princeton University Press, 1973).

15. See, for instance, Barry Barnes, *Interests and the Growth of Knowledge* (London: Routledge and Kegan Paul, 1977), Chapter 3, where the "problem of imputation," i.e., the problem of how to capture the links between social interests and thoughts and beliefs, is raised as a central issue for sociology of knowledge. Here and elsewhere Barnes is clear that some such thesis is part of his program, though he is usually careful to avoid crude and over-direct formulations.

16. Paul Forman, "Weimar Culture, Causality and Quantum Theory," *Historical Studies in the Physical Sciences*, Vol. 3, 1971, pp. 1–116.

17. See David Bloor, *Knowledge and Social Imagery* (London: Routledge and Kegan Paul, 1976), p. 26.

18. Forman, "Weimar Culture, Causality and Quantum Theory."

19. Of course, there are circumstances in which many scientists have and will do the "socially expedient" thing, rather than what is epistemically justified. Galileo, under severe threats, avoided interpreting the phenomena of astronomy in Copernican terms, despite being clearly convinced that this was indeed the epistemically preferable way to do astronomy. And during Lysenko's political dominance of Soviet biology, few biologists dared to question the Lamarckian views defended by Lysenko. But these sorts of cases surely don't help the strong program's general thesis! I suppose it might be argued that Galileo was concerned to promote the social interests of some group which could benefit from the collapse of the traditional astronomical metaphor for the social order. But the burden of showing that this rather than epistemic concerns motivated Galileo seems a heavy one indeed!

5

Changes of Rules, Issue-Circumscription, and Issue-Processing

David Braybrooke

The logic of rules may be joined, as Braybrooke proceeds to show, with the logic of questions to treat deliberated changes in settled social rules in a perspective that gives special prominence to what he calls "issue-processing." He goes on to consider how far the same perspective, defined by the same combination of logics, can be used to track changes in rules that fall short in various degrees of being deliberated changes. If one accepts that it can be so used, the perspective can be identified with the perspective on changes of rules that can be ascribed to logicians and philosophers and as well to anthropologists and sociologists.

"Logic on the track of social change"—whatever success the Dalhousie project obtains under this banner, logic is not going to catch up with all forms of social change. Not all that happens in society falls under settled social rules. In the general population, whether to jog or not, indeed whether to exercise, does not; and the proportion of joggers in the population may rise or fall over time without coming under a rule old or new. Some will think—even though I have set no limit to the variety of behavior left outside rules—that this allowance for shortfall in the logic is far from being ample enough. They will hold that sustained deliberation is rare in human affairs; and that even when it does occur it is hardly ever deliberation that conforms to logical standards. I have a good deal of sympathy with this position. However, I think that the extent and frequency with which people behave in conformity with logical standards is a question for empirical investigation, which we would be unwise to try to decide a priori. It is, moreover, a question that can hardly be given a serious empirical investigation until we develop a logic suitable for tracking social change when and if it does conform to logic; and construct with this logic models of change with which we can compare in a great number of particular historical instances the real courses that change has taken.

Issue-processing is a way of characterizing by the joint use of the logic of questions and the logic of rules (here and now the hyperdeontic logic developed by the Dalhousie team) social change at the pole where deliberated choices are to be found, if they are found at all. The characterization can be usefully carried through—I cherish the belief that it was usefully carried through in my little book on traffic congestion[1]—in the face of a great deal of disorder in the social process of deliberation. In what we might define as logically complete debate, the participants, turn by turn, raise proposals and invoke arguments for them; and the other participants deal with all the proposals and answer all the arguments not their own; thus as the issue moves toward resolution, every participant is aware at every stage of every ingredient still current in the debate—every proposal outstanding; the arguments still pressed on its behalf; the distribution among the participants of favor for the various proposals and of opposition to them, and as well the distribution of conviction respecting the various arguments and of doubt. Thus when the issue is resolved, say by a majority voting to adopt a certain set of proposals, every participant, whether in the majority or in the minority, will have the same complete information about the track that the debate has taken. But we do not need to find logically complete debate, so defined, for an issue-processing model to be descriptive, for it can be asserted to apply as an idealized synopsis of the program of debate that the collectivity—the decision-making body—as a whole has followed: these were the proposals raised by these participants and debated by some others; those were the reasons that in the end prevailed, of those advanced by one participant or another; they were the reasons that favored the proposals adopted.

The sort of fit that subsists between the model and logically complete debate will come true, approximately at least, we may hypothesize, when we have a well-defined decision-making body in which participation has been continuous and which has been continually preoccupied with the same issue for a considerable period of time. This was the case with the debate over the abolition of the British part in the Atlantic slave trade that took place in Parliament between the passage in 1788 of the Slave Trade Regulating Act and the passage in 1807 of the act abolishing the trade.[2] In 1807— maybe well before 1807—a formula for abolition emerged neatly answering to all the considerations that in the end Parliament wanted attended to; and by that time Members of Parliament were fully acquainted with all these considerations and with others that had been rejected. In its final phase, therefore, the processing of this issue should bring up short anyone who lightly maintains that deliberation never follows a logical track and invite instead a decent respect for the logical powers of Parliament and its members.

The technical details of the issue-processing approach are simple. It takes over from the logic of questions[3] the distinction between "which" (better, "what") questions and "whether" questions; and uses the first category for issue-circumscription questions: e.g., "What shall we do to reduce or eliminate human suffering caused by the slave trade?" The second category of question embraces issues simpliciter: "Shall the conditions of transportation be healthier or shall the slaves be enabled to have family lives and enough leisure to raise children or shall importation of slaves from outside the West Indies be stopped or shall all trading in slaves be abolished pending general emancipation a quarter of a century hence?" Each of the proposals that figure in the disjunction of proposals that make up an issue simpliciter is there because it purports to make some headway with the problem raised by the corresponding issue-circumscription question. Hence the issue-circumscription question serves as a test of the relevance of proposals. Note that as presented the proposals that make up a given issue may not be mutually exclusive. It is logically easy to reformulate a set of such proposals so as to produce a set of mutually exclusive ones, which economists, decision-theorists, and social choice theorists usually assume;[4] but to do so is to take a step away from issue-processing as it is carried on in the real world.

What is the logical character, now not of the issue itself, but of the proposals that make up a given issue? Here the issue-processing approach brings in a logic of rules (here and now, the Dalhousie logic of rules) and identifies the formula of every proposal as the formula of a social rule (as I have done, taking "shall" in its imperative sense, in the example above). Thus the issue-processing approach treats the presence or absence of social rules as what is subject to change as a result of the debate. That is one role for the logic of rules. But the issue-processing approach gives the logic another role, that of formulating the rules that govern the processing and of showing how these rules come to bear in the rejection or selection of the rules proposed in the issues simpliciter. Rules governing processing are of two general types: rules of procedure, of which I shall say no more here; rules of higher order (invoked in the arguments of the participants) bearing on the character of the other rules. In the debate on the slave trade, one such rule (not accepted by every participant) was the rule that Christian morality prohibited trading in slaves; another was the rule that preventing British subjects from making use of their property was prohibited; a third was the rule that no measure which was both idle and expensive should be adopted—i.e., that every such measure was prohibited. The first of these rules combined, as it happened, with the second to produce a quandary in which it was both prohibited not to enact abolition of the slave trade and prohibited to enact it; and (at one stage) the first rule combined with the third to the same effect, a quandary produced by other means. No enactment could therefore occur until one or the other of the two last-mentioned rules was repudiated (the fate apparently, in this connection, of the rule about property) or ceased to apply (the fate, in this connection, after slave-traders of other powers had been swept from the ocean, of the rule about idle expenses).

Does the issue-processing approach give too much weight to rules? One way of at least mitigating the charge is to point out that the approach leaves a good deal of room for giving weight to costs. Costs enter in at least three ways. First, the issue-circumscription question may have come up because the costs of certain social practices had become intolerable—though if we are thinking of money costs alone, this is not a plausible assertion in the case of the issue about abolishing the slave trade. Second, some of the rules coming to bear upon the proposals may bring in cost considerations. In the debate over the slave trade, the prohibition against idle and expensive measures brought in cost considerations. In other debates, this would be done by a rule against incurring expenses exceeding the amount a budget had appropriated for dealing with the problem. Third, costs would come in as affecting the actual amount appropriated to carry out and enforce the proposals finally adopted. This is the stage at which the real commitment to the legislation is often tested.

I think we must take care not to reduce processing to a matter of costs, on the model of cost-benefit analysis. I say this without wishing to deny cost-benefit analysis an important role during processing, for example, in showing that of two proposals roughly equal in expected effectiveness one costs considerably less. But not only are some costs—like the cost of human suffering—hard, I would think, impossible, to measure in money terms; some convictions are not such as to be overborne by monetary compensation. Madison, we may reasonably suppose, would not for any amount of money have sold his mother into slavery or prostitution. We shift to a problem of a different character if we fantasize offering Madison a choice between selling his mother and a unique opportunity to relieve famine throughout the world. Even then he might well resist selling his mother; and people ordinarily act so far within the opportunity-cost horizon (all costs, money and otherwise) posed by either sort of problem that the hypothesis of their conduct's often being determined by rules which they adhere to seems secure.

At the other pole from deliberated social change there is the sort of change that occurs without any deliberation at all and maybe without any attention on the part of the people affected. The Dalhousie team, as it happens, has not worked up any examples of application that fall close to this pole, but I am not prepared to renounce the claims of the logic to tracking some changes in this region, too, and not only in the minimal (though still substantially useful) sense of supplying the means of formulating the rules in the status quo ante and for comparison the rules in the status quo post. Perhaps I can stake out a temporary claim by mentioning some trivial examples: the shift in the United States from the rule before World War II that an appropriate regular tip for a waiter was 10% of the bill to the rule that has prevailed since the War calling for 15%; the declining frequency among North Americans of the word "me" in what used to be distinguished as the accusative case by the expression "you and me" ("That will not affect you and me"); another linguistic example, the resurrection and spread in printed English of the word "albeit," which Doctor Leavis taught me to regard as no longer belonging in the vocabulary of anyone making fully sensitive use of the living language. The change in the rule prescribing tips was something that the people affected, person by person, were aware of; but it was not subject to any collective decision. In the two linguistic examples, there was no collective decision; nor were the people who adopted the changes aware of what they were doing (that was just Leavis's point). But in all of these cases there was, we may suppose, a period in which an old rule and a new rule were in conflict; and a higher-order rule (such as "Conform to the local practice") may have played a part in resolving the conflict, so far as it has been resolved.

Some further strength can be drawn for the claim to the region of non-deliberation from the applicability of the logic to cases that we can find on the way as we move from pole to pole. Why should we suppose, as we treat one case succeeding another with success, that the way will be blocked before we get to the end? Even in cases near to the pole of deliberated changes we may suspect the operation of non-deliberating processes in a penumbra surrounding the debate. I said that the formula of abolition adopted in the Act of 1807 neatly answered to all the outstanding considerations that Parliament wanted attended to; but this may be true only for the considerations that MP's then had in mind as outstanding, not for all the considerations, some of them still unanswered, that had been brought up in the preceding debate and remained logically relevant. In the 1790s rules about respecting the property of slave holders and allowing them to make use of it if compensation was not to be paid to them in view of the difficulties that abolition would create for them had stood, according to one close student's account (namely, Porter's[5]), as the chief barriers to abolition. Porter mentions nothing that reduced their relevance; so, logically (by his account), they were still outstanding in 1807; but evidently they were ignored, a fact that Porter does not notice or explain. I suspect the explanation has something to do with the transformation in Parliament's eyes of the British West Indies from the source of imperial wealth that they still seemed in the 1790s to the economic basket cases that they had apparently become after 1800. I suspect, too, that there were rules at work— perhaps rather ignoble rules, which MP's did not desire to acknowledge adhering to, rules that called for ignoring the property rights of people who were now supplicants for charity rather than sources of revenue for the Crown; but these are matters that have yet to be brought to light.

Cases in which rules are adopted after some deliberation, but have unintended consequences, cases which we meet farther on the way from pole to pole, supply further examples of non-deliberated processes affecting changes in rules and yet lending themselves to some extent to tracking by the logic. Recall the Ruthenians, who lived successively under Polish, Russian, and was it Hungarian? rule, hence under several different regimes, with different religious practices. I once read that they adopted all the holidays observed under each successive regime, and kept them up after the regime changed, with the consequence that they did not have enough working days left to get the crops in. Perhaps it was one of their lesser difficulties that this put them in a position of having to choose between conforming to the rule of celebrating this or that saint's day and conforming to other rules dealing with the support of their families or with paying taxes. Again, in societies, of which I seem to recollect Ireland for some time was one, where the rule of inheritance was to divide a peasant's holdings equally among his sons, after a while this led to some peasants' not having enough land to subsist on; but long before they began to starve, they must have been in difficulties about conforming to all the other rules bearing upon them. Changes in the rules effectively in force would have occurred before the problem got legislative attention: the rules prescribing the payment of tithes might have been the first to go, followed after a time by rules about taxes.

Another, even more spectacular example, this time from the present century, can be found in the attempt to impose Prohibition upon the American population, drinking or not. Among the unintended consequences of adopting this rule was not only (it has been asserted) some general weakening in respect for laws and law-enforcement, but also the entrenchment of organized crime on a large scale, with the lapse, at least for significant periods of time, of serious attempts in many jurisdictions to enforce various rules. Those rules then fell—without deliberation in the rule-making bodies—into abeyance. Moreover, in their place grew up a system of rules informally licensing various sorts of corruption and assigning the licenses to various groups, but keeping any of them from going so far as to create public clamor or disorder.

In one, maybe more than one, of the cases worked up by the Dalhousie team as an application of the logic, our inevitable reliance on specific historical works, which already have imposed a scheme of intellectual order upon the primary data, may have led to an ambiguous result. Is the logical story that we have arrived at the story of a deliberative process or of a non-deliberative one? Consider, for example, the attempt of the French revolutionaries to abolish hospitals and faculties of medicine. Following Foucault,[6] we have portrayed this attempt as running up immediately against a rule of protecting the public against substandard medical practice and thus creating a quandary that was resolved only by keeping the hospitals, to be sure under a different plan and in a different relation to medical research and medical teaching. But was the collision clear to the people involved much before the crisis came to an end in this form of resolution? Was there a rule against substandard medical practice (distinguished in the public mind from the licensing provisions upheld by the *ancien régime*) going into the crisis, or was the rule called into being during the crisis as a means of bringing it to an end? I am not reporting a failure in the application of the logic. Further historical research should be able to disambiguate the logical story, and show how far it represents a deliberative process, how far a non-deliberative one. The logic applies either way; and the ambiguity is a question that the logic usefully poses to historians, as well as a piece of evidence that the logic can track non-deliberative processes.

Not all unintended consequences are distressful. Some of them create, not crises about rules, but solutions or part-solutions for long-standing difficulties. Such is the case, on Lawrence Stone's account, with the Hardwicke matrimonial act of the mid-18th Century.[7] The Act, which sharply reduced the opportunities for elopement and a marriage ceremony unauthorized by parents, looked on the face of it a reassertion of parental control over the choice of marriage-partners. The actual effect, however, was to allow young people in the propertied classes much more freedom of association with each other (since parents no longer had to fear elopements); and this in turn encouraged the young people to assert choices of partners. Having more eligible partners in view, there was more chance of finding one without having to resort to a veto on either the children's or the parents' side. Thus here we have, in the sequel to the deliberated act, if we put the sequel in the perspective of the long conflict about children's freedom to choose their marriage-partners, a non-deliberative process proceeding toward resolution, in a way that the logical tracking makes clear.

Closer yet to the pole of non-deliberated processes we shall find cases in which rules change by the accumulation of exceptions, exceptions of a sort that first strike people as deviations from a standing rule, yet after a while—maybe only after some generations, but sometimes more quickly—become accepted on all sides as normal, with the implication that the former rule has vanished. To my earlier examples of tipping and of two points of linguistic usage I would now add a more substantial example: how it has become respectable to live in sin. Forty years ago it was almost unheard-of in respectable American families for their children to live with members of the opposite sex openly and continuously without being married. Now it is taken for granted, and even approved as a useful experiment preceding marriage, as it often turns out to be.

What accounts for this change? People will say, "The Pill," but that answer, though it no doubt has a part to play, overlooks both the existence before the Pill of other effective and tolerably convenient methods of birth control; and overlooks, too, the change implied in the present ready acceptance of the practice of prescribing the Pill. It was a big deal for one of Mary McCarthy's Vassar graduates, a woman, unmarried but making her way as an independent adult in New York City, to go to be fitted with a diaphragm.[8] Changes in rules, occurring by the accumulation of exceptions, are an indispensable part of the explanation. In particular, the rule against bearing children out of wedlock has waned (waned now to the point of its now being respectable for women to choose to bear children on their own). This, historically, was one of the main grounds for the rule against fornicating (to use a word that has become more archaic even than "albeit") even casually, and through the rule against fornication of the rule against living in sin. Jean Fourastié, who has written illuminatingly of the connections between traditional morality and economic circumstances, has given a telling account of how crucial it was in French villages right up to the latter part of the 19th Century to make sure that every child who came into the world came with a man and woman assigned the responsibility to bring it up.[9] The assumption was that resources were and always would be stretched thin.

There are more resources to spare nowadays, in France and elsewhere. Is the waning of the rule against bearing children out of wedlock to be given a wholly economic explanation? But the rule survived for several generations after resources had become more abundant. Moreover, another factor in the waning, one might argue, has been the widespread decline in religious belief and practice, and, for most people, with it, any vivid idea of sin. Has this decline, too, an economic explanation? I would not deny an economic explanation some part. Perhaps several economic explanations can play a part, among them one that cites economic insecurity as an important condition for having the fears reflected in a sense of sinfulness, though this would be as much a psychological explanation as an economic one.

However this may be, it should be clear that a logic of rules has a claim—a well-nigh inexorable claim—to giving kinematical accounts, that is to say, accounts that trace the path of changes like these, near the pole of non-deliberated processes. With the logic the accounts can show both what alternatives were considered at each juncture and some of the alternatives that were ignored; what relations these alternatives had to one another; and how they related to more general considerations, including higher-order rules. For reasons already given, furthermore, I think that it is implausible to suppose that conforming to rules can be reduced to a matter of costs; and if that it is true, it will be hard to deny that the rules that the logic treats also act not merely as signs of costs, but as dynamic causes of change, pushing for more or less rapid change along one or another of the paths that the kinematic accounts are prepared to trace.

Notes

1. *Traffic Congestion Goes Through the Issue-Machine* (London: Routledge, 1974).

2. In an elaborate application of the logic of rules, treated in the Dalhousie book (*Track*, Chap. 10), following the accounts by David Brion Davis in *Slavery and Human Progress* (New York: Oxford University Press, 1984) and Dale H. Porter, *The Abolition of the Slave Trade in England, 1784–1807* (Hamden, CT: Archon Books, 1970).

3. As set forth in Nuel D. Belnap, Jr., and Thomas B. Steel, Jr., *The Logic of Questions and Answers* (New Haven: Yale University Press, 1976).

4. See, for example, the article on "Political Evaluation" by Brian Barry and Douglas Rae in Fred Greenstein and Nelson Polsby, eds., *A Handbook of Political Science* (Reading, Mass.: Addison-Wesley, 1975), Vol. I, pp. 337–401; and Kenneth Arrow, *Social Choice and Individual Values, 2d ed.* (New York: Wiley, 1963), p. 12.

5. See note 2.

6. Michel Foucault, *La naissance de la clinique* (Paris: Presses Universitaires de France, 1963) [English translation by A. M. Sheridan, *The Birth of the Clinic* (London: Tavistock Publications, 1973)], treated in *Track*, Chapter 8.

7. Lawrence Stone, *The Family, Sex and Marriage in England 1500–1800* (New York: Harper & Row, 1977), p. 35. I am indebted to my research assistant Elizabeth Harper for a substantial correction of my text at this point.

8. Mary McCarthy, *The Group* (New York: Harcourt Brace Jovanovich, 1954).

9. *Essais de morale prospective* (Paris: Editions Gonthier, 1966), pp. 16–17.

6

The Nature of Customary Law in the Manor Courts of Medieval England

Lloyd Bonfield

Was there issue-processing in the manorial courts of medieval England? At first sight, Bonfield seems to be holding that there was deliberation, but it was not deliberation about what rules to apply to individual cases or what rules to adopt for application, but rather a sort of oscillation between ad hoc remedies for particular cases. If so, what he is describing represents a sort of zero-stage both of the application of rules and of changes of rules through issue-processing. Certainly we should not take it for granted that we shall have application of rules or issue-processing wherever we have deliberation.

Lawyers and historians have given little consideration to the internal dynamics of the manor court as a forum in which private matters between villeins were settled as distinct from an institution in which seigniorial interest was enforced. In the absence of such studies, and in the absence of concentrated attention to the legal nature of customary law, rather "modern" notions of the operation of the customary legal system (based on a number of what a legal theorist might call *jurisprudential assumptions* or more simply principles that governed the resolution of civil—that is, inter-peasant—disputes in the manor court) have been inferred.

The purpose of this essay is to articulate and then test these assumptions. We shall construct a model derived from my perception (as a lawyer) of what must be historians' conception of the nature of customary law as it governed inter-peasant disputes (if litigation recorded in the court rolls can be used as a measure of cultural norms).[1] To test the viability of these assumptions, we shall apply them to a particular debate: the controversy over the nature of peasant marriage in medieval England. Finding these jurisprudential assumptions unfulfilled, I shall tentatively offer an alternative hypothesis on the operation of the customary legal system and liken it tentatively to a modern alternative dispute resolution forum. Before embarking upon our discussion of customary law, I should like to set out the framework that the debate over the legal nature of customary law has assumed.

The Function of the Manor Court

Some consideration of the function of the manor court must precede a discussion of litigation therein. This is not a straightforward task. The manor court was a curious institution for a number of reasons. In the first place, the word *court*, in its modern sense, is a somewhat misleading term, for the tribunal's function greatly exceeded that of its judicial role. The manor court directed the affairs of those subject to its jurisdiction to a far greater extent than a modern court. It established and enforced village by-laws, elected local officials, enquired into disturbances of public order, resolved disputes between villeins, and performed the function that historians regard as its *raison d'être*: the monitoring of payment of fines and the performance services owed to the lord. A second peculiarity of this court, and perhaps a more significant one, was that those subject to its jurisdiction were in a rather awkward legal position, because common law regarded them as property of the lord whose steward presided over court proceedings.[2]

It is no surprise then that the primary area of debate regarding the nature of law in the manor court has been focused around a single question posed before the turn of this century by F. W. Maitland, when he edited a volume entitled *Select Pleas in Manorial and other Seigniorial Courts*: "How far was 'the will of the lord' tempered or controlled by 'the custom of the manor'"?[3] Maitland's very preliminary investigation into manorial records led him to conclude: "It is a true jurisdiction, an administration of the custom of the manor; it is no mere exhibition of the will of the lord who is the owner of villein tenements and the owner of the villeins—no decent lord treats it as such."[4] Maitland, in a fashion uncharacteristic for him, failed to bring forward evidence to substantiate his position. He neither attempted to document the restraint that "decent lords" exhibited, nor did he estimate a seigniorial "decency ratio" (the percentage of lords who treated the system of customary law as a limitation on their ability to exact services from their villeins). Since Maitland's book, many more court rolls have been examined in detail. While some scholars have broadly supported Maitland's position and have marvelled at seigniorial self-restraint,[5] others, less convinced, point instead to the economic balance between lord and peasant which ebbed and flowed in the course of the later middle ages as the factor that mediated the relationship.[6]

The extent to which the lord was able to control the process of establishing the burdens of villeinage is a crucial component in understanding the structure of medieval English rural society. The manorial court rolls are an important source to gauge the relationship, yet they are difficult to use, and the opaqueness of the record produced further fuels the controversy. An eldest son inherits according to the custom of the manor; the widow enjoys her free bench (customary law's equivalent to common law dower) according to the custom of the manor; the customary tenants, refusing to convey the lord's millstone for repair, deny that such transport at their own expense is in accordance with the custom of the manor.[7] What shall we make of these references to custom? Does custom limit or control seigniorial action? If so, how are its principles deduced, or is the phrase "according to the custom of the manor" merely a formalistic legal convention dutifully parroted by the scribe? Likewise, how comprehensive is customary law? When, as in the case of the transportation of the millstone, the customals are searched, and no authority is found, does the lord have his way? Does the decision make custom?

Unfortunately, it is easier to pose questions regarding the workings of the manor court than it is to answer them. The insight into the relationship between lord and peasant gleaned from the records in large measure supports Maitland's view. To ponder the extent of seigniorial control we must isolate areas of relations that have a legal component and in which the lord has an interest (for example, carting the millstone) from areas of supervision and administration (for example, land transfer and inheritance). While lords may have wanted to monitor the latter realm to insure the payment of heriots and entry fines, the exact rule of succession or the quantity of land constituting free bench did not have a direct impact on incidences of lordship. Indeed, extant customals dealt mostly with villein obligations; they were largely written recitations that set out in some detail the services required of villeins.[8] While the lord may have established the quantity and type of service owed, the mere fact that obligations were committed to record suggests some limitation upon seigniorial ability to extend them arbitrarily. Moreover, evidence exists to suggest that the breadth of customary service was at times challenged by villeins. Take, for example the following case:[9]

> It is noted that the customaries of Bury withdraw and do not plough, and have not given when they ought, the accustomed ploughing services owed to the lord, namely one ploughing service on a Friday or Wednesday or every week. At the same time these same customaries plough their own land or even land of others, and for this ploughing of outsiders they are paid in cash. However, these customaries expressly state that they are not obliged to perform any ploughing services for this same lord once their own land has been completely ploughed. A day is arranged for them to discuss this matter with the lord and his officials, namely the next Sunday after the feast of Saint Lucy the Virgin at Ramsey, at which time all are obliged to appear there under penalty of one-half mark.

Indeed, lords themselves may have recognized that written record provided protection. In the summer of 1408, a petition was sent to the Bishop
of Chichester, lord of the manor of Amberley in Sussex, by nine of his customary tenants asking that they be relieved of the obligation of building a
new hay loft because they were burdened[10] "with so many other costs and
charges that they have not the power among them to complete the building. ..."

The Bishop granted the petition; but it was noted on the reverse that
relief was granted "on condition that it shall not serve as a precedent in
time to come." That the Bishop felt compelled to protect himself against
his concession having the enduring effect of extinguishing an element of
customary service suggests a limitation in seigniorial power (if services
could be arbitrarily imposed why be concerned with the implications of a
release?); and the reference to "precedent" likewise implies some notion of
a regularized system of governing and binding the legal relations between
lord and villein.

This point cannot be pursued far on the basis of scattered references,
and I do not mean to suggest that equality of bargaining power existed
between lord and villein. There is evidence of a legal order that established
obligations in the realm of seigniorial relations and recognized procedures
for adjudicating differences regarding them, yet can this conception of
manorial court jurisprudence be translated to the civil side of manorial
court jurisdiction? Even if the extent of seigniorial power was limited by a
notion of law—no doubt hazy but still recognizable to the modern lawyer—it does not necessarily follow that the manorial court took a similar
legalistic approach to resolving relationships among peasants, as has been
assumed by medieval historians who wish to use decisions of the manor
court as indices of cultural norms.

Caution is advisable here. It is important to recall the nature of the manor
court and its multifarious functions. The bulk of the manor court's business did not relate to disputes at all. As Maitland, the legal historian, remarked, court rolls are basically economic documents; the primary purpose of the court was to regulate an agrarian economic system.[11] A large
proportion of court business was concerned with the recording of transfers
of villein land. "Civil" litigation revolved around disputed inheritances
and unfulfilled personal obligations (debt and contract). In these cases,
substantive law of a complex nature was often absent.

Take for example the common situation of litigation over maintenance
agreements. Elaine Clark has drawn attention to the frequency with which
villeins entered into a contract so that the land of an aged peasant could be
conveyed to his child, a relative, or a stranger in return for maintenance at
a prescribed level. The terms of this early form of retirement or "social
security" as she has termed it were recorded in the manor court rolls.[12]

There is evidence that some individuals failed to adhere to the arrangements recorded (at least to the satisfaction of the retiree), and the retiree brought the defaulting party to the manor court. In such cases, however, the dispute did not actually turn upon issues of law. Whether an individual adhered to a maintenance agreement, for example, was an issue of fact. The court rolls would have had to have been searched to find the terms of the arrangement, and the evidence of performance assessed. It remains uncertain exactly how the forum determined these issues of fact; perhaps the homage (a jury of the lord's tenants) was presumed to have personal knowledge regarding the transaction or possessed the means to obtain it. Because of the unsophisticated system of pleading, it is difficult to ascertain either the facts in detail or the considerations directing the resolution of a case. As S.F.C. Milsom has noted in discussing legal evolution in the royal courts, substantive law is forged through a detailed consideration of facts.[13] In England, this movement occurred as the system of pleading matured; a similar development appears to have been absent in manorial courts.

Finally, it is difficult to ascertain the extent to which manor courts were governed by what may be thought of today as extralegal factors in reaching a decision, for example, on equitable concerns arising from the circumstances of a particular case. It must be remembered that inter-peasant disputes arose within a community in which the decision-making body possessed a wide array of knowledge about the character of the litigants and perhaps even the issue in controversy. These factors, particular to civil cases, suggest a very different legal context from the one that obtained in matters concerning the lord. Medieval historians, I would argue, seem to ignore external factors and use disputes in the court rolls between peasants as if they were dealing with cases in a modern legal system that attempts to separate relevant facts bearing on the dispute from those deemed, at least at law, immaterial. It is to an analysis of their assumptions that we may now turn.

The Assumptions Underlying Manor Court Practice

Above it has been argued that little attention has been devoted to the legal nature of the customary court in so far as it settled disputes between individuals.[14] Historians have been preoccupied with discerning the nature of customary law as it regulated the relations between lord and villein. Their conclusions have been carried over to the civil side with historians assuming that manor courts adjudicated disputes between peasants in a similar, adversarial fashion. In this section, I shall play the role of a legal theorist by positing three jurisprudential assumptions that must have been elements of manor court practice if principled adjudication obtained, thus enabling historians to use the resolution of cases to distill rules of law reflective of cultural norms.

Three interrelated premises inform their analysis. First, in attempting to extrapolate cultural norms from resolutions of disputes in the court rolls, historians have, consciously or otherwise, assumed that conflict was adjudicated in the manor court through the articulation of what modern lawyers would call principles of substantive law and that the application of some of these principles created rights in a modern sense. Using the debate regarding marriage formation (which I shall elaborate upon later in my discussion) as an example, it has been suggested that for purposes of inheritance customary law recognized that trothplight (an out-of-church but nevertheless ceremonial exchange of promises to marry) rather than actual church solemnization created a marriage; that is to say, a child born after trothplight but before church solemnization was considered legitimate and therefore had a right of inheritance as heir in areas of primogeniture (or partible inheritance), a position contrary to common law.[15]

Likewise implicit in the historians' use of the resolution of particular court roll cases must be a second assumption; that manor courts were governed by a notion of precedent; that is, similar cases were evaluated by similar reasoning with similar decisions. In short, rules of customary law were either immutable or altered through some legally recognized manner. The finding that the seigniorial courts operated in such a fashion might startle historians of common law, because it would mean that manor courts had adopted the concept of precedent centuries before that of the royal courts.[16] Moreover, because manor courts were local courts, the recognition of rules would have to have superseded jurisdictional boundaries, because those historians who use cases resolved in individual manor courts tend to argue they are indicative of national norms.

Finally, historians assume *due process* (of the substantive variety to be technically correct) and *equal protection* existed; that is to say, the decisions reflect a proper application of customary law regardless of the status of the parties involved and the equities of the dispute.[17] In my marriage example, the first-born inherits regardless of extraneous factors like the respective positions of power in the community between himself and his brother; only if there was a recognized, applicable exception to the rule of substantive law would the general principle not be applied.

The resolution of disputes can provide evidence of cultural norms only if these three assumptions in large measure control dispute resolution in the manor courts. With some or all of them lacking, the resolution of disputes would not be the result of principled adjudication. Decisionmaking would not exhibit the requisite regularity to use law as a barometer of values, and the window into medieval society framed by the manor court would appear rather more opaque than some historians are willing concede. The problems that plague the quantitative studies would pale in comparison to the qualitative. Let us now turn legal theory into legal history, and scrutinize this model in the context of a current debate over the use of court rolls to understand the nature of peasant marriage.

The Debate over the Nature of Peasant Marriage

Perhaps the most lively debate utilizing evidence derived from manor court rolls to draw inferences regarding customary norms is in the realm of the nature of peasant marriage. A recent thoughtful article by Richard Smith entitled "Marriage Processes in the English Past," takes issue with a particular characterization of peasant marriage and offers a counter-hypothesis. Smith argues that the depiction of popular marriage as informal by a number of medieval historians, in particular R. H. Hilton and Zvi Razi, who arrive at their conclusion in part through the marshalling of court roll evidence, does not accord with Alexandrine reforms in the area of marriage formation.[18] Simply stated, the rules that Pope Alexander III established through the issuance of a series of decretal letters in the late twelfth century held that words of present consent to marriage, or alternatively words of future consent followed by sexual relations were sufficient to create a valid marriage; solemnization at the church door was unnecessary.[19] Smith believes that these rules were implemented by the church courts and accepted by the peasantry; this conjunction of church law and peasant cultural norms brought a great amount of certainty to the process of marriage formation. Further, Smith disputes the interpretation of evidence from manor court rolls that substantiate a view of the informality of peasant marriage, in particular, cases of *lyrewite* (fornication) or *childwite* (bastard bearing).[20]

Our interest in the debate is not so much in resolving the dilemma of the nature of peasant marriage, as in using the controversy to understand the historians' concept of customary law and how it was employed in the manor court. Our goal requires a detailed discussion of the substance of Smith's argument. In attempting to cast doubt on the position of Hilton and Razi, Smith suggests that the decisions in a number of inheritance cases (particularly one in Wakefield) in which an elder child born after trothplight[21] but before church solemnization prevails over his younger brother born after marriage at the church door demonstrate that "in the eyes of the hallmote, trothplight was the act that established the marriage."[22] Because these courts fixed a right in property at customary law at a particular point in the process of the formation of a union, Smith believes that at this point, trothplight, was tantamount to marriage in the minds of "the middling layer of the tenantry."[23] By fixing such a juncture, marriage was therefore neither "flexible," "fluid," "uncertain," nor "unstable."

Smith's exercise provides a useful example of an attempt to extrapolate a societal norm (when people are married in the eyes of the peasantry) from the articulation of a point of substantive law (trothplight constitutes a valid marriage) in cases in the manor court against which we can test our jurisprudential assumptions. In Smith's view the resolution of this case (and a number of others) evidences the collective view of peasant culture on marriage formation.[24] In arguing that it was recognized that trothplight was the event that formed marriage from the cases that he has observed, Smith must consider the case to have (consciously or otherwise) fashioned a rule of substantive law applied similarly in similar cases regardless of the status of the claimants.

In applying our first "jurisprudential assumption" (that the cited cases are resolved by the application of a rule of substantive law), let us begin by conceding that the pronouncement of the jury clearly resembles one of substantive law. Then we must ask further what is the extent and relevance of the decision to the particular question of marriage formation, because substantive law is created by and limited to the facts of an instant case. Thus the factual context of the litigation is crucial. Is the litigated issue one of marriage formation (and therefore perhaps indicative of the cultural value for which Smith argues) or is the issue one of inheritance rules? I would argue the latter. As Maitland noted, secular law had no legal doctrine regarding marriage formation: "It had often to say whether a woman was entitled to dower, whether a child was entitled to inherit. About these matters it was free to make what rules it pleased."[25]

Smith's cases are ones in which the primary issue is inheritance and not marriage formation. Thus, returning to the cases cited by Smith, the rule of law as articulated in these cases applies to one narrow issue touching inheritance law: The child born after trothplight but prior to a solemnization in church has priority over younger brothers in inheriting customary land. The court made no decision on the point at which marriages are valid.

My point is not merely a doctrinaire quibble for lawyers. Modern law is quite specific in delineating the requirements for a valid marriage. In some cases the benefits of marriage are conferred, even though a valid marriage has not been contracted. For example, the Social Security Act in the United States extends the surviving spouse benefits to women who are not legally married because of some technical defect in the marriage process.[26] Likewise, a recent Louisiana case held that a person may be entitled to the civil effects of marriage (ability to receive alimony) even though the marriage was void.[27] In short, the law creating a status can be separated from laws conferring the incidences of that status. More simply, though no doubt odd to the non-lawyer, one may be considered married for a particular purpose, although unmarried according to marriage law.[28] Accordingly, the manor court in Wakefield could possibly have sought to protect the property interest of the son born after trothplight regardless of (or perhaps despite) whether they believed a valid marriage had occurred. One would need more information to be persuaded that the court rendered its decision because it was bound to implement the church court's view of marriage and that such a view was imbedded in the psyche of the peasantry. Alternatively, one would need to see Smith's principle that trothplight is equivalent to marriage operating upon land in other situations in which marriage creates a right in property. Corroboration might come from an analysis of free bench (customary law's equivalent to dower) where the outcome affects not property relationships between brothers but removes land temporarily from heirs and allows the widow to hold it. Smith has been unable to find examples of women claiming free bench on the strength of trothplight rather than church solemnization.[29] The failure to find such occurrences may suggest that Smith's cases are isolated examples of the resolution of inheritance disputes and not broad acceptance of ecclesiastical marriage formation rules.

Our second jurisprudential assumption requires regularity of application of customary law; that similar cases are decided by similar reasoning, similarly. This assumption raises two issues when applied to medieval English manor courts. The first is the extent to which the same manor court followed rules set down in resolving earlier cases in disposing of subsequent cases with similar facts. A second issue is whether the jurisprudence in one manor court also applied in others so that, for example, the Wakefield pronouncement can be taken as evidence of a national cultural norm. It must be conceded on the first issue that there could be fairly rapid reversal on points of what were arguably points of substantive law within a manor court. For example, in Brigstock in Northamptonshire, there was a swift turn-around on the issue of the sale of free bench by a widow. In 1297 the homage ratified a sale of land by a widow; five years later an inquisition determined that a widow could not alienate any part of her free bench.[30] Moreover, the manor court could alter previously accepted practice by claiming, disingenuously, conformity with established custom. Change in custom might be implemented through the process of inquisition. An example is found in the court rolls of High Easter in Essex dealing with an out-of-court transfer by a customary tenant on his deathbed. The transfer should have been invalid, but an inquisition by the jury claimed that such transfers *in extremis* were according to custom, and it was accepted though no previous examples appear in the court rolls.[31]

Likewise, there was inconsistency within individual manor courts when enforcing broad legal principles. The legal status of women provides a useful example. In a recent book, Judith Bennett argues that customary law followed the common law in considering that a married woman's legal personality was subsumed within that of her husband. The approach of the court varied with regard to procedure:

In some cases, the Brigstock court insisted that both husband and wife had to be present for a joint plea to proceed. In 1314, for example, Walter Helkok and his wife Emma successfully postponed their case against William Hayroun by Emma's essoin; the court determined that Walter could not respond in Emma's absence. In another court of the same year, Sarah the wife of Hugh ad Crucem lost her case against Richard Westwode and his wife Godwyne because she inadvertently dropped Godwyne from the plea. But in other cases, the court was completely indifferent to the participation of wives in joint pleas. When Robert Molendinarius sued Richard Aukyn and his wife Margery in 1343, he dropped Margery after the first statement of complaint, and the case proceeded as if Margery had never been involved. In 1331, Emma the wife of Richard Suig essoined in their joint pleas against Egidius le Faber, but her husband concorded the case despite her absence.[32]

Moreover, women who were apparently married were found to transfer land without having their husbands joined in the conveyance[33] and are fined as individuals under the Assize of Bread and Ale, even though such practice violates the principle of legal incapacity.[34] Indeed, closer on point in our discussion, we see how tenuous principles articulated in customary courts may have been. Thirty years after the now famous pronouncement in Wakefield on the effects of trothplight cited by Smith, a somewhat similar marriage case arose there. The court was so uncertain about the law regarding the inheritance rights that they referred the case to the Earl's advisors.[35]

Our second point regarding precedent in the manor courts deals with the ambit of the jurisdiction. Manor courts were local courts, administered by stewards with juries comprised largely of peasants holding customary land in a circumscribed geographical area. Under such circumstances, we must ask whether a decision in one jurisdiction was likely to be reflective of national societal norms. Smith seems to regard it as such because he argues that an acceptance of canon law marriage formation rules obtained throughout England. Such a proposition is at best dubious, but Smith's argument would be more persuasive if it could be demonstrated that customary rules in general were in force throughout the realm. Manor courts held diverse positions regarding inheritance and adhered to different positions on a range of legal issues.[36] A case from the Chertsey Abbey manor of Stanore suggests that the position articulated in Wakefield and the Court Book of Park in Hertfordshire by Smith may not have held there. The court rolls record that one John de Tothale was the bastard son of Ralph and Alice and held a meadow by a surrender of his parents "In the time of Edward II." The land was taken into the hand of the lord because John was "born before marriage, so he *by the laws of England* is a bastard, to whom no serf-land can descend."[37] The court seems to adopt and confirm the common law rule here regarding inheritance rights of children, and the reference is to marriage rather than trothplight as the crucial event conferring heirship rights. This is not because the homage was unaware of the linguistic distinction; the court rolls are peppered with references to "betrothal."[38]

Indeed, diversity rather than consistency appears to mark the approach of manorial courts in resolving disputes regarding inheritance and illegitimacy. In the Chertsey Abbey manor of Chobham it would appear that a bastard could not receive villein land through *inter vivos* transfer, a position that differed from Halesowen.[39] Moreover, in Wakefield, it may have been possible for an illegitimate to inherit without even a prior arrangement. In court of 26 February 1333, Alice Peger died, and it is noted that she was a bastard and "died without heirs." Curiously though, one Robert Peger was admitted.[40] Are we to assume the similarity of surname is coincidence or was an illegitimate's collateral relative allowed to inherit at Wakefield? Indeed, John Beckerman has found a number of cases in which bastards were allowed a right to inherit.[41] Richard Smith, in arguing that illegitimate women of villein parentage were free and therefore did not pay *merchet*, cites an example of a woman born out of wedlock assessed a merchet of 5s.[42] These examples suggest that customary rules regarding illegitimacy and inheritance varied widely from jurisdiction to jurisdiction, as well as within jurisdictions, and caution should require the historian to provide an array of uncontradicted examples before assuming a nation-wide rule indicative of a national cultural value.

At the same time, customary law was malleable. An example of the way it could be changed can be observed by considering the adoption of deathbed transfer of land.[43] Customary land, at least in theory, could only be transferred by a surrender and admission in the manor court or by descent. In the course of the fourteenth and fifteenth centuries, the courts of some manors allowed a tenant on his deathbed to declare in front of witnesses the persons to whom his land should pass upon his death. The recognition of these *in extremis* transfers allowed a customary tenant in effect to will land, yet the acceptance of this ability and its ambit was uneven. In some manors it appears never to have been recognized, while specific rules were developed in other manors to limit and control the practice.

Thus it seems dubious that pronouncements of customary law as well as the resolution of cases were sufficiently uniform for us to assume that similar cases were decided similarly throughout the kingdom.

Our final jurisprudential assumption is that concepts of due process and equal protection were recognized so that relative positions of power within the community did not affect the result. Unfortunately, this point is perhaps the most difficult to discern and awaits further investigation of series of court rolls and examinations of the social relations within the community from other sources. It is important to recognize that attempts to extrapolate cultural values from the decisions in the manor court presume even-handed justice. It is therefore relevant to note the increasing economic differentiation amongst the peasantry and the movement towards removing the lesser tenantry from decisionmaking with the increasing use of the presentment jury in the fourteenth century.[44] This discussion of the jurisprudence of the manorial courts is not a textual exegesis to fashion a contrary rule of the substantive law of marriage at customary law by citing a different formulation between Smith's cases and other manorial court judgments such as the one at the Chertsey Abbey manor. In my view, recourse to linguistic interpretation with regard to manorial court cases is unsatisfactory. First, it has been demonstrated that some pronouncements by the manor court are incorrectly or incompletely formulated. As Eleonore Searle has argued, the statement frequently found in manor court rolls ("He is unable to give his daughter in marriage without the license of the lord") cannot mean what it literally seems to mean because controlling ecclesiastical law allowed for marriage formation by exchanging promises.[45] The pronouncement really means that the lord could require a merchet to be paid. Second, the nature of adjudication highlighted by the comparison of cases to our jurisprudential assumptions underscores the difficulties presented to historians who wish to consider statements in the court rolls as tantamount to pronouncements of substantive law in a modern, highly developed legal culture from which cultural norms of medieval English peasant society may arguably be extrapolated.

Conclusion

The purpose of this essay has been to suggest that recent work attempting to extrapolate societal norms regarding marriage or other areas of the law of family relations from decisions in manorial courts may ultimately rely upon a perception of customary law that is flawed. There is little direct evidence to suggest that the conceptions of jurisprudence governing transactions in court encompassed the regularity of application of rules either within a jurisdiction or throughout the kingdom required to support an argument that any decision reflected the collective cultural position on a particular aspect of the regulation of family relations. Our preliminary sketch of cases suggests that the outcome of disputes touching fundamental issues of customary law seem to vary. I am not arguing here for contrary positions on individual issues of law but rather that law in its modern sense may be absent, regardless of how judgments are articulated.[46]

I do not wish to advocate the position that principled adjudication was absent in the manor court. It must be recognized that legal orders can assume a variety of forms consistent with the requirements of their culture. In short, different sets of jurisprudential assumptions could have been in force that would have resulted in principled adjudication, even though the system was not directly governed by principles of substantive law or protection of rights as in modern western European or American law. Tentatively, and with some trepidation, I shall proffer an alternative hypothesis that a very different jurisprudential assumption guided the manorial court: The manor court as a civil forum resolved disputes based upon factual equities rather than on substantive law.

To develop further my theory we must return to the operation of the forum. Manor courts basically concerned themselves with questions of administration rather than adjudication. Even when they were resolving interpersonal disputes like the enforcement of maintenance agreements the court was basically supervising the execution of agreements. Compliance was merely a question of fact to be deduced by recourse to straightforward evidence. Substantive law was not created when a child was required to furnish his aged parent with another quarter of corn or a promisor or debtor was ordered to perform.

The manor court did, as we have seen in the area of inheritance, go beyond the supervision of contracts and actually adjudicate disputes. While its usual role was that of fact finder, it would have been necessary to have resolved the cases discussed in the previous section by having the jury (consciously or otherwise) come to terms with what we know as abstract legal rights. This is not to say that juries were directed or controlled by them, or that they were custodians of a body of substantive law systematically distilled from societal values that were to be routinely and even-handedly implemented to resolve disputes. Rights articulated by substantive law may not have been elevated to the same position as in modern Western society. The local community may have preferred to come to what they perceived was an equitable result regardless of legal right. This was arguably the cultural norm directing dispute resolution in medieval English village communities.

My argument is bolstered by the legal nature of the court. Indeed, the court was well-adapted to ascertain what the community regarded as a just result. It had an informal procedure (certainly relative to common law), and resolution was made by individuals who were likely members of the same community as the parties and who therefore were informed of the basis of the dispute. Ability to inquire was present and certainly was not limited by the structure of the proceeding like a modern trial. In short, a very different economic and social order may have produced a legal order that regarded consistency maintained by rules of substantive law as less appealing than a "just result" in a dispute between neighbors. Perhaps medieval historians should not envisage the manor court as if it were a rudimentary modern court that purports to undertake adjudication on a case-by-case basis with regularity, applying similar rules to similar fact situations similarly. In short, the court's goal may have been to craft equitable resolutions of disputes than to enforce rights. This, I would argue, was the cultural norm that informed the customary legal system.

Rather than a formal court that adhered to my jurisprudential assumptions articulated above, the manor court may be akin to an informal dispute resolution (and prevention) forum, an alternative dispute resolution forum (ADR) as modern law theorists term it.[47] If so, the endeavor of historical sociologists to extrapolate cultural norms from customary law becomes extremely difficult, because ADRs look to a range of external factors beyond formal law and are not tribunals in which precedent is regarded as controlling.[48]

The analogy of manor courts to alternative disputes resolution forums is indeed an attractive one.[49] While contemporary proponents of ADRs in our highly developed legal culture often stress its cost-effectiveness[50] and therefore the accessibility of these alternate mechanisms, focus is also upon the benefits of "communitarian" rather than formal dispute resolution.[51] Doubtless modern lawyers do not envisage the manor court when they ponder the advantages of ADRs, but it is interesting that arguments about its effectiveness under two particular circumstances strikingly parallel the reality of medieval English communities. First, alternative dispute resolution forums are able to reach underlying problems that separate parties with an ongoing relationship, rather than upon merely focusing on the formalized legal issue that is framed in formal litigation by lawyers.[52] Second, ADRs either promote compromise or fashion a remedy that may avoid the all or nothing outcome of traditional adversarial litigation: Parties in the context of ADRs may work together towards a creative resolution of a conflict that neither party regards as a defeat.[53]

An example from the past might be the following dispute from the court rolls of the Chertsey Abbey manor of Sutton:

> Adam, who held a virgate in Sutton, died leaving a widow and two sons; the widow Matilda came into court asking that her younger son, Robert be admitted in accordance with the current custom of Borough English; the homage then asked for the custom of inheritance to be changed to primogentiure; the alteration was then approved for a fine of 40s; and Matilda was instructed to send her elder son William on next court.[54]

The modern rights-oriented lawyer would be aghast. The change in custom was retroactive. An interest in property had descended to Robert at Adam's death, and the court transferred it to William. The manor court appeared to have no compunctions about interfering with Robert's right. Like the Wakefield trothplight case previously discussed, the court chose between brothers and perhaps was confident that an arrangement would be worked out, if and when the two brothers reached majority. Indeed compromise rather than judgment more often settled disputes in the manor court. Few cases were actually decided.

Although the manor court may have been organized along the lines of alternative dispute resolution forum, this does not necessarily mean that it was the medieval equivalent to an ADR. Yet if systems of adjudication are placed upon a continuum from the most structured and rule-bound to the least formal, elements of the manorial courts—such as the relative (to modern or contemporary common law) informality of procedure, the factbound nature of the litigation, the close relationships of the parties in dispute and the fact that the arbiters were neighbors—suggest that the manor court was closer structurally to the informal end of the spectrum.

If the manor court resembled what modern lawyers have called alternative dispute resolution forums, historians must more fully understand the dynamics of litigation within that context, rather than focus on statements of custom to employ cases to fathom social relations in medieval English peasant society. The intractable problems raised by the legal nature of the customary court underscore the need for broad-based community studies to explain the operation of customary law, and, with regard to disputes between villeins, the view of the legal nature of manorial courts proffered here would require caution before assuming that particular judgments incorporate points of substantive law that reflect culture norms. In short, the process by which disputes were adjudicated in the manor courts may be a more fertile focus of inquiry than seeking to discover substantive "customary law."

Yet why manor courts chose at times to articulate rights in technical language, as in the much-quoted Wakefield pronouncement on trothplight, is indeed intriguing. Only a systematic study of a range of court rolls— advocated, but never completed, by Maitland—will illuminate the nature of the customary legal system. Until then, reliance upon the occasional reference to law in the court rolls to extrapolate the culture norms that directed medieval English society may be misplaced.

Notes

Another version of this paper has been published under the same title in *Comparative Studies in Society and History*, Vol. 31, No. 3, 1989, pp. 514–534. Copyright 1989, Society for the Comparative Study of Society and History. Reprinted with the permission of Cambridge University Press. A more complete study of the manor court has been undertaken and will be published by the Selden Society in 1996. Some of my own conclusions in this article may have to be modified, though the central theme remains, in my view, viable.

1. I regard it as sufficiently reckless for an early modern legal historian to jump headlong into the turf of medieval social histories without further invading the discipline of legal anthropology. My use of the term means simply that behavior is

prescribed by a particular society and somehow embedded in the collective consciousness. Peter Laslett terms them "noumenal normative rules" and defines them as "programmatic principles embedded in collective attitudes." See his "Demographic and Microstructural History in Relation to Human Adaptation: Reflections on Newly Established Evidence," in D. J. Ortner, ed., *How Humans Adapt: A Biocultural Odyssey* (Washington: Smithsonian Institution Press, 1983), pp. 343–370.

2. For a general discussion of the law of villeinage, see Paul Hyams, *Kings, Lords and Peasants in Medieval England: The Common Law of Villeinage in the Twelfth and Thirteenth Century* (Oxford: Clarendon Press, 1980).

3. Selden Society, London, 1889, Vol. 2, p. xi.

4. Maitland, *Select Pleas*, p. ix.

5. E. Searle, "Merchet in Medieval England"; Jean Scammell, "Freedom and Marriage in Medieval England," *Economic History Review,* 2d Ser., Vol. 27, 1974.

6. See for example, R. H. Hamilton, "Freedom and Villeinage in England," in R. H. Hilton, ed., *Peasants, Knights and Heretics: Studies in Medieval English Social History* (Cambridge: Cambridge University Press, 1976), pp. 174–191.

7. J. A. Raftis, *Tenure and Mobility* (Toronto: Pontifical Institute of Medieval Studies, 1964), p. 108.

8. See for example the printed Sussex customals: W. D. Peckham, ed., *Thirteen Customals of the Sussex Manors of the Bishop of Chichester,* Vol. 31(Lewes: Sussex Record Society, 1925); R. C. Redwood and A. E. Wilson, eds., *Customals of the Manors of Laughton, Willmingdon and Soring,* Vol. 55 (Lewes: Sussex Record Society, 1961). The dispute over the millstone was to be resolved by a search of "the register of their customs and services" (Raftis, *Tenure & Mobility,* p. 108).

9. Raftis, *Tenure and Mobility,* p. 69.

10. Peckham, ed., *Thirteen Customals,* p. 55.

11. Maitland, *Select Pleas,* p. xlv.

12. Elaine Clark, "Some Aspects of Social Security in Medieval England," *Journal of Family History,* Vol. 7, 1982, pp. 307–320.

13. S.F.C. Milsom, "Law and Fact in Legal Development," *University of Toronto Law Journal,* Vol. 17, 1967, pp. 1–19.

14. The notable exception is John Beckerman's unpublished 1972 University of London Ph.D. thesis, "Customary Law in English Manorial Courts in the Thirteenth and Fourteenth Centuries"; see also R. M. Smith, "Some Thoughts on 'Hereditary' and 'Proprietary' Rights in Land under Customary Law in Thirteenth and Early Fourteenth Century England," *Law and History Review,* Vol. 1, 1983, pp. 95–128.

15. R. M. Smith, "Marriage Processes," in L. Bonfield, et. al., eds., *The World We Have Gained* (Oxford: B. Blackwell, 1986), pp. 52–63. R. H. Hilton, *The English Peasantry in the Later Middle Ages* (Oxford: Clarendon Press, 1975).

16. I recognize that precedent in historical context may have rather a different technical meaning than its present one. In the instant context, I mean simply that the manor court felt compelled to reach a decision in a particular case because a previous case with similar and indistinguishable facts was decided in a given way.

17. For a discussion of the concepts of substantive due process and equal protection, see Leonard Levy, Kenneth Karst, and Dennis Mahoney, eds., *Encyclopedia of the American Constitution,* 4 Vols., Vol. 2 (New York and London: Free Press, 1986), pp. 2, 589–590, 640–647.

18. Smith, "Marriage Processes," p. 52, citing R. H. Hilton, *The English Peasantry in the Later Middle Ages;* and Barbara Hanawalt, *Crime and Conflict in English Com-*

munities (Cambridge, Mass.: Harvard University Press, 1979). Maitland was the first historian that I could find who refers to marriage in this vein. Frederick Pollock and F. W. Maitland, *The History of English Law Before the Time of Edward I*, 2d ed., 2 vols., Vol. 2 (Cambridge: Cambridge University Press, 1968), p. 369. Smith's view of peasant marriage is strikingly similar to that of George Homans, *English Villagers of the Thirteenth Century* (New York: W. W. Norton, 1941), pp. 163–166.

19. For a fuller discussion, see R. H. Helmholz, *Marriage Litigation in Medieval England* (Cambridge: Cambridge University Press, 1974), pp. 26–31; and Charles Donohue, Jr.'s two interesting articles: "The Policy of Alexander the Third's Consent Theory of Marriage," in Stephen Kuttner, ed., *Proceedings of the Fourth International Congress of Medieval Canon Law*, (Vatican City: 1976), pp. 251–281; and "The Canon Law on the Formation of Marriage and Social Practice in the Later Middle Ages," *Journal of Family History*, Vol. 8, 1983, pp. 144–158.

20. Smith, "Marriage Processes," p. 52.

21. Although Smith equates trothplight with marriage in the minds of English villagers, he never defines it. Because he makes the argument that the villagers' view conformed to the Alexandrine position, I am assuming that he considers the vergal requirement in its broadest sense as promises to marry using either words of present consent or future consent. For the latter to bind would require intercourse, and as a practical matter, it is difficult to see how the community perceived it. It is relatively easy to envisage a community norm that regarded words of present consent as binding. In this sense a promise to marry is treated no differently than any other contract or undertaking to pay a debt. On the other hand with promises of future consent the words themselves have no binding effect. It was the act of intercourse, of which presumably they might be ignorant (at least for a while), that would transform the promises into marriage. One might argue that the manor court made decisions based upon evidence of what had previously transpired but does this mean that it was a court judgment which created the marriage in the mind of the villager?

22. Smith, "Marriage Processes," p. 57.

23. Smith, "Marriage Processes," p. 69.

24. To some extent, his process of deduction is questionable. In the first place, Smith, while arguing on the one hand that conceptions of entrance into marriage are fixed and therefore marriage is not informal, concedes that many cases of fornication must be attributable to uncertain trothplights. Regardless of which ceremony prevailed in the minds of medieval villagers as tantamount to a formal union, the argument that exactly what constituted entrance into marriage was uncertain is surely substantiated if significant numbers of villagers misunderstood the ceremonial mechanics required in its formation, be it trothplight or church solemnization. Moreover, if the Alexandrine position had captured the hearts and minds of the peasantry sufficiently to affect property relationships, present consent or words of future consent followed by sexual intercourse rather than plighting troth (which did not establish a valid marriage under Alexander's rules) should have been the event that established a valid marriage.

25. Pollock and Maitland, *The History of English Law*, Vol. 2, p. 374.

26. For the reference to the Social Security case, see 42 United States Code Annotated, Sec. 402, 416(a); see also *Chlystek v. Califano*, 599 F.2d, 1270 (1979).

27. In *Super v. Burke*, 367 So.2nd 93 (La. App. 4th Cir. 1979) a man sought to annul his marriage on the grounds that a foreign divorce that he obtained from his

first wife was invalid. While the court held the second marriage null, the woman was entitled to alimony under the Louisiana Civil Code.

28. Further examples, as provided for me by Professor Harvey Couch include Oregon Rev. Stat. 656.226 (although a person is unmarried, the partner and his/her children will receive workman's compensation payments); and *Estate of Borax v. Commissioner*, 349 F.2d 666, 2nd Cir. 1965 (although a man's Mexican divorce was invalid and therefore his second marriage void, the man and his partner would be considered married for tax purposes).

29. Smith, "Marriage Processes," p. 64, esp. n. 78.

30. Judith M. Bennett, *Women in the Medieval English Countryside* (New York: Oxford University Press, 1987), p. 165.

31. *PRO.DL30.65.817 (10 May 1361): Ad istam curiam venit Thomas Bowyere bedellus domini cum Galfridus Poynaunt in sua magna egritudine tamen sanus mente secundum conseutudines manerij ut dicitur et reddidit tria quarteria terre customarie cum suis pertinentiis vocata Yonges boven et modo in ista plena curia venit predictus Thomas et sursumreddit in manum domini predicta tria quarteria terre ... ad opus Johannis Poynaunt ... et quia videtur seneschal curie quod nullahs tenens ad voluntary domini posit Se disintered de terries et tenements ... Basque licence domini et hoc in plena curia prefatory reductio ... non allocator seed pro nullah denature ... et static venit cummunitas villate de Alta Estre et similiter cummunitas de Valtham et dicunt quod est consuetudo usitata in utraque villata et a tempore quo non existat memoria ... quod quilibet nativus domini et quicumque tenens in bondagio domini eger et languens non potens ire ad curiam ... potuit reddere in manum praepositi seu bedelli villatarum predictarum tenementa sua ... ita quod ipse praepositus aut bedellus in curia ... sursum redderet illud tenementum in manum domini ad opus perquisitorum. ...*

I owe this reference to Professor L. R. Poos, with whom I am engaged in a study of marriage and family law in manorial courts 1300–1550 which is to be published by the Selden Society.

32. Bennett, *Women in the Countryside*, p. 109.

33. Bennett, *Women in the Countryside*, p. 112.

34. Bennett, *Women in the Countryside*, p. 124.

35. The case is noted as follows:

The land held by John, s. of Nicholas Kenward, to be seized into the lord's hands, because he is dead. And as Nicholas, his elder son, was born before marriage, and Thomas, his younger son, after,—counsel is to be taken thereon with the Earl's advisers [consuland' est inde cu' consilio di'ni Com'].

Admittedly, the roll does not state whether Nicholas was born before marriage or after trothplight; but if the court was so uncertain here, how strong could have been their understanding of marriage formation rules? Lister, ed., *Court Rolls of the Manor of Wakefield: from October 1331 to September 1333*, Vol. 3 (Yorkshire Archeological Society, 1982), p. 91.

36. It is generally accepted that inheritance customs varied in English manors. Homans, *English Villagers;* and Rosamond Faith, "Peasant Family's and Inheritance Customs in Medieval England," *Agricultural History Review*, Vol. 14, 1966, pp. 77–95.

37. E. Toms, ed., *Abstract of Chertsey Abbey Court Rolls*, Vol. 21 (Surrey Record Society, 1937), pp. 151–152.

38 . Toms, ed., *Chertsey Abbey Court Rolls*, pp. 22, 28, 29, 30, among others.

39. Toms, ed., *Chertsey Abbey Court Rolls*, pp. 151–152; Zvi Razi, *Life, Marriage and Death in a Medieval English Parish* (Cambridge: Cambridge University Press, 1980), pp. 65–66.

40. J. W. Walker, ed., *Wakefield Court Rolls*, Vol. 3, pp. iii, 161.

41. John Beckerman, "Customary Law in Manorial Courts in the Thirteenth and Fourteenth Centuries" (Ph.D. thesis, University of London, 1976), pp. 156–157.

42. Smith, "Marriage Processes," p. 58, n. 52.

43. For a fuller discussion, see Lloyd Bonfield and L.R. Poos, "The Development of the Deathbed Transfer in Medieval English Manor Courts," *Cambridge Law Journal*, Vol. 47, 1988, pp. 403–427.

44. Smith, "Some Thoughts," pp. 106–107.

45. Searle, "Merchet in Medieval England," p. 6.

46. In his comment to a version of this article presented at the Social Science History Conference, Professor Dewindt suggested that historians might better avoid the use of the term "customary law" and refer to the governing principles as "custom." It may be salutary advice. It is well worth recalling Father Raftis's remark that "customary law was far too vital ... to require exposition in the court rolls" (*Tenure and Mobility*, 1964), p. 55.

47. The literature on alternative dispute resolution is nearly boundless. The American Bar Association has published a bibliography: *American Bar Association Special Committee on Alternative Means of Dispute Resolution, A Selected Bibliography* (Washington, D.C., 1982).

48. "Paths to Justice: Major Public Policy Issues of Dispute Resolution: Report of the Ad Hoc Panel on Dispute Resolution and Public Policy," National Institute for Dispute Resolution (1983), reproduced in Leon Kanowitz, *Cases and Materials in Alternative Dispute Resolution* (St. Paul: West Publishing, 1986), p. 26.

49. For an historical discussion of "communitarian" dispute resolution in America, see Jerold Auerbach, *Justice Without Law* (Oxford: Oxford University Press, 1980). See also, William E. Nelson, *Dispute and Conflict Resolution in Plymouth County, Massachusetts, 1725–1825* (Chapel Hill: University of North Carolina Press, 1981).

50. Kanowitz, *Cases and Materials*, p. 13.

51. H. T. Edwards, "Hopes and Fears for Alternative Dispute Resolution," *Williamette Law Review*, Vol. 21, 1985, p. 425; Paul Wahrhaftis, "Non-Professional Conflict Resolution," *Villanova Law Review*, Vol. 29, 1984, p. 1466.

52. Kanowitz, *Cases and Materials*, pp. 12, 14.

53. Robert McKais, "Civil Litigation and the Public Interest," *Kansas Law Review*, Vol. 31, 1983, pp. 355–376.

54. Toms, ed., *Chertsey Abbey Court Rolls*, pp. 105–106.

7

Worries About Quandaries

Richard W. Miller

Miller comes forward at this point to challenge application of the Dalhousie logic of rules to procedures for using different technologies; and to challenge as well the importance that the logic of rules, taken together with a generalized issue-processing perspective, attributes to quandaries, indeed, to rules. The basic causes of social change, he argues, are to be found in other matters.

Among most English-speaking social scientists, there is a strong inclination to suppose that an accurate description of a social structure will refer to elements that would, through their interaction, reproduce themselves forever, if outside forces did not intervene. Basic change always comes about from outside the basic structure. Indeed, this conservative expectation is suggested by the dead metaphor of "structure" itself. Since the first and most important step in understanding large-scale social phenomena is supposed to be the identification of the structure in which they occur, this expectation influences most social inquiry.

I think that the standard conservative expectation is wrong, even though the emphasis on location in an underlying social structure is right. Often, though not always, the most accurate description of a structure would describe a system of elements that are bound to give rise to fundamental change in the system as a whole, even in the absence of outside forces. The systems of large-scale phenomena that reproduce themselves, through their effect on conduct, motive, and resources, inevitably produce the means of their own destruction and are followed by a basically different system. In this sense, there is a contradiction in the structure.

Here, of course, I am agreeing with the Dalhousie team, and the agreement is much more fundamental than any of the doubts and worries I will express. Also, I think that their investigation of quandaries and cases in which obedience to rules gives rise to quandaries provides extremely powerful warnings against the dogmatic separation of structural description and the identification of sources of change. If there is any style of structural description that fulfills the expectation of no internal causes of change it is, one would suppose, the identification of rules which are followed in a rule-abiding society. If the conservative expectation is a useful working hypothesis, it ought to provide excellent guidance when it is applied to systems of social rules. By that token, the Dalhousie team's examples of contradictory systems of social rules are good evidence that this expectation, explicitly proclaimed by Durkheim, Parsons, the major British social anthropologists, structural-functionalists in American political sociology and many others, should be discarded.

Against the background of these agreements, I will present some doubts about the Dalhousie project. These doubts are not meant to question the project, but to contribute to its development. I'm sure that the mechanism of rules and quandaries does sometimes operate and is sometimes the most important cause of change. I'm less sure how important rules and quandaries are in the whole process of social explanation and description, properly conducted. My questions are meant to help to define the terms of the Dalhousie project and to assess its proper scope. They concern the nature of rules; the nature, prevalence, and explanatory role of quandaries; and the importance of rules in basic distinctions of social type.

Rules and Beyond

It is important to distinguish rules from goals (including interests, desires, concerns, and commitments) and from maxims, i.e., rules-of-thumb employed in the interest of quickly or conveniently finding the way to reach goals. I am sure that this is not a disagreement with the Dalhousie team. Rules, goals, and maxims constitute virtually every source of reasons for action. The statement that change results from conflicts among reasons would be too true, too uncontroversial to yield a distinctive program. No doubt, what puts social change on the agenda is sufficiently acute frustration of groups with sufficient resources, i.e., their frustration in their goals by others, motivated by conflicting goals, goals which may be implemented by consulting maxims. If a large-scale, relatively stable social system is changed, many must be motivated by disruptive goals and strategies to violate rules in which they were brought up. No one disputes this. So, while allowing (as the Dalhousie team does) that rules need not be legislated, precise or explicit, some way must be found to distinguish them from goals and maxims, the other main reason-providers. I'm not sure how the distinction can be made without excluding many important cases that are supposed to fall within the logic of rules. For example, there are a number of suggestions in *Track* that the Industrial Revolution might have resolved contradictions between rules concerning the division of labor, where perhaps a rule permitting the assignment of tasks according to a pre-industrial division among specialized handworkers conflicted with a requirement to exploit the potential of machine production as effectively as possible.[1] But such principles strike me not as rules, but maxims. (At one point in *Track*, they are called "technical norms.") Treating them as rules is risky in two ways. The rules model may be absorbed into the mere truism that people abandon old ways for new when the old ways frustrate them in important interests. Also, the struggle for power in the face of conflict may be portrayed, instead, as the confusion of people committed to conflicting rules. Certainly, this is a danger when Marx's account of the Industrial Revolution is fitted onto the model of conflicting rules. In Marx's view, the Industrial Revolution occurs long after guild restrictions and other sanctioned or morally imperative rules regulating the division of labor had passed from the scene. Machines are introduced, and new kinds of jobs are assigned by employers, to overcome the resistance of skilled workers, by eliminating the bargaining advantages they derive from their special skills. Workers fighting with some success, not rules, are on the other side of the conflict in which the new division of labor eventually prevails. Marx quotes Andrew Ure with complete (intellectual) approval. "Speaking of an invention for dressing warps [Ure writes]: 'Then the combined malcontents, who fancied themselves impregnably behind the old division of labor, found their flanks turned and their defences rendered useless by the new mechanical tactics, and were obliged to surrender at discretion.'"[2]

Quandaries

Assessing the role of quandaries is a somewhat separate project from determining the scope of rules (though only partly so, since one still wants to avoid the assumption that any conflict between a practice and a goal is a conflict among rules). In the fundamental account of hyperdeontic logic, a quandary is said to be a situation in which every course of action is forbidden for an agent. In the most general descriptions of the new explanatory strategy, the need to resolve quandaries is often presented as the central explanatory mechanism. I'm worried by the number of conflicts in the case studies that turn out not to involve true quandaries. It isn't clear how much departure from literal quandary can be allowed, if the explanatory strategy is to be distinctive. (This is not meant as a coy way of rejecting the project, but as a description of a part of it that may need more definition.)

Consider the quandary ascribed to the people dispossessed by the new nobility.[3] We are told that "the consequences of actions dictated by one rule ... were prohibited by another rule." The prohibition is against begging. The other rule, I take it, is the rule permitting the new nobility to "drive those who have labored on the land off it." But surely, the permission did not dictate any action. Perhaps what is intended, here as elsewhere, is that the system of rules permitted actions that put people in quandaries, actions which were actually engaged in. And of course, "Starve or be whipped for begging," is a quandary in a broad but all-too-real sense. But it would not seem to be a quandary in the special sense of the logic-of-rules proposal. "Don't starve" is an extremely important goal and a wise maxim for those who want to live. But it is not a rule in any other way. Again, it would be too true, too uncontroversial to propose that what puts change on the agenda is a situation in which the old system permits actions that frustrate people so long as they remain loyal to the system.

David Braybrooke, in his paper on the logic of the succession of cultures,[4] emphasizes a quandary-generating conflict that is certainly important if it existed, the conflict between a rule giving ownership over a thing to whomever contributes labor to its production and a rule giving ownership to the owner of the tools used in its production. But I don't think this conflict existed, or that Marx or Engels thought it did. Braybrooke acknowledges that in the countryside, landlords owned land and crops to which only their tenants contributed labor. Contrary to Braybrooke's distinction, I think that such arrangements were acceptable under rules that governed the production of goods in towns as well. Wage-labor existed in feudal society, though it was not important in the material and social life of feudalism as a whole. Indeed, Marx, a close reader of Aristotle, knew that there had been wage-labor in ancient Greece, although there, too, its role was peripheral. Also, Marx vividly portrays the domination of guild masters and the great merchants of the medieval towns as rule-sanctioned surplus-extraction, conveying ownership of products to people other than the producers. In the Manifesto, "guildmaster and journeyman" are listed with "lord and serf" as "oppressor and oppressed" in the history of class struggle. Marx fully appreciates the reactionary role of masters in chartered guilds and royally-privileged merchants, locating them squarely in the old regime.

Elsewhere in *Track*, when rules cause trouble (or get into trouble) the trouble is that obedience to the rule makes it hard to pursue one's goals efficiently while respecting another rule. Or actions permitted by a rule ultimately put people in situations where they have sufficient motives for disdaining other rules. These aren't quandary states, so there is a need to consider whether the explanatory appeal to such conflicts should be regarded, broadly speaking, as an appeal to the model of quandary and resolution.

My final worry about quandaries concerns their explanatory power. As the Dalhousie team are well aware, the resolution of a quandary can favor one or the other rule or neither. Moreover, a quandary isn't the death of a system of rules. The result may simply be that people sometimes eat forbidden fruit. So, in the explanation of the change in rules that does occur, one must appeal to interests in bringing about the change and resources for influencing change. Once this explanation has been developed, will there be any further point in appealing to the existence of a quandary? There won't be, I take it, if the interests and resources would have led to the same result, say, a capitalist rule, even if there had not been a quandary, posed, say, by a contrary feudal rule, which was overcome. Even if Braybrooke is right about feudal property principles,[5] his quandary doesn't explain the change if it was wholly due to the new resources that the bourgeoisie came to enjoy in their pursuit of power. On the other hand, the quandary plays an explanatory role if the removal of quandary as such is part of the mechanism without which change would not have occurred. Two main possibilities of such causal involvement come to mind. People might be stimulated to crucial actions by a desire to avoid quandaries. Or the quandary might have produced so many difficulties in social coordination, that the shared need for more order at the level of rules made change necessary. So, in assessing the project, we may need to consider whether a threatened need for orderly rules as such, as against, say, a desire for increased power, or hatred of oppression or a fear of competitive losses, has played a pervasive role in the dynamics of social change.

Kinematics and Social Type

As the Dalhousie team points out, kinematics, the description of changing states, has its own role to play, independent of dynamics, the description of causes of change. Indeed, every great scientific revolution, certainly including Galileo's, Darwin's, and the quantum-mechanical revolution, has depended on the development of new means for merely describing the states that change. My final question concerns the use of the logic of rules to describe basic large-scale changes in social type.

Of course, the replacement of one set of rules with another is a change. But part of the kinematic proposal is, I take it, that the contrast between society before and society after the changes that are usually regarded as epoch-making is often most usefully presented as a contrast between the rules obtaining before and after. I think that this model of description may underrate the importance of purely quantitative differences, affecting social power but not the content of the rule books.

Engels says, at one point, that pure feudalism (which did have highly distinctive rules, e.g., distinctive requirements for corvée labor) only existed in certain self-righteously traditional Crusader kingdoms in Palestine. Marx takes the English Civil War and the French Revolutions to be great watersheds separating feudal and capitalist societies; but the rules current in sixteenth century England are not, as he actually describes them, very different from those current in eighteenth century England. Indeed, when Volume III of *Capital* is read along with Volume I, Tudor England looks very much like eighteenth century England in its book of rules. Money rent has replaced corvée labor; increasingly, peasants work land they farm on long-term leases; and so forth. No doubt, one can point to certain distinctions between the Tudor rule book and Queen Anne's that make the latter less feudal than the former. But insisting that the character of one of these systems of rules is, by its nature, feudal, the other, capitalist, would require criteria as perverse as those that make Japan or Singapore socialist on account of the extent of state intervention. The rule normally broken in the Tudor process of dispossession was the capitalist rule to respect leases. The squires of *Middlemarch*, over a century into capitalism, are guided by paternalistic obligations to tenants.

What is feudalism then, in the Marxist typology that the Dalhousie team is often exploring? I think it is best understood as a system in which the extraction of a social surplus mainly depends on relatively direct access to military or political power, or privileges granted by those who have such access. Capitalism is best understood as a system in which the exploitation of the advantages in the labor market of those who control means of production, confronting sellers of labor power who don't, is the main basis for extracting a surplus. "Main basis" is a bit misleading, here, since one doesn't look at percentage of domestic output (which is dominated by petty-production in nearly all societies preceding industrial capitalism). Rather, the main kind of surplus extraction is the kind that provides an effective basis for determining the main features of political and ideological institutions. No doubt, the transition from one of these structures of power to another will be marked by changes in rules. But there may be no general characterization of the sort of rule book associated with one or another general type of structure. And the change in rules need not be fundamental whenever the change in social type is.

If my previous worry about technical norms and rules is well-placed, there is an even more striking departure from rule-kinematics when manufacturing capitalism is distinguished from industrial capitalism. The change, as such, is a shift from production by muscle-driven tools, typically depending on special skills directing the muscles, to production by tools driven by inanimate forces, supervised by unskilled and semi-skilled people. There simply is no change in rules, as opposed to maxims.

A Basis for Skepticism

These doubts about the kinematics presuppose type distinctions derived from Marx, and even interpret them in a controversial way. I think that similar doubts based on other non-Marxist type distinctions, might be directed at other examples offered to illustrate the logic of rules. In addition, the Marxist examples happen to be good illustrations of an alternative view of order, conflict, and power that would be the principled grounds for denying that quandary and its resolution are exceptionally important in social change, and for denying that contrasting rule books are especially important in the description of the beginning and end of change. I'll conclude by sketching this alternative attitude. One of the many ways in which the Dalhousie project is clarifying is by providing a contrast that illuminates such important differences in the framework in inquiry.

I have to ask myself why rules and quandaries do not seem as important to me, in the process of large-scale social change, as they do in *Track*. After all, respect for rules is, I know, an exceptionally important motivation for socially significant conduct. Without such motivation, social power would too largely depend on the barrel of a gun, and it would collapse, as Mao and even Hobbes would have conceded.

Still conceding that social stability would be unattainable if respect for rules were not a part of the human psychological repertoire does not require assigning this motivation a system role, in general, among the various causal factors determining the long-term history of social systems. Suppose that a system is dominated by an elite, whose interests have ceased to be the interests of most people (or weren't to begin with). In particular, suppose that the major political and ideological institutions tend to operate in the interests of the elite, and that the elite have special resources for system politics and ideology so that new institutions and new rules will tend to arise and to serve those interests when old ones no longer can. As for people outside the elite, suppose that their violation of the rules sustained by respectable institutions is almost always risky, often putting hopes for one's career in jeopardy, and, in crucial cases putting liberty or life at risk. Finally, suppose that the dominant elite will not be persuaded to give up their dominance by superb arguments, even superb arguments from rules they sincerely profess. The old dominance only ends when people, acting in ways that the dominant rules permit, arrive (or produce descendants who arrive) in situations that give rise to the motivation and the means to take the resources for dominance from the old elite, in a process in which the dominant rules are broken.

In the situation that I have described, some of the agents of change will probably find themselves in genuine quandaries, generated by rules that they have acquired from the ideological apparatus together with rules arising in a subculture reflecting their own subordinate social interest. But it is not likely that the existence of these quandaries will be an important basis for socially transforming action. The resolution of quandaries as such is not likely to motivate people to take the risks required for changing society. The effective desire is, not to remove the quandaries and eliminate disorder, but to create a new order in pursuit of the new goals. Some of the dominant elite may be loyal to the most traditional rules, and find themselves in a quandary when new rules are introduced to defend old prerogatives. But these traditionalists are not apt to be effective opponents of change. The explanation of large-scale social change, if it comes about, will be the explanation of how initially permitted actions gave rise to eventually subversive interest, motives, and resources. Finally though the rules of the old society will be different from the rules of the new one, a characterization of the different interests, motives, and resources of the respective dominant groups will best capture the basic difference between the old and the new.

Despite all my coy "supposes," I think that this situation is typical of historical societies. I have stated the hypothesis with broad talk of dominant minorities to make it clear that one needn't be a Marxist to give the needed emphasis to power and resources outside of rules. One could give primacy to political or military factors, in the style of Bloch's *Feudal Society*, or primacy to elites as such, in the style of Pareto. This framework for explaining and describing social change is compatible with the general drift of Weber's *Economy and Society* (though the routinization of charisma might be understood as the resolution of a quandary).

There is an approach to social explanation in which respect for rules is given the social efficacy I have denied and stability is divorced from minority domination. This is the structuralist approach of Durkheim and his intellectual heirs which I mentioned at the start. Here, the social system is seen as a system of rules, each effectively guiding social conduct and to serving the function of maintaining the whole rule system. My deep agreement with the Dalhousie team is that this conservative structuralism is wrong, that it distorts social inquiry along with the pursuit of more humane political possibilities. My deepest worry may be that the new model of rules, despite its usefulness in undermining the old structuralism, may require too many of the old assumptions about the role of cultural orderliness in social action. But perhaps this worry depends on a narrow view of rules and quandaries which further discussion will broaden.

Notes (by the Editor)

1. Such rules are illustrated above in Chapter 1.
2. Karl Marx, *Capital*, Vol. I, Chapt. 15, Sec. 5.
3. Miller is referring here to the rules relating to vagabondage, reproduced in Chapter 1.
4. See above, Chapter 1, for the relevant extract from the paper that Miller is referring to.

5. Among other things at issue here is the feudal rule for disposing of the social surplus, as against the rule under capitalism, which assigns it to capitalists for investment. See Chapter 1.

8

Rules and Resources: The Legitimation of Political Parties in France and the United States

Ronald Aminzade

Aminzade, though perhaps readier in discoursing about history than Miller to focus on rules and changes in rules, holds like Miller that the causes of change lie in other matters—like class interests—rather than in the conflicts captured and exposed by a logic of rules. He undertakes to make this point by a comparative study of the rise of political parties to legitimacy in France on the one hand and in the United States on the other.

Late eighteenth century French and North American republicans shared an intense hostility toward political parties. "Every party is criminal. ..." proclaimed Saint-Just, "Every faction is thus criminal. ... All faction attempts at undermining the sovereignty of the people."[1] Across the Atlantic Ocean, the founders of the American Republic expressed similar sentiments. "If I could not go to heaven but with a party," wrote Thomas Jefferson, "I would not go there at all."[2] By the end of the nineteenth century, both French and American political leaders had drastically revised their assessments of parties, which they came to accept as legitimate components of a democratic political order. The timing of this change varied, however, with American political elites reconciled with organized mass party competition several decades before their French counterparts. This paper explores the sources of this difference in the timing of changes in normative rules governing competition for state power.

The quandary facing late eighteenth century French and American political leaders was the same: how to reconcile the rule that governing bodies should be chosen in a process of electoral mobilization with a norm rejecting the party institutions necessary to accomplish this task. In both cases, a republican political culture proclaiming the unity of the nation and the "general will" was at odds with the practical exigencies of political mobilization. The timing of the resolution of this quandary, in the form of new norms governing organized political competition, differed due to variations in processes of class and state formation.

The transformation of political rules cannot be understood in terms of a desire to eliminate logical inconsistencies in established rules. Rule changes, I argue, were a result of the ways in which large-scale processes of class and state formation altered the interests and capacities of social classes and state managers and the ways in which conflicting interests were articulated with rules of the political game. In both France and the United States, political elites and dominant class members learned how to realize their interests under the rules of parliamentary politics, but the differing character of working-class and state formation in each country meant that ruling groups faced different practical tasks for the realization of these interests.

The first section of my chapter suggests that late eighteenth century rules which defined acceptable means of political competition in terms of the "general will" and national unity were closely linked to both the political project of replacing feudalism with capitalist forms of property and the task of establishing an emergent nation-state in a secure position within an unstable international state system. Early republicans in France and the United States repudiated organized political dissent because such a rule fostered both the class interests of wealthy property owners and the interests of the political leaders of a nation at war. The second part of this paper explains the difference in the timing of party legitimation in France and the United States. The pivot of my explanation is conflicting interests implicated in political rules rather than the logic of rules themselves. In both France and the United States, success in wars and periods of relative peace fostered the legitimation of mass party organizations competing for state power. In France two core obstacles to the realization of consensus over new rules of the political game played a more important role than in the U.S.: landed elites looking backward to feudalism; and, after 1830, revolutionary workers looking forward to socialism. Only after these critical challenges were definitively blocked was it possible for governing elites to acknowledge the legitimacy of organized party competition, to agree upon a common set of rules of the political game which tolerated organized dissent but prevented political contenders from taking advantage of state power to destroy existing rules that guaranteed a republican form of the state and bourgeois property rights. Mass parties gained legitimacy only after the opposition parties that incorporated workers into the electoral arena were willing to take bourgeois property rights as a given and only after competing elites became reconciled to a republican Constitution. The concluding section of the paper suggests that to move beyond identifying contradictory rules to the task of explaining the consequences of such contradictions and how the quandaries posed by conflicting rules are resolved, we need to pay attention to resources as well as rules, interests as well as norms, and learning as well as deliberative processes.

The Legitimation of Political Parties in France

Republican leaders of the French Revolution, from Danton to Robespierre to Condorcet, routinely equated parties with factions and used the term party leader (*chef de parti*) to denounce their opponents. The antipathy of early French republicans to political parties was in part a logical consequence of their rejection of the corporate order of the Old Regime, which was based on privilege and particularism. French Republicans espoused a liberal individualist ideology[3] which envisioned a new social order based on the legal equality of individuals sharing the status of citizens. In repudiating the corporate order, early republicans envisioned the creation of a new "one and indivisible" republic in which numerous corporate bodies, each enjoying a particularistic status before the law, would be replaced by the absolute sovereignty of "the nation." They embraced a vision of politics as rational consensus in the pursuit of a "general will," the emergence of which, as Rousseau taught, was impeded by parties or factions representing particularistic interests.

Early French Republicans espoused a unitary view of politics, which saw the Republic as a means for subordinating conflicting interests to the larger common good of the nation, rather than an adversarial view in which political institutions exist to express or regulate conflicting interests. Their doctrine of a general will directed toward the common good was rooted in an understanding of democracy which assumed that citizens have a single common interest. According to this view, "People who disagree do not vote; they reason together until they agree on the best answer. Nor do they elect representatives to reason for them. They come together with their friends to find agreement. This democracy is consensual, based on common interest and equal respect. ..."[4] Jacobin, Girondin, and sans-culottes Republicans contested the meaning of the "common good" and disagreed about which rules of political representation could best facilitate the pursuit of the general will of the nation. Early French Republicans combined their unitary political vision with two competing notions of political representation,[5] both of which were justified as compatible with the sovereignty of the general will.

The sans-culottes advocated a view of political representation centered around the notion of imperative mandates—i.e., of elected officials as delegates subject to recall if they failed to adhere to their specified mandates.[6] The sans-culottes reconciled their simultaneous adoption of a unitary political vision of France (i.e., the "general will") and an imperative mandate view of representation by the convenient fiction that the people of Paris were the French nation. Although the Parisian sans-culottes' neighborhood assemblies adopted a view of elected representatives as delegates (*mandataires*), such a Rousseauian understanding of representation was soundly repudiated by the National Assembly in 1789, at the very outset of the Revolution.

Jacobin and Girondin republicans espoused a view of representation which favored allowing elected officials considerable discretion to achieve the undivided general will of the nation. The imperative mandate, in their view, was a device that tied elected officials to the particularistic interests of regions or corporate groups rather than to the general interests of the nation. It was therefore at odds with the creation of a one and indivisible republic.

The Republican equation of organized dissent with conspiratorial threats to national unity was in large part a result of continuing royalist challenges to the French republican experiment, in the form of foreign invasion and aristocratic counter-revolution. Given the continued presence of a relatively large landed aristocracy and a clergy with strong monarchist inclinations, French republicans were reluctant to accept organized dissent that might threaten the constitutional foundations of a republican form of government. For the Girondin Republican leaders of the Directory, the threat posed by the Jacobins after 1795 provided an additional justification for refusing to tolerate organized political dissent.

During the years from 1795 to 1799, annual national elections prompted the formation of nascent political parties and the first attempts by French republicans to legitimize political parties. Although the Constitution of 1795 guaranteed freedom of association, it forbade both affiliation and correspondence among clubs, outlawed collective petitions, banned the label "société populaire" that most Jacobin clubs had adopted, and forbade associations from holding public meetings or imposing conditions of admission and eligibility upon their members.[7] The language of the Constitution was sufficiently ambiguous, however, to allow circumvention. In 1797 royalists organized "philanthropic institutes" to mobilize grass roots electoral support, which brought them an electoral triumph. Leading royalist deputies caucused at the Clichy Club to devise a parliamentary strategy.[8] The royalists' continuing connections to counter-revolutionary émigrés and British agents enabled the Directory government to destroy this early attempt at party formation in the so-called Fructidor coup, in which royalist deputies were purged from the Assembly. During the 1798 election campaign, Republican leaders of the Directory faced a different threat, from Jacobins who had developed strong local party organizations centered around clubs and newspapers as well as a national parliamentary leadership. The Directory's leadership responded by taking initial steps toward building a political party, despite their continued opposition in principle to political parties.[9] After the Jacobin victory in the 1798 election, the Directory government annulled the election of Jacobin deputies. "The painstaking work of building up a constitutional party of opposition," writes Isser Woloch, "was arbitrarily canceled out and stigmatized as subversive. It was not simply the individual candidates who were the objects of this arbitrary purge, but the nascent party formations themselves."[10]

Despite the repression, the Jacobin club network persisted, playing an active role in the elections of 1799. By 1799, write Hunt, Lansky, and Hanson, "The left and party organization as a political tool were indissolubly linked together, so much so that the Jacobins began to defend themselves explicitly as a party. ..."[11] These neo-Jacobins of 1799 portrayed themselves as a loyal opposition and acknowledged the legitimacy of organized political dissent as long as it occurred within the boundaries of commitment to a republican form of the state. This initial eighteenth century effort at party formation, and the early glimmerings of a republican defense of the legitimacy of parties by Jacobin democrats, was brought to an abrupt end with Napoleon Bonaparte's coup d'état. In voiding the results of elections, Republican leaders of the Directory discredited parliamentary politics and paved the way for the downfall of the French First Republic.

Early French Republicans' unitary vision of politics was inconsistent with the organized dissent generated by the popular political participation accompanying expanded suffrage rights and frequent elections. This dilemma was the basis for a quandary: republican leaders accepted rules of governance—including expanded suffrage rights and competitive elections—which gave rise to organizations resembling early political parties but they simultaneously rejected parties as illegitimate. Although the creation of a parliamentary republic during the 1790s generated the first "proto-parties," these organizations existed in the inhospitable context of a political culture informed by notions of national sovereignty that denounced political opposition as a threat to the newly created indivisible nation.

By 1848 French republican leaders uniformly regarded party organizations as legitimate vehicles of organized political opposition. After seizing state power and proclaiming universal male suffrage in 1848, Republicans proceeded to create a mass party and allowed their political opponents to create party organizations that actively contested nation-wide elections.[12] Viewed from the vantage point of 1789, this is a rather surprising development. It signaled French republicans' rejection of a unitary vision of politics in favor of an adversarial view, which regarded politics as an arena for the expression and regulation of conflicting interests. The growth of competing parties representing different interests belied the notion of a general will reflecting the shared interests of all citizens. It fostered a revival of the view that elected officials should be held accountable to the particular constituencies that elected them. When mid-nineteenth century republican leaders rejected the notion of a universal will embodying a common good, they also embraced a view of representation more consistent with an adversarial vision of politics, one in which elected officials should be held accountable to their constituents via party organizations and platforms.[13] An explanation of why and when this change in normative rules governing competition for state power took place requires attention to the conflicting interests represented by competing political parties.

The leadership of the republicans' electoral opponents—Orleanists and Legitimists—accepted political parties as legitimate actors on the political scene in 1848 but remained wary of associational and suffrage rights and uncommitted to a republican form of the state. They were convinced that a monarchy, rather than a republic based on universal male suffrage, could best assure public order and the protection of property rights. The earliest French proponents of parties—constitutional monarchists like Benjamin Constant—espoused liberal individualist principles but remained steadfastly opposed to suffrage extension. Constant recognized from his parliamentary experience under the constitutional Bourbon monarchy of 1815–1830 that the toleration of dissent could limit rather than exacerbate political conflict, as long as political participation was sufficiently restricted to property-owning elites. The toleration of political parties by French governing elites from 1815 to 1848 was based on the recognition that parties might serve to reduce conflict by negotiating intra-elite conflicts. Such toleration was premised on the existence of restrictions on associational and suffrage rights which guaranteed that party organizations excluded workers and prevented the emergence of any mass party challenging dominant class interests. After 1830, when workers attracted by early visions of socialism that challenged capitalist property relations embraced the republican cause in growing numbers, this liberal tolerance was quickly replaced by political repression.

The establishment of an Orleanist constitutional monarchy in 1830 was followed by widespread strikes, working-class insurrections in 1832 and 1834, and republican political agitation, all of which led to the passage of repressive laws limiting the right to association.[14] After 1834, liberalism became closely associated with an undemocratic and politically repressive constitutional monarchy, thereby temporarily dissociating liberal and democratic traditions and fostering a close tie between republicanism and socialism in France. The workers' insurrections of the early 1830s and the rapid spread of early socialist ideologies among artisans during the 1840s made French political elites wary of associational and suffrage rights. These became two key goals in the struggle to re-establish a republican form of the state. The Revolution of 1848 inaugurated a regime based on universal male suffrage and a competitive party system. However, Orleanist and Legitimist party leaders were unwilling to tolerate organized political dissent that threatened private property or public order while republican leaders remained hesitant to tolerate political dissent that threatened the Republic. After a growing Republican party with a strong socialist wing expanded its electoral base into the countryside and threatened to capture the French presidency in 1851, Louis Napoleon launched a coup d'état. The coup was followed by intense repression which temporarily destroyed the Republican party and put an end to the party system of the Second Republic. It was not until after the violent repression of the working-class challenges of the revolutionary communes of 1870–1871 and the establishment of a conservative Republic on firm foundations by the Constitution of 1875 that organized mass party competition become fully legitimated in the eyes of French political elites.

Political Party Legitimation in the United States

Like their French counterparts, the Founding Fathers of the American Republic, including James Madison, Alexander Hamilton, and George Washington, denounced political parties as factions, as divisive and disloyal threats to national unity. Although they disagreed as to whether parties should be abolished or tolerated as unavoidable evils, late eighteenth century American political leaders shared an aversion to political parties.[15] Among the founders of the American Republic, a political discourse which invoked "the public interest," rather than the "general will of the nation," was used to elaborate a unitary vision of politics. Although national party organizations existed at the beginning of the nineteenth century, neither Federalists or Republicans recognized their opponents' right to existence. The early Federalists unsuccessfully attempted to eliminate their rivals with the Alien and Sedition Act of 1798. This legislation equated organized political opposition with subversion and established criminal penalties for criticism of the government or its officials.[16] The political repression facing Jeffersonian Republicans did not lead them to embrace the need for organized political parties. In resisting Federalist attempts to destroy them, Republicans defended free speech but not free association or the legitimacy of party organizations.[17] The War of 1812 sealed the defeat of the Federalists and established a one-party system which lasted until 1828. "The best effect of the war," wrote Thomas Jefferson, "has been the complete suppression of party."[18] As was the case in France, war and the threat of war provided rival political leaders with opportunities to charge their opponents with conspiracy, disloyalty to the nation, and allegiance to foreign powers. Wars enabled political leaders to pose as men who were "above parties" and could therefore unite the nation. In short, the international conflicts that accompanied early nation-state formation were not a propitious context for the legitimation of organized political dissent.

In the United States, political leaders began to defend parties as beneficial institutions during the 1820s and 1830s. The expansion of the suffrage to include most adult white males as well as the adoption of a new system of presidential elections, in which popular votes rather than legislatures chose presidential electors, fostered the growth of state-level party organizations designed to mobilize popular votes.[19] In contrast to the Federalist and Jeffersonian Republican parties, which were coalitions of notables,[20] the Jacksonians created mass-based party organizations. The expansion of the electorate, alongside Jacksonian reforms which increased the number of public offices subject to popular election and shortened the terms of office, created a new group of professional party leaders. These men espoused a different view of the legitimacy of parties after 1828.[21] This precarious tolerance and acceptance was soon tested by violent sectional rivalries which culminated in the American Civil War. Prior to the Civil War, many political elites accepted organized national party competition as an alternative to sectional rivalries.[22] The failure of such competition to peacefully resolve the conflict ultimately reinforced rather than undermined the legitimacy of organized mass party competition as a central rule of the political game.

Explaining the Timing of
Party Legitimation in France and the United States

Political parties gained widespread acceptance among governing elites earlier in the United States than in France and mass parties arose at an earlier date. Two key factors help to explain the different pattern: intra-elite consensus on the form of the state and the timing of suffrage extension to the working class. In contrast to France, the U.S. experienced an earlier and more firmly established republican form of the state. The issue of monarchy or republic was resolved in the United States by the end of the eighteenth century while in France it continued to animate political antagonisms and conflicts until the final decades of the nineteenth century. In the United States, Republicans of the 1790s, including Madison, Jefferson, and Monroe, accused their Federalist opponents of conspiring to restore a monarchy. Federalists in turn charged their opponents with advocating a French-inspired version of democracy that threatened private property and public order. However, the republican form of government in the U.S. did not face the same threats to its existence that it did in France, where proponents of monarchy triumphed in 1815 and remained politically formidable until late in the nineteenth century. There was a relatively early and widespread consensus among American political elites on the form of the state and the constitution. Such a consensus was not shared by French Legitimist, Orleanist, Republican, and Bonapartist leaders. In France, rival groups did not acknowledge being bound by the same rules of the game, hence their resort to coups d'état (in 1799 and 1851) and revolution (in 1830 and 1848) and their denial of legitimacy to their opponents' goals. As long as republican political leaders regarded their opponents as a threat to the republic and their opponents defined the republican challenge as a threat to constitutionally protected property rights, neither side was willing to clearly differentiate between organized political opposition and sedition. In short, the absence of intra-elite consensus on the form of the state, which was inhibited by the presence of a powerful landed aristocracy and revolutionary workers challenging capitalist property relations, prevented acceptance of a norm acknowledging the legitimacy of organized political dissent.

Differences between France and the U.S. in the timing of legitimation of political parties suggest a second key factor, the timing of suffrage extension to the (male) working class. Whereas American political elites became reconciled to democracy and accepted universal male suffrage relatively early, their French counterparts feared the consequences of popular political participation and remained wary of extending the vote to propertyless workers. The intensity and violence of political conflicts during the First French Republic explains their hesitancy. Although the early years of the American Republic were marked by considerable social turmoil, including an armed insurrection [i.e., the Whiskey Rebellion of 1794], the founding of the American Republic was not marked by regicide, guillotines, and civil war. Nor did it culminate in a military dictatorship. The violent revolutionary experience of 1789 combined with the violent class conflict of the early 1830s and the rapid spread of early socialist ideologies among artisanal workers during the 1840s made French political leaders wary of associational and suffrage rights. The workers' insurrections of the early 1830s convinced most French political leaders that voting and associational rights posed a serious threat to property rights and public order.[23] In contrast, American political elites had early evidence that freedom of association and expanded voting rights could serve to control and regulate popular protest. In the United States, early democratic politics did not give rise to a national political party with a strong socialist wing. In France, socialist workers played a key role in Republican party politics during the 1840s and many socialists found their way into positions of local, and to a lesser extent national, state power after the revolution of 1848.

The relatively early extension of male suffrage rights in the United States had important consequences for the character of party formation. The early acceptance of universal male suffrage by American political elites resulted in mass parties that were less class oriented, more patronage-based, and posed less of a threat to established property relations than the Republican party of mid-nineteenth century France. The first mass political parties in the U.S. were founded by elites who occupied positions of power within the prevailing regimes and undertook to mobilize a popular following. The first mass party in France was established by political outsiders who organized a mass following in an effort to expand access to the electoral system for their working-class supporters and replace the existing constitutional monarchy with a different form of government, a parliamentary republic.

Conclusion: Political Change and the Logic of Rules

The history of party legitimation in France and the United States suggests that people are perfectly capable of justifying and adhering to seemingly contradictory rules. During the French Revolution, norms concerning the illegitimacy of parties conflicted with a political rule which rewarded those most capable of creating organizations that could mobilize large numbers of voters with public office. This contradiction created the anomaly of the founders of the earliest parties ardently denouncing the very institution they were helping to create. French republican leaders' rejection of parties did not prevent the emergence of nascent parties, in the form of Jacobin clubs, that contested national elections. Similar norms in the United States did not prevent the formation of the Federalist and Republican parties. Political leaders did not resolve this quandary by choosing between the rules in conflict, i.e., by either rejecting electoral competition or failing to organize parties. They resolved the quandary by defining their own organizations and activities, which they regarded as pursuing the general will of the nation, as falling outside the definition of parties, which they continued to equate with factions. In France the quandary was temporarily eliminated in 1799 by Napoleon's coup d'état, which altered electoral rules and established a military dictatorship, but revived with the establishment of a constitutional monarchy in 1815. The subsequent resolution of the quandary entailed a redefinition of the meaning of parties so as to distinguish them from factions.

Peoples' capacity to embrace seemingly contradictory rules is also evidenced by the sans-culottes' espousal of an imperative mandate rule of representation. This did not prevent their adherence to the contradictory rule that elected officials must pursue the general will of the entire nation rather than the demands of any particular constituency. They simply defined the nation as the people of Paris. These examples suggest that the internal contradictions of ideologies are not always perceived by people and that even when they are, people are quite capable of holding incompatible ideas. Political behavior is not rigidly determined by rules because divergent courses of action can be made to accord with the same rule.

The Dalhousie group identifies three ways in which people confront quandaries: (1) newcomers working under one rule may appear and displace those people working under an incompatible rule; (2) people may confront the incompatible demands of two sets of rules by openly defying one in favor of the other; (3) people may feel obliged to obey both rules and experience a moral dilemma. The first response appears to describe the process of party legitimation in the United States, where party professionals emerged as a new political elite during the 1830s. But none of these three responses adequately capture what happened in the French case, which suggests a fourth possible response. People may reinterpret rules by redefining either their own activities or the rules designed to govern them so as to resolve, in their own minds at least, the quandaries they face. Given that political rules are often defined by vague concepts—e.g., the nation, the general will, liberty—that are open to multiple contested interpretations and that normative rules are subject to less systematically enforced sanctions than legal rules, this device of reinterpreting the terms that define rules to accord with interests and goals may be a common response to quandaries. Whose interpretation prevails will depend less on the logical consistency of competing rules than on the unequal distribution of resources and the differential capacities for collective action of contending groups.

Deontic logic is undoubtedly useful for clarifying and specifying conflicting rules and the quandaries they produce, such as early republicans' simultaneous rejection of parties and acceptance of electoral and parliamentary rules that fostered organized political dissent. However, the various resolutions of such conflicts cannot be derived from logical considerations alone; understanding the different forms these resolutions took requires historical research. Such research is valuable not only because it can elucidate past rules and rule conflicts but, more importantly, because it can situate rules and rule changes in the context of larger historical processes, such as the emergence of nation-states in an international state system and the formation of the working class in a developing capitalist economy and political system. Studying logical inconsistencies in the writings of prominent political leaders, or in texts like the Constitution, and studying change in terms of before and after snapshots may help us to identify quandaries. But if we want to understand the sources and resolutions of quandaries, we must look beyond texts to contexts, beyond specific events to large-scale and long-term processes.[24]

The character and internal logic of long-term processes—like capitalist industrialization and state formation—impart systematic tendencies and particular trajectories to political institutions. Although I share with the Dalhousie group an appreciation of the centrality of contradictions in deciphering these trajectories, I am not convinced that contradictions rooted in rule conflicts are the central source of political change. Political elites were not motivated to reassess parties by a desire to eliminate the logical inconsistency between rules—i.e., between a rule of suffrage rights which fostered party organization and norms concerning what constituted legitimate political activity. Their need to resolve this rule conflict appears to have been less the product of a desire for logical consistency than the result of a need to achieve certain goals—such as the incorporation of French workers into the polity via organizations that would not challenge established capitalist property rights or the creation of American political organizations that could prevent sectional loyalties from becoming central lines of political division.

In France the resolution of the quandary concerning political parties awaited the dissociation of republicanism and socialism, the repression of the revolutionary communes of 1870–1871, and the establishment of a stable conservative republican form of the state. In the U.S. case, the resolution depended on the growth of a bureaucratic party organization which displaced class-based interests and goals with the patronage politics of ethnically-oriented local political machines.[25] In both cases, politically transformative action was motivated less by a desire to resolve quandaries so as to attain normative order and consistency than by political elites' pursuit of certain goals and interests. Changes in political rules cannot be explained in terms of a desire to eliminate logical inconsistencies in established rules. They are a result of the antagonistic interests and differential capacities for collective action of social actors.

The comparative study of party legitimation suggests that if we wish to move beyond merely identifying quandaries and rewriting them in the language of formal logical notation to the more difficult task of explaining their consequences and the determinants of their different resolutions, we need to be attentive to unequally distributed resources as well as rules, interests as well as norms, and learning as well as deliberative processes. Deliberative processes in which considerable attention is devoted to the logic of rules undoubtedly play a role in political change. Yet the weight that deliberators give to logical considerations is arguably less significant in the dynamics of change than the weight they give to geopolitical and socio-economic interests. If deontic logic is to contribute to historical understanding, it will have to be attentive not only to deliberative processes and the norms that govern them but also to the interests and resources of social actors who, in pursuing conflicting goals with varying capacities for collective action, transform political rules.

Notes

1. Giovanni Sartori, *Parties and Party Systems* (Cambridge: Cambridge University Press, 1976), p. 11.
2. Richard Hofstadter, *The Idea of a Party System: The Rise of Legitimate Opposition in the United States* (Berkeley: University of California Press, 1969), p. 123.

3. For a discussion of the central features of classical liberal ideology, see Stuart Hall,"Variants of Liberalism," in James Donald and Stuart Hall, eds., *Politics and Ideology* (Milton Keynes: Open University Press, 1985), pp. 34–69.

4. Jane Mansbridge, *Beyond Adversary Democracy* (New York: Basic Books, 1980), p. 3.

5. For an analysis of conceptions of representation in late eighteenth century French political culture, see Keith Michael Baker, "Representation," in K. M. Baker, *The French Revolution and the Creation of Modern Political Culture* (New York: Pergamon Press, 1987), Vol. 1, pp. 469–91.

6. "The sans-culottes," writes William Sewell Jr., "reduced the notion of representation almost to the vanishing point. As opposed to the Girondins, who saw the individual citizen's chief role as casting a vote to choose members of a representative body, who would then rationally determine the general will and enact it into law, the sans-culottes believed that the people as a whole, acting through their local sectional assemblies, should constantly, collectively, and unanimously express their general will, maintaining continual surveillance over the 'mandatories' and immediately replacing those who deviated from the general will. ..." "Ideologies and Social Revolution: Reflections on the French Case," *Journal of Modern History*, Vol. 57, 1985, p. 76.

7. Isser Woloch, *Jacobin Legacy: The Democratic Movement Under the Directory* (Princeton: Princeton University Press, 1970), pp. 16-17.

8. Woloch, *Jacobin Legacy*, pp. 273–74.

9. "In effect," writes Isser Woloch, "the Directory was building its party from the top down by means of official propaganda, patronage, electoral funding, and a relatively restrained use of intimidation. On balance it was contributing to the crystallization of parties by its response to the Jacobin challenge, regardless of its theoretical opposition to parties. Democrats and conservatives both seemed to be following the logic of their positions rather than the conventional wisdom of political theory." *Jacobin Legacy*, p. 280.

10. Woloch, *Jacobin Legacy*, p. 310.

11. Lynn Hunt, David Lansky, and Paul Hanson, "The Failure of the Liberal Republic in France, 1795–1799: The Road to Brumaire," *Journal of Modern History*, Vol. 51, 1979, p. 755.

12. These political organizations were not disciplined, bureaucratically structured, professionally administered national organizations, but they qualify as parties in the sense of political groups sharing a recognized label and general principles that elected some of their members to local and national office. Most definitions of political parties focus less upon organizational structure, ideology, or ultimate goals than upon functions (e.g. representation, expression of interests). They typically include electoral criteria and often some organizational criteria, such as the requirement that the group have a label, share some general principles, or be cohesive enough to elect some of its members. See, for example, Leon Epstein, *Political Parties in Western Democracies* (New York: Praeger, 1967), p. 9 and Giovanni Sartori, *Parties and Party Systems* (Cambridge: Cambridge University Press, 1976), p. 63.

13. The concrete organizational mechanisms for assuring this accountability did not develop until later in the nineteenth century, although local electoral committees served this function during the late 1860s.

14. At the beginning of 1834 new laws were enacted which prohibited all associations with sections of more than twenty people, a provision directed against the Republican Society of the Rights of Man. The laws required all organizations of more than twenty members to apply for a revocable governmental authorization. The law also extended the liability for unlawful association from leaders to members and to the owners of property on which illegal meetings took place.

15. Richard Hofstadter notes that the creators of the first American party system, Federalists and Republicans, both regarded parties as "sores on the body politic." *The Idea of a Party System*, p. 2. For statements by James Madison, George Washington, and Thomas Jefferson on the dangers of parties, see Noble Cunningham, ed., *The Making of the American Party System* (Englewood Cliffs, N.J., 1965), pp. 6–11, 14–20.

16. On the Sedition Act, see Norman L. Rosenberg, *Protecting the Best Men: An Interpretive History of the Law of Libel* (Chapel Hill: University of North Carolina Press, 1986), pp. 79–101.

17. Hofstadter, *The Idea of a Party System*, p. 113.

18. Hofstadter, *The Idea of a Party System*, p. 182.

19. Hofstadter, *The Idea of a Party System*, p. 210.

20. "During the period extending from the emergence of the two parties [Federalists and Jeffersonian Republicans] in the 1790s through their collapse in the 1820s," observes Martin Shefter, "the level of political participation in most areas of the country was low, party organizations were weak or nonexistent, elective offices were monopolized by local notables, and these officials appointed their associates and clients to positions in the bureaucracy. ..." "Party, Bureaucracy, and Political Change in the United States," in Louis Maisel & Joseph Cooper, eds., *Political Parties: Development and Decay* (Beverly Hills: Sage, 1978), p. 214.

21. "The shift from tolerating parties as necessary evils to accepting them as positive goods," writes Ron Formisano, "took place primarily among political leaders, of course, and especially among those whose careers were becoming like those of professional politicians ...," *The Transformation of Political Culture* (New York: Oxford University Press, 1983), p. 17.

22. Eric Foner contends that Martin Van Buren, one of the architects of the "second" party system, was motivated by a recognition that in the absence of two-party competition, sectional divisions would constitute the central lines of political division. "Van Buren and many of his generation of politicians," writes Foner, "... saw national two-party competition as the alternative to sectional conflict and eventual disunion. ..." *Politics and Ideology in the Age of the Civil War* (New York: Oxford University Press, 1980), p. 38.

23. Alexis de Tocqueville, in his observations on the United States, questioned the fears of his fellow French liberals. "Freedom of association in political matters," he wrote, "is not so dangerous to public tranquility as is supposed, and possibly, after having agitated society for some time, it may strengthen the state in the end." *Democracy in America*, Vol. 2, ed. by P. Bradley (New York: A. A. Knopf, 1945), pp. 126–27.

24. Charles Tilly, *Big Structures, Large Processes, Huge Comparisons* (New York: Russell Sage Foundation, 1984).

25. See Martin Shefter, "Trade Unions and Political Machines: The Organization and Disorganization of the American Working Class in the Late Nineteenth

Century," in Ira Katznelson and Aristide Zolberg, eds., *Working Class Formation: Nineteenth Century Patterns in Western Europe and the United States* (Princeton, N. J.: Princeton University Press, 1986), pp. 197–276.

9

Synoptic Comment on Applications of the Logical Theory of Rules

David Braybrooke

Braybrooke reasserts the relevance of the logic of rules and the issue-processing perspective. He acknowledges the truth of some of the things that Bonfield, Miller, and Aminzade have had to say, but argues that these things only bring forward matters that operate in the history of changes of rules in addition to considerations of logic. The Dalhousie team has not contended, or even suggested, that a logic of rules can express the whole story about changes in rules. Nor does it contend that what the logic can express is sure to be, or even likely to be, the most important part of the story. It is still a part worth illuminating.

If any doubts about the frequency with which social rules operate in history had survived to this point, the historical illustrations brought up by Aminzade, together with Sayre-McCord's constructed examples, should have laid them to rest. Bonfield's finding that the foundation for imputing to manor courts rules applied under modern jurisprudential assumptions is doubtful serves almost equally well to demonstrate that rules are at issue in history; the logic of rules applies just as much to define particular rules that are discovered not to have been current as to define the rules that were. Sayre-McCord's examples also suggest the variety of ways in which rules can, both directly and indirectly, affect people's behavior. But this variety must be multiplied by the great variety of subjects, forms, and purposes to be found in different rules. Can the case for a logic of rules include in this variety technical norms, for example, norms that in effect instruct people in the most efficient use of machinery? Miller would set them aside as "maxims" and worries that if these are allowed to collapse into rules we shall have an uncomfortably diminished accommodation for the variety of reasons that affect human conduct. So long as a robust category of goals—Miller's third category for reasons—is kept up, however, plenty of accommodation would remain, one might think; and while in one connection or another it may be useful to distinguish between rules proper and technical norms, in other connections the distinction may be best suppressed for the time being. Hence, without repudiating the distinction, it may be best to preserve a certain amount of freedom in applying it.

Some arguments for this approach can be found in the treatment of Marx's account of technical change (which is what Miller has specially in mind). That a certain way of dividing labor to use new machinery is the most productive way of using it does not imply that there is a rule prescribing such a division, or even a permission for carrying it out. Moreover, if the division does happen to be the most effective way of reducing workers' bargaining power by eliminating the demand for their traditional skills, this is not a result from logic; logically, things might be otherwise. The employers' interest in reducing the workers' bargaining power might be best served by insisting on a less productive organization of work; and at least as a short-run measure clearing the way for larger appropriations of surplus value in the future, the less productive organization might not conflict with the employers' interest in deriving the maximum benefit from productivity. Competition from other employers may not allow any employer the liberty to choose short-run measures separately from long-run ones; competition may require them all to adopt the most productive division of labor rightaway. But then some cause besides present competition must be found for explaining why the most productive division is also the one that does most to reduce the employees' bargaining power. Some changes in technology, after all, create new skills; and, for the employer, greater dependence on highly skilled labor. In all these cases, it is significant that a rule prescribing the most productive division holds, if it does hold. For that it holds implies that some things that might have been expected to preclude its holding have not had that effect. The same thing can be said of the employers' having a permission to carry out the most productive division, which is what is at issue in the discussion in *Track* that Miller refers to. Further significance attaches to the permission from the fact that not just considerations of power and profit, but one or more rules that have prevailed hitherto might have been expected to run contrary to the permission.

What, however, would be the point of having a rule that the most productive division of labor should be applied to new machinery if employers are under pressures sufficient already to carry this division out? There would be very little point. However, in the real world, competition is not so unremitting as to supply sufficent pressure; nor are employers always fully up to their jobs. The rule might emerge first as a maxim of prudence. It will become something more immediately some social responsibility is ascribed to employers to make the best use of machinery. Pressing the rule upon employers could make sense even under a regime of private property. (One might recall Locke's campaign to have English landowners make better use of the arable in their possession.[1]) Even in a society that relies more on the market than on central planning it may make sense to press the rule; attempts to do something of the sort have occurred from time to time during the last half-century in Britain and in the United States in public complaints about the lack of enterprise in manufacturing firms. In these connections, the rule has without ceasing to be a maxim of prudence become at least a candidate for being a fully-fledged social rule, though perhaps it cannot go all the way to becoming one unless socialism comes in and makes the employers managers of public enterprises.

Another example of maxims or technical norms becoming rules proper expressing a public interest and something rising toward full moral force can be found in the maxims that employers follow in dealing with a strike. On the one hand there is a maxim calling for them to put as much pressure as possible upon the strikers, making the strike so uncomfortable that the strikers will be eager to settle rather than continue it. On the other hand there is a maxim calling for the employers to avoid measures that do more to anger the strikers than to put pressure upon them. For examples nearer at home at the moment of writing than I would like, consider a university administration that cuts off striking faculty from access to their incoming mail, or attempts to sequester research grants that faculty members have won on their individual merits from outside sources. Such measures will not only heighten the strikers' militancy; they will make it more difficult than need be to restore cooperative relations once the strike is over. The latter maxim, like the first, begins as a counsel of prudence. Does not abiding by it soon become, however, a feature of what the strikers and the public expect as reasonable behavior on the part of the employers? But in becoming a standard for reasonable behavior the maxim has become a full-fledged social rule prohibiting merely irritating measures. If employers were perfectly prudent, there would, again, be no point in having such a rule; but they are not, and the rule, upheld by judges or arbitrators or alert members of the general public, serves to bring employers made reckless by anti-union zeal or rage into line with standards of civility applying to both sides of the strike.

Nothing in our conception of the logic of rules implies that all rules are applied with the jurisprudential assumptions respecting rights, attention to precedents, due process, and equal protection which Bonfield suspects may be absent in the manor courts. Rules establishing rights are only a small subclass of rules; and rules may exclude due process (calling, for example, for immediate execution on the battlefield of anyone suspected of intending to desert; or calling for secret procedures without counsel for the defense) and demand unequal protection (for example, sparing the nobility any liability for taxes, or any liability to stand trial in ordinary courts). Even attention to precedents in the strict sense of deliberately making sure that present applications of a rule are consistent with past ones is not a necessary condition of a rule's existing, though there must in upshot be parallel results on parallel occasions. The rules that govern the sort of "alternative dispute resolution" that Bonfield thinks may be ascribed to manor courts instead of legal processes answering to the jurisprudential assumptions seem to be a case in point, for the central rule seems to be, settle a given dispute not with regard to precedents for this topic of dispute but with regard to what has most promise of placating these particular disputants. One can hardly find an intentional pattern in what the manor courts—or any other historical agents—do without imputing to them some rule expressible in the logic of rules with appropriate exactness (no more and no less).

Miller does not direct his challenge against claims that the logic (with its notation) may make attention to rules more precise and with the precision raise new questions about the relations between rules. He questions the importance of rules in causing social change. Does this belie his readiness to look for sources of change internal to social structures? It does move too quickly, one might think, to dismiss rules and difficulties with rules as internal sources. This would leave no internal sources to operate if social structures are identified as structures of rules. However, there is the alternative, which Miller may prefer, of identifying them as structures that combine rules with distributions of interests and of resources among the people living under the structures. Given this view of structures, the case for the importance of rules would have to be made by comparing their operation as internal sources with the operation of those distributions as conditions for the activities of the people in question. In this regard, Miller can be seen to have raised an interesting and immensely complex question for empirical social theory. We should not try to settle it a priori or exclude a priori the possibility that rules will turn out to relatively unimportant, compared to the causal weight of interests backed (when they are backed) by resources sufficient to defend and advance them. They might even approach being epiphenomenal: People might be found always to do what they conceived to be in their interest, sometimes succeeding, sometimes failing; and the rules might just confirm the prevalence for the time being of certain interest-driven patterns of behavior. Marxists will recognize this possibility as answering to a certain view of how the economic basis determines the superstructure of laws and other expressions of ideology.

We cannot settle this issue. We can say something to reduce expectations that it will be resolved in a way that discredits the causal efficacy of rules. Miller's remarks about the persistence into capitalistic times of rules familiar under feudalism beg some questions—which the logic of rules might be called in to assist with—about whether they are in fact the same rules. The Queen observes certain rules in her relations with Parliament that look the same as rules observed by James the First; but they are, one might say, only the same in form. They are no longer equivalent to rules in which the power and judgment of the monarch count for something. Those rules have given way to rules under which the monarch must not defy the advice of her Prime Minister. Something similar has happened to the rule under which the stockholders in a corporation can decide what use the management of the corporation shall make of their property in it; the rule is still there in form, but in substance the managers (given wide diffusion of the stock over a large number of stockholders) are no longer bound by it. The case for the efficacy of rules need not fail because rules can cease to correspond to the realities of behavior. It should make its stand upon rules that do correspond.

All along, both the obstacles to personal defiance and to the social policy of abandoning the rule are consistent with the rule being a creation of a set of human beings, which would vanish if they behaved sufficiently differently. Transconventional rules, it is true, would not vanish, but they, too, could be defied both by persons and by whole populations; to say that they were still present would be only to say that the confusion created by the defiance was inescapable.

Aminzade makes the point that people often carry on in spite of confusion, contriving to live somehow with blatant contradictions. This is true, and raises the question how far people are attached to the rules of logic, including the rules of logic brought to bear by a logic of rules. Their attachment, like their attachment to the rules not of logic that the logic of rules treats, may be expected to be variable. Is it at all plausible to suppose, however, that it often falls to zero, or is more often than not negligible? People do not relish finding themselves at odds in attempting to communicate with others whose cooperation they wish to obtain; they find it hardly more agreeable to have their aims and their actions continually out of accord. So, even if not all of them have become so far aware of the rules of logic as to identify implications, contradictions, and non sequiturs, and attach themselves to some extent to abiding by the rules insofar as the rules are at stake in such identifications, they may be expected to give some heed to logic— to back into heeding it unaware of the rules—because the alternative is confusion, even chaos. Thus they would be attached to logic in a way touched upon by Miller, as an instrument for avoiding confusion; though attached to it unawares, as Sayre-McCord implies that people may be attached to transconventional rules. Now suppose that they are made aware of the rules and recognize that, while flouting them breeds confusion, abiding by them prevents it. Will not people who get this far in their logical education value logic as a means of preventing confusion? We must not take for granted that this value is widespread; an educated awareness of the rules of logic is not widespread. We must not take it for granted, on the other hand, that there are not some people who continually make a good deal of logic, while there are few that heed it not at all.

Rules other than rules of logic—the rules arising from human invention, which vanish when human beings no longer accept them, the rules whose presence, operation, and supersession the logic of rules enables us to identify and track more precisely—awaken only variable attachment, too. Conflicts—quandaries, and conflicts short of quandaries—that might otherwise trouble people greatly may fail to do so just because the attachment to one or another of the rules involved is so weak that the rules collapse in favor of other rules once the conflicts arise. Sometimes—very often—people patch over conflicts in some such way as Aminzade portrays the revolutionary citizens of Paris, professing attachment at once to having their delegates bound by their mandates and to having them express the unified will of the whole French nation, and reconciling the two rules implied by persuading themselves that the citizens of Paris express the will of the nation. They thus—not always, of course, so blatantly—"reinterpret rules by redefining either their own activities or the rules designed to govern them so as to resolve, in their own minds at least, the quandaries they face" (Aminzade, above). If we do not, in *Track* give fully systematic attention to this as a common way—it may even be the most common way—of dealing with quandaries, it is nevertheless treated explicitly at several points.[2] We do have some prime illustrations to offer: most spectacularly, perhaps, on a topic of Aminzade's own, the move made by Madison and other early "Republicans" to redefine what they organized not as a party or faction—the sort of thing that they had been so vigorously denouncing—but as an organization defending the national interest from other people's parties.[3] A subtler case can be found in the readiness with which British MP's in the 1790s accepted an end to the slave trade some years hence, after a rising tax would have made it unprofitable, as close enough to abolishing the trade to satisfy the rule under which abolishing it was prescribed to them.[4]

Do not these very redefinitions, in their way—something like the way in which hypocrisy pays tribute to virtue—manifest some attachment both to the rules in question and to the rules of logic? If people take steps to avoid conflicts among rules, including quandaries, the conflicts enter into the explanations of these very steps; and the steps can be counted as evidence that the rules have some efficacy. Part of the answer to Miller's question about whether quandaries ever have important roles in social change lies in their being logical disasters that, foreseen it may be only dimly, people take some pains to avoid. They are sufficiently attached to the rules that are leading them into quandaries to want to find formulas under which they can persuade themselves they can conform to all the rules at issue. We do not agree, however, that quandaries are always anticipated, and avoided, if not by deliberated relegislation, by some stratagem of redefinition. Indeed, if we are ready to say that a quandary has come to pass in some instances before it becomes an issue to be resolved by debate in which the quandary is fully recognized as such, Aminzade's example of representation as conceived by the citizens of Paris and our own example of Madison and his allies evading their own rule against parties will serve as examples of quandaries that have not been anticipated and dealt with while they remain only incipient. Miller denies that the quandary that I found represented in Engels's account of the consequences for appropriating surplus value of changing from having workers and toolowners the same people to having them different classes of people was a real one.[5] I think his quarrel is rather with Engels than with me. I agree that Engels's account is suspiciously oversimplified and subject to just the sort of objections about exploitation by guild masters that Miller can find in other texts of Marxism. I agree, too, that side by side with whatever pattern of appropriation prevailed among urban artisans, there was wage labor in agriculture; indeed I cite this as offering a model for resolving the quandary that I find in Engels's account.

There are, I think, further quandaries represented in Marx and Engels's account of history; they are treated in the chapter of *Track* devoted to the role of justice in Marxist theory, and include as the most important examples the quandaries about respecting in turn feudal claims to the social surplus and capitalist claims once the classes concerned cease to make useful social contributions. Standing in the way of Miller's giving due weight to these quandaries may be his belief, which I do not share, that Marx and Engels do not make use of the concept of justice and in particular do not consider that capitalism has become unjust (as feudalism had become after its heyday). However, an obstacle equally, perhaps more important, is, again, Miller's inclination to think—as Aminzade does—that it is not the rules or difficulties with the rules that account for important social changes, but the distribution of interests and the distribution of resources. (Aminzade speaks of interests and capacities.) Again, I have no intention of refusing these things more causal weight—possibly, very much more causal weight—than rules or conflicts between rules. However, can interests and capacities (or resources) be treated separately from rules? Rules assign resources; thus (if for no other reason) people have an interest in having some rules upheld. Rules guide their use of resources; and in this connection help define their interests (e. g., given certain rules, it will be in their interest to save in one form rather than another). Goals, which both Miller and Aminzade cite as alternative explanatory considerations, are equally intimately intertwined with rules: on occasion, people have as their goals the legislation or the enforcement of certain rules; and, again, their goals commonly reflect the prevailing rules and the extent to which their uses of their resources are circumscribed by those rules. It would be wholly implausible to suppose that rules are efficacious independently of people's attachment to them, and this attachment depends on their interests and their goals, while the upshot of the attachment depends on their resources. Is it not equally implausible to suppose that interests, goals, and resources operate in ways that are not consequences also of rules?

Notes

1. See Richard Ashcraft, *Revolutionary Politics and Locke's Two Treatises of Government* (Princeton: Princeton University Press, 1986), p. 271.

2. See, e.g., *Track,* Chapter 1, Chapter 9, Chapter 11.

3. See the discussion in *Track,* Chapter 9.

4. See *Track,* Chapter 10.

5. See my article, "The Logic of the Succession of Cultures," in Howard E. Kiefer and Milton K. Munitz, *Mind, Science, and History* (Albany: State University of New York Press, 1970), in which I discuss some theses of Engels's in *Socialism: Utopian and Scientific.*

PART TWO

Transition

10

Do We Know Enough About Legal Norms?

Charles Silver

With Silver's contribution, the discussion of changes in rules continues, but Silver is concerned specifically with how information about changes—changes in laws made by the decisions of lawsuits—is diffused. He takes an economic approach to this question and challenges a current theory according to which lawsuits will be brought in numbers sufficient to maintain an optimal flow of this information.

Introduction

Some people obey laws intentionally. They act as they know laws require. Some people disobey laws intentionally. They act as they know laws forbid. Both sorts of people have one thing in common: they know something about law. A person who obeys intentionally knows what actions laws permit, and a person who disobeys intentionally knows what actions laws forbid. A full explanation of intentional obedience and disobedience to law must therefore include an account of how people learn about law.

Nor is a single account of this learning process likely to suffice, if only because information about law travels by a variety of routes. It spreads by both market and nonmarket means. Because different information networks may have different structures, they may have to be modeled in different terms.

William Landes and Richard Posner modeled one network in an effort to explain the growth of information about common law norms, the norms judges in common law countries are said to create when they decide cases in court. The model, which they propound in several articles and books,[1] predicts that lawsuits will maintain the flow of information about common law norms at an optimal rate. To communicate the intuition behind their account, Landes and Posner ask readers to [s]uppose ... a completely

"

new statute has just been enacted. There are no precedents indicating how the statute is to be applied. ... Initially, therefore, there will be great uncertainty as to the practical meaning of the statute. The uncertainty will increase the private costs of negotiating out-of-court settlements of disputes resulting from attempts to apply the statute because the outcome of litigation over the meaning of the statute will be difficult to predict. Hence a good deal of litigation can be expected to occur and, as a by-product, precedents defining the precise meaning of the statute will be generated. As the stock of legal knowledge relating to the statute is built up, uncertainty will fall, and with it the amount of litigation and hence the production of additional precedents. But uncertainty will not be eliminated; as changing social or economic conditions generate new kinds of disputes over the application of the statute the stock of prior legal knowledge will depreciate, inducing litigation that will produce fresh precedents.[2]

If Landes and Posner are correct, lawsuits maintain an efficient flow of information about law because people sue when laws are cloudy and settle when laws are clear.

Landes and Posner's account of the connection between uncertainty, lawsuits and information has sparked few flames. A small number of scholars have questioned it, one has embraced it, and it has drawn little attention on the whole.[3] For example, although many scholars and judges have complained of the rapidly rising litigation rate in the United States, to my knowledge only Posner has seen a need to explain why the decline in the settlement rate has failed to correct itself, as the model suggests it should.[4] Nor has any scholar or judge been concerned that reforms designed to discourage litigation would reduce the flow of information to a suboptimal rate, although this too is a possible implication of the model. Because Landes and Posner's views are rarely permitted the comfort of obscurity for long,[5] it is surprising that so few people have taken notice of their opinion on an issue of importance.

I think a careful assessment of Landes and Posner's model will show that the possibility of a shortage of information about law is real. That, at any rate, is what I shall try to prove here. I will first explain the model, and the economic analysis of litigation on which it is based, in detail. By doing so I hope to introduce Landes and Posner's work to an audience of readers who are likely to find it important and interesting. I also hope to further the aims of the Dalhousie University project on the logic of norms, the project that gives this volume of essays its occasion and point. Even if Landes and Posner are mistaken, as I think they are, they force one to think seriously about the means by which information about laws and other norms is produced.

After the expository sections—sections 2 and 3—are complete, I will explain why I think the prediction of optimality is unwarranted. My objection is simple. It is that information about law is a public good and that litigants therefore lack incentives to produce information about law at an optimal rate. After I set out this complaint, I will explain why Landes and Posner's reply, which relies on the fact that lawsuits are subsidized by the public, is insufficient.

The Economic Model of the Decision to Sue

As mentioned, Landes and Posner claim that uncertainty breeds litigation and thereby maintains an optimal flow of information about law. An inefficient increase in the level of uncertainty prompts a corresponding and correcting change in the rate of litigation, and efficient levels of certainty and litigation are restored.

The basis for Landes and Posner's claim is a simple economic model of the decision to sue. The intuition the model embraces is that conflicts settle when disputants can agree on a price. For example, if an injurer will pay up to $10,000 to avoid litigation and a victim will accept $9,000 or more, the dispute will settle out of court. Otherwise, "if the plaintiff won't settle for less than $10,000 and the defendant won't settle for more than $9,000, settlement negotiations will fail."[6]

Not everyone accepts Landes and Posner's simple exchange model of settlements, and in some respects I think their critics have the upper hand.[7] My purpose, however, is neither to defend their model nor to reject it. It is to show that even if the exchange-based account of settlements is correct, the conclusion that lawsuits maintain an optimal level of information about law is not. I will therefore assume that lawsuits occur for the reason Landes and Posner suggest, that is, because litigants are unable to effect mutually advantageous exchanges out of court.

Given that parties settle when they can agree on a price, it remains to determine how people who are involved in disputes form maximum offers and minimum demands. Under the American system where each party pays his own costs and taxpayers bear the expense of running the courts, the conventional wisdom is that settlement offers and demands reflect the influence of three factors: the probability that the plaintiff will win; the size of the award the plaintiff will receive if liability is imposed on the defendant; and the difference between the the cost of litigating and the cost of settling before trial. A plaintiff's minimum demand "is the judgment if he wins discounted by his estimate of the probability that he will win" *minus* the net of his litigation and settlement costs. A defendant's maximum offer "is the judgment if he loses discounted by his estimate of the probability of losing" *plus* the same net amount.[8] It is only when a plaintiff expects to win more than a defendant expects to lose that a trial will take place.

The condition for litigation is, then:

$$P_pJ - C + S > P_dJ + C - S, \tag{1}$$

"where J is the size of the judgment if the plaintiff wins, P_p is the probability of plaintiff's winning as estimated by the plaintiff and P_d is the defendant's estimate of that probability, and C and S are the costs of litigation and settlement, respectively, of each party."[9] The right side of inequality (1) represents a defendant's maximum offer. The left side represents a plaintiff's minimum demand. When the latter exceeds the former, the parties will be unable to settle and a trial is predicted to occur.

It may be helpful to work through an example.[10] Suppose a plaintiff and a defendant both think the plaintiff will win $10,000 if the plaintiff prevails at trial (J = $10,000), and both estimate the plaintiff's chances at 50% (P_p = P_d = .5). Now suppose each party will have to pay $1,000 in litigation costs (C) if the case goes to trial and $500 in settlement costs (S) if it is resolved out of court.

Under these assumptions, a settlement will be reached. The plaintiff will expect to receive a discounted award of $5,000 at trial, $1,000 of which will be used to defray costs, leaving a net return of $4,000. To this amount the plaintiff will add $500, the cost of negotiating a settlement, for it is only when this cost is covered that the plaintiff will be indifferent between settling and going to trial. In the case imagined, then, the plaintiff will demand no less than $4,500 in settlement.

By contrast, the defendant will pay up to $5,500 to get rid of the case. This figure reflects the defendant's discounted loss of $5,000 at trial, the cost of defending at trial ($1,000), and the cost of negotiating a settlement agreement ($500). In this case, then, the defendant's maximum offer exceeds the plaintiff's minimum demand and settlement is the predicted result.[11]

This is shown by returning to inequality (1). By plugging in the appropriate values, we get

$$.5(10,000) - 1,000 + 500 < .5(10,000) + 1,000 - 500, \tag{1'}$$

or

$$4,500 < 5,500.$$

Thus, the model predicts that the parties will resolve their differences on their own. It is no accident that the parties are $1,000 apart. This figure can be derived from inequality (1). By rearranging the terms of the basic model we get

$$(P_p - P_d)J > 2(C - S). \tag{2}$$

When parties agree on the plaintiff's chances of winning, as they do here, $P_p = P_d$ and the left side of (2) goes to \$0. In this situation, any excess of C over S will create room for the parties to negotiate an agreement.

A condition for litigation is, then, that the parties' estimates of the plaintiff's chances at trial differ by some amount. The extent of the difference required is a function of the amount to be lost or won, as shown in inequality (3).

$$P_p - P_d > 2(C - S)/J. \tag{3}$$

As the stakes increase, ever smaller differences of opinion about a plaintiff's prospects at trial will prevent people from settling. In the example described above, the required divergence is specified by (3').

$$P_p - P_d > 2(1{,}000 - 500)/10{,}000, \tag{3'}$$

or

$$P_p - P_d > 0.1 \tag{4}$$

In other words, a trial will occur only if the plaintiff's estimate of the probability of winning at trial exceeds the defendant's estimate of the probability of losing by more than 10%.

Uncertainty and Litigation

"In general, then, litigation will occur only if both parties are optimistic" and only if they are optimistic by more than a specifiable amount.[12] But why might a difference greater than 10%, or any difference at all, come about? If plaintiffs and defendants have equal resources, equal intelligence, equal representation, etc., will their estimates ever diverge?

If the answer to this question were no, all disputes would be expected to settle. And, in fact, most do, which means that a predicted 100% settlement rate would not be very far from the mark. But trials do occur—more and more often of late—and an acceptable model of the decision to sue will have to explain why.

Standing alone, the economic model says nothing about why an excess of P_p over P_d might arise. It says only that trials occur when P_p exceeds P_d by a sufficient amount, and it treats the process by which P_p and P_d are formed as a black box. To explain why litigants' assessments of their prospects may differ, one must look outside the economic model of the decision to sue.

The difficulty of accounting for mutual optimism is increased if one keeps in mind that disagreements over facts rarely prompt appeals, the kind of lawsuits from which most important opinions of law emerge. The standard of review in force in the United States requires appellate courts to uphold all but clearly erroneous findings of fact. Because this standard is easily met, "[C]ivil appeals are relatively infrequent unless there is some uncertainty about the applicable law. ..."[13] If disagreement over facts is eliminated as a potential source of optimism, only disagreement over law remains.

Nor is disagreement over law by itself enough. Even if appeals typically ask courts to decide disputed questions of law, it must still be explained why uncertainty about law would prompt opposing litigants to predict favorable results. They might predict unfavorable results instead.

George Priest and Benjamin Klein have offered an account of the decision to sue on which uncertainty about law causes opposing parties to be optimistic a predictable part of the time.[14] They start with the model Landes and Posner use and they posit that litigants make mistakes. Plaintiffs misestimate P_p and defendants misestimate P_d, both as a predictable matter of chance. When their mistakes are sufficiently great and in the proper direction, trials take place. Because Landes and Posner would probably follow Priest and Klein's lead, I will explain this approach in detail.[15]

Suppose a person is involved in an accident and incurs a loss of \$10,000. The victim is familiar with the facts, but is unsure that the injurer will be held liable at trial because the law governing the accident is unclear. The victim has read the appropriate statutes and cases, but ambiguity remains even so. Although the facts enable the victim to know precisely how negligent the injurer was, the prospect that the injurer will lose at trial is uncertain because the victim is unsure what level of negligence is legally sufficient to establish guilt.

The injurer confronts the same predicament. The injurer knows the facts and the degree of negligence the facts reveal. But the injurer is unsure that the victim will win at trial because the legal standard a court will apply at trial is unclear.

What will the disputants do? Will they settle or take their case to court?

The answer turns on how they handle uncertainty and risk.[16] Priest and Klein hypothesize that litigants deal with uncertainty by making educated guesses about the legal standard a court will apply and by acting on their estimates in the way risk neutral persons would. To represent this process symbolically, first define N. as the minimum level of culpability a court will require before holding an injurer liable for a victim's loss. Then define N_p and N_d as, respectively, the plaintiff's and the defendant's estimates of N.. We then have

$$N_p = N. + e_p \tag{5a}$$

and

$$N_d = N. + e_d \tag{5b}$$

where e_p and e_d, the error terms associated with the parties' estimates, are assumed to be independent random variables with zero expectation and identical standard deviations. On the Priest/Klein approach, then, disputants form unbiased but potentially mistaken estimates of the legal standards courts apply to disputes.

Having located N_p and N_d, the disputants then ask themselves two things: (1) Given my estimate, N_p or N_d, do I expect to win or lose?; and (2) How confident am I that the answer to question (1) is correct? This two stage reasoning process is represented in Figure 10.1.

How will a litigant answer question (1)? By assumption, each party knows N_f—the level of culpability revealed by the facts. So each party will answer question (1) by comparing N_p or N_d with N_f. For example, if N_p exceeds N_f, the plaintiff will expect to lose because the injurer will seem less culpable than the law requires. By contrast, if N_f exceeds N_p, the injurer will appear to be more culpable than the law requires and the plaintiff will therefore expect to win.

The injurer will answer question (1) the same way. If N_f exceeds N_d, the injurer will expect to lose because the facts indicate a level of culpability seemingly sufficient to hold the injurer responsible at law. But if N_d exceeds N_f, the injurer will expect to win. In this event, the law will seem to require a higher degree of culpability than is revealed by the facts.

In Figure 10.1, N_f is located so that $N_p < N_f < N_d$. This means that the victim (the plaintiff) thinks the injurer is more culpable than the law requires while the injurer (the defendant) disagrees. On this ordering, each party expects to win.[17]

With their answers to question (1) in hand, the parties will then consider question (2), which asks how confident each is in the predicted result. To answer the second question, the parties must examine the distributions of e_p and e_d, the error terms associated with N_p and N_d. These distributions, which are shown at the bottom of Figure 10.1, map the probabilities that N_p and N_d differ so much from N. as to fall on the wrong side of N_f. The shaded area to the right of N_f in the distribution centered about N_p represents the probability that $e_p > N_f - N_p$, in which event the victim will lose even though he or she expects to win. The shaded area to the left of N_f in the distribution centered about N_d represents the probability that $e_d > N_f - N_d$, in which event the injurer will lose even though he or she

Figure 10.1

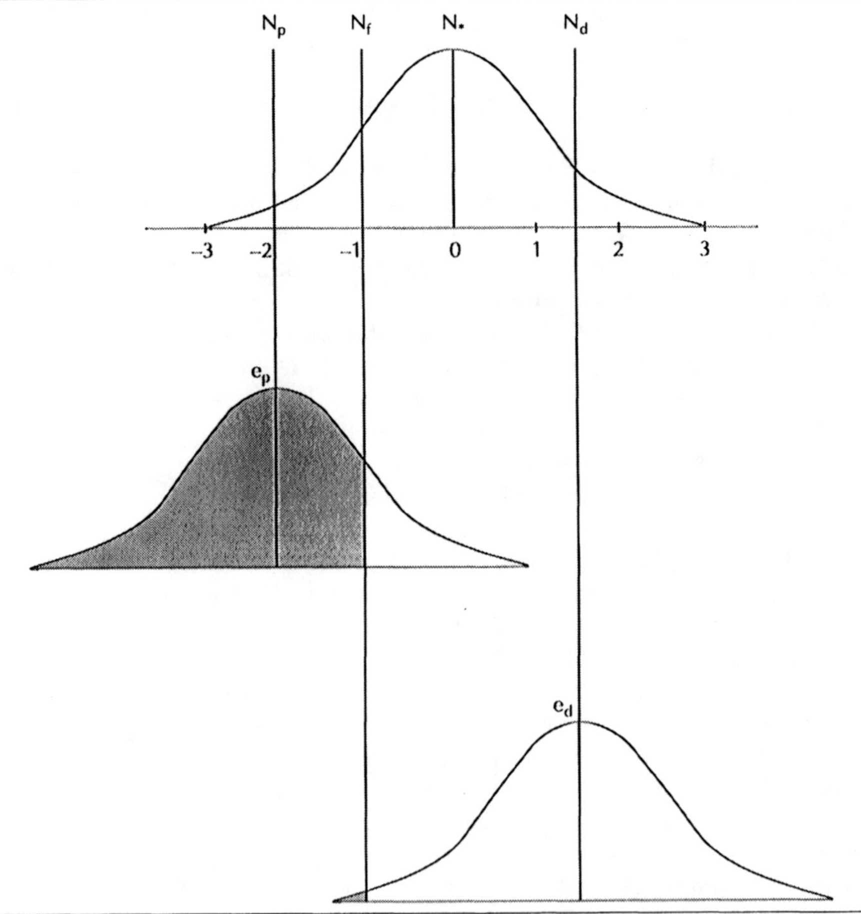

expects to win.[18] The size of the shaded areas indicates that each party thinks
the probability of losing is small.

The parties' actual confidence levels can be assessed only by assigning
numbers to N_p, N_d, and N_f. In Figure 10.1, N_p is set at −2, N_d at +1.5, and N_f
at −1. Assuming that the distributions of e_p and e_d are standard normal
curves, the disputants' confidence levels are determined by finding the
cumulative densities of e_p and e_d left of N_f (the shaded areas at the bottom
of Figure 10.1). The larger the cumulative densities, the higher the parties'
estimates of the likelihood that the plaintiff will win.

Given the values for N_p, N_d, and N_f assigned in Figure 10.1, the plaintiff's
estimate of the probability of a pro-plaintiff verdict is .84, while the

defendant's estimate of the same probability is less than .01. In the example, then, the parties are far apart. As mentioned, the condition for litigation is

$$P_p - P_d > 0.1 \tag{4}$$

Here, the condition is easily met.

Thus, according to Priest and Klein, trials occur as a matter of chance. When plaintiffs and defendants read laws differently and to some extent erroneously, trials occur a predictable part of the time. It remains to be seen, however, whether this stochastic process can generate realistic probabilities of litigation, and whether changes in the level of uncertainty about law affect those probabilities in the manner Landes and Posner's theory predicts. To answer these questions, we will have to consider Priest and Klein's model again.

Given the values assigned to C, S, and J in the example described in Figure 10.1, the probability that a victim and an injurer will take a case to court is determined by calculating the likelihood that P_p will exceed P_d by 10%. In this case, I was unable to calculate the probability of litigation exactly, so I simulated the problem on a computer. The program paired 1000 samples of N_p with 1000 samples of N_d, all 2000 samples having been drawn randomly from standard normal curves. It then calculated P_p and P_d for each pair of estimates and determined whether P_p exceeded P_d by more than .10. For this set of paired estimates, the threshold for litigation was met 34.3% of the time.

Since the trial rate observed in the real world is generally agreed to be less than 5%, a probability of trial greater than 34% seems high. The discrepancy may be accounted for in large part by the values assigned to C, S, and J. It is commonly thought that a great deal of money can be saved by settling early on, so that in the real world the difference between C and S is often large. In the example, however, the excess of C over S was $500, a fairly small amount. It also seems likely that the stakes at issue in many disputes are small, as when the source of contention is a bent fender, a broken arm, or a bruised ego. By contrast, in the example J was set at $10,000, a sizeable amount. In the real world, then, P_p may have to exceed P_d by far more than 10% if a case is to be taken to court.

When the litigation threshold is raised, the probability of litigation falls fairly fast. For example, in only 17% of the cases created by the computer did P_p exceed P_d by more than .30. In only 8% of the cases was a threshold of .5 met. When the litigation threshold is raised, Priest and Klein's generates a realistic result.

A second reason that may explain some of the discrepancy between the predicted and observed litigation rates is that in the real world many disputes are cut-and-dried affairs. As the distance between N_f and $N_.$ grows, the likelihood of litigation falls for any given level of uncertainty about N_*. For example, when N_f was placed at -1.3, slightly farther to the left of N_*, the observed frequency litigation at thresholds of .1 and .3 were 30% and 12%, respectively, down from 34% and 17% when N_f was set at -1. If actual disputes often involve gross culpability, Priest and Klein's model can again predict a more realistic litigation rate.

By saying that Priest and Klein's model can generate realistic results, I do not mean to suggest that the model explains worldly behavior. My aim is not to defend the model at all. It is only to explain how the model works and to show that it is not implausible on its face.

Even so, one question remains. Does Priest and Klein's approach relate changes in the level of uncertainty about law to changes in the rate of litigation in the manner Landes and Posner's model requires? As stated above, their model predicts that the litigation rate will rise and fall as uncertainty about law grows and declines. Does Priest and Klein's model generate the same result?

The answer to this question is unclear. It may depend on the way changes in the level of certainty about law are represented in the model. If greater uncertainty increases the variance of N_p and N_d but leaves everything else unchanged, the litigation rate will rise, as Landes and Posner predict. In this event, the distributions of N_p and N_d will be less densely packed about N_* than before. This is shown in Figure 10.2, where the curve at the top of the figure, which has a standard deviation of 1.2, is wider and flatter than the corresponding curve in Figure 10.1. When the simulation was run using the distribution in Figure 10.2, 35.9% of the cases met a litigation threshold of .1 and 22.6% met a threshold of .3. The rates at those thresholds were 34.3% and 17% above. If only the variance of N_p and N_p is affected by changes in the level of uncertainty about law, then Priest and Klein's model and Landes and Posner's model are in accord.

If increased uncertainty about law increases the variance of e_p and e_d, however, agreement between the models may break down. An increase in the variance of the e_p means that N_p is a less reliable indicator of N_* than before, and an increase in the variance of e_d means the same with respect to N_d. In other words, as the variance of the error terms grows, the parties' confidence that N_p and N_d fall on the proper side of N_f may decline and their desire to settle may increase. For example, when the standard deviation of e_p and e_d was raised from 1 to 1.2, the simulated rate of litigation was 36.2% at the .1 threshold, 14.9% at the .3 threshold, and 4.2% when the threshold was set at .5. The original rates were 34.3%, 17%, and 8%, respectively. If this way of building changes in uncertainty into Priest and Klein's model is correct, then the correspondence between their model and Landes and Posner's is mixed.

Figure 10.2

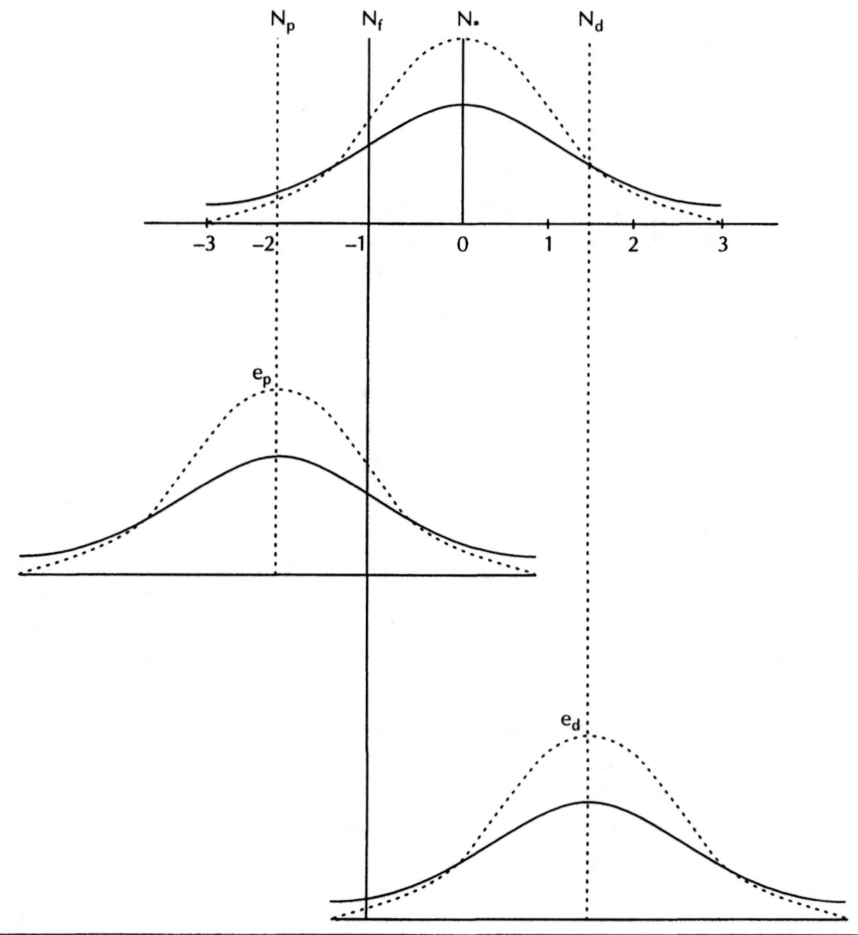

What if changes in uncertainty affect the distributions of N_p and N_d and the distributions of e_p and e_d at the same time? Will the probability of litigation grow or decline?

The answer to this question is also unclear. When the standard deviations of both sets of distributions were set at 1.2 at the same time, the simulated litigation rates were 33.7%, 17.7%, and 7.9% at thresholds of .1, .3, and .5. These rates are virtually the same as those observed when the variances were set at 1. For this simulation, then, the changes were offsetting. Although the level of uncertainty changed, the litigation rate neither fell nor grew.

The question, then, is: What is the right way to reflect changes in the level of uncertainty about law in Priest and Klein's model? As changes in the variance of N_p and N_d? As changes in the variance of e_p and e_d? Or as changes in both at the same time? The second option provides little support for Landes and Posner's approach, and from their point of view the third option must also seem mixed. Only the first option helps them unambiguously. Because the idea of representing changes in uncertainty as changes in the variance of N_p and N_d is intuitively plausible as well, I will therefore assume the first option is correct. When information about law is scarce, the distributions of N_p and N_d become more widely dispersed about N. and the probability of litigation grows as a result.

Is the Supply of Information About Law Optimal?

Many objections can be made to the views described in the preceding two sections.[19] Landes and Posner's model of the decision to sue can be questioned because it assumes solely economic motivations, because it distorts the incentive structures of multi-party and public interest lawsuits, and because it ignores conflicts between lawyers and clients that may affect the settlement rate. Priest and Klein's account of reasoning under uncertainty may be suspect as well. Plaintiffs and defendants may form biased estimates of their chances at trial, both because the adversarial structure of litigation tends to drive parties apart and because people use flawed decision heuristics when dealing with uncertainty instead of analyzing problems as probability theory suggests they should.

Although these objections have considerable force, I do not wish to address them here.[20] My aim in the prior sections was to explain one account of how the relationship between litigation and uncertainty works. I will therefore be content at having related the views of Landes and Posner and Priest and Klein correctly—assuming I have—even though their views may be objectionable on many grounds.

My aim in this section is to explain the public goods objection to Landes and Posner's claim that lawsuits provide an optimal amount of information about law. To be clear, I do not mean to deny that lawsuits are important sources of information about law. England's common lawyers knew that many years ago, and the fact is as obvious today as it was then. I mean to deny only the idea that, "by a process analogous to Adam Smith's 'invisible hand,'" lawsuits provide an optimal amount of information about law.[21] It is one thing to say that an equilibrium between uncertainty and litigation is reached when a certain amount of information about law is produced. It is another thing to assert that the equilibrium reached is efficient. The first claim is correct. The second, perhaps not.[22]

To determine whether an invisible hand is at work, one must know something about the way judicial opinions are produced. The first thing one must realize is that judges do not publish opinions in every case. In the United States, for example, judges write opinions in the minority of cases they decide, and they publish opinions in fewer cases still. Cases decided by unpublished opinions "are not frivolous. ... They call for an opinion and they get it, but it is not published ... [and] may not ... be cited by counsel as precedent. ..."[23]

Because so many cases are decided either by unpublished opinion or without any writing at all, comparatively few cases produce information about law for the public at large to use. An interesting but unresolved question is whether judges correctly decide which opinions to print. Although judges are well placed to appreciate the potential value of precedents, they may make mistakes, both by failing to publish valuable opinions and by publishing opinions no one reads. Both mistakes entail social costs, and the former, if made often enough, may impair the balance between litigation and uncertainty as well.

The second thing one must know about the publication process is that judges publish opinions in profusion, even though they do so in the minority of cases they decide. According to Posner, who as a judge of the United States Court of Appeals is in a position to know, writing opinions for publication is an appellate judge's most time consuming task. He estimates that judges on the Courts of Appeals published an average of 42 majority opinions each in 1983, for a total of 169,000 words per judge and 5,572 opinions nationwide. He also estimates that the aggregate capital stock of appellate precedents that year was 76,547, an increase of 20% over the past ten years.[24] Thus, even though cases decided by published opinion are the exception, not the rule, courts supplement society's stock of information about law at an impressive rate.

It is because opinions are published so frequently that Landes and Posner believe lawsuits keep the level of uncertainty efficiently in check. When information is needed, litigants are likely to go to court and a judge is likely to meet the need by writing an opinion and permitting it to go into print. The process contains a certain amount of slack, most obviously in the form of a lag between the time a need for information arises and the time a published opinion appears. But if Landes and Posner are right, important needs will be met over the long haul. This explains, they contend, "how it has been possible for the Anglo-American legal system to rely, for almost a thousand years, on the uncompensated efforts of litigants to create most of the legal rules administered by the legal system."[25]

The question remains, however, whether the flow of information about law is great enough. Might it not be? Are there reasons to doubt that lawsuits produce information at an optimal rate?

Several reasons to question Landes and Posner's prediction of optimality have already come up. One was just discussed. If trials occur because of uncertainty about law, then a presumption would seem to exist in favor of publishing opinions whenever trials take place. A trial, and especially an appeal, is prima facie evidence that uncertainty about law exists and may be widespread. Therefore, whenever a trial occurs, the publication of an opinion should be presumed to promote efficiency on balance. This presumption may be overridden, as it might be when there is reason to think that only the actual litigants are likely to encounter a particular question of law, but the presumption itself seems correct.[26]

A second reason to question Landes and Posner's prediction is that trials occur only when optimists collide. When pessimists collide, they always settle out of court. If optimists collide infrequently, as they do when the litigation threshold is high, a need for information may escape the courts' attention for some time.

A third reason to question Landes and Posner's prediction is that the incentives people have to sue change independently of changes in the cost of producing information about law. For example, federal courts in the United States recently adopted certain cost shifting rules in an effort to discourage litigation. If these rules have the desired effect, they may alter the rate at which information about law is produced as well. The incentive to sue has also occasionally been strengthened, as it was in the United States during the 1960's when laws entitling victorious civil rights plaintiffs to attorneys' fees were adopted. Because disputants' incentives change in exogenous ways, the flow of information about law is likely to be optimal only some of the time, if at all.[27]

A fourth reason to question Landes and Posner's prediction, the reason I will discuss in detail here, stems from the fact that information about law is a public good. It benefits litigants and nonlitigants alike. Because litigants receive no compensation for the external benefits information about law provides, they ignore those benefits when assessing the attractiveness of litigation and they lack incentives to sue at socially optimal rates.[28]

Landes and Posner agree that published opinions are public goods. They write that "much of the social benefit of litigation, viewed as rule-creating activity, is received by people who may never be involved in any litigation."[29] Published opinions benefit nonlitigants because nonlitigants are free to read them and because the information they contain is valuable and may be available from no other source.

By describing information about law as a public good, I mean to say that it is in joint and nonexclusive supply. The supply of information is *joint* because no one's use of a published opinion restricts its availability to anyone else, in the way, say, that one person's bite of an apple precludes the same bite being taken by anyone else. The supply of information is *nonexclusive* because information about law is available to most people at fairly little cost. People who work with law on a daily basis, for example, lawyers, law professors, and judges, have access to law reports in the same way most people have access to newspapers, magazines, radios, and broadcast television programs, albeit at somewhat greater marginal cost.[30]

The fact that information about law is a public good also affects the conditions for its optimal supply. In an economy of private goods—goods like hamburgers that can be consumed by one person only—an optimum is reached when the marginal cost of producing the last unit of a good equals the marginal value the person consuming that unit enjoys. For example, if it would cost $1 to produce a hamburger and someone is willing to pay $1 for it, the hamburger should be made. Otherwise, if no one would pay more than 99 cents, it should not.

The theory behind the optimum supply of public goods is the same. It is that an additional unit of a public good—a good like a published opinion that everyone can enjoy—should be produced only if the sum of the value all consumers would derive from that unit exceeds its cost of supply. So, if 100 accident victims would pay $100 apiece for a judicial opinion clarifying their legal rights, the opinion should issue if it can be written and published for $10,000 or less. "[A]t the optimum, the marginal cost of supplying the last unit of [a public good] ... just equals the sum of the marginal benefits that all users of the increment of [the public good] simultaneously obtain. ..."[31]

The point, in other words, is that a level of unsatisfied demand for public goods is not necessarily bad, just as an abudance of unwanted hamburgers is not necessarily good. From an economic standpoint, demand for hamburgers should be met only when the cost of producing them is lower than the price consumers are willing to pay, and the desire for greater certainty about law should be met only when the value of additional information exceeds its social cost.

Landes and Posner's claim, as I said above, is that lawsuits keep information about law in optimal supply. They ask the reader to:

> [s]uppose that the stock of legal capital, and hence the flow of information on the likely outcomes of potential legal disputes, were temporarily below the desired (long-run equilibrium) level. ... With the resulting increase in uncertainty, ... litigation would increase. The result would be a temporary increase in the production of precedents until the discrepancy between actual and desired capital was eliminated.[32]

For Landes and Posner, the "desired" amount of capital is the socially optimal amount.[33] If they are right, private lawsuits will meet the demand for information about law whenever that demand can efficiently be met, that is, whenever the social value of additional information exceeds the social cost of production.

The idea that private parties will produce an optimal supply of information about law runs counter to the presumption that economically rational persons lack incentives to supply public goods at optimal rates. Such persons care about benefits they personally derive from goods they produce, not about benefits they confer on others free of charge. Consequently, they refuse to supply additional units of public goods when the private cost of doing so exceeds the private gain, even though the social value of those units may exceed the social cost by far. Because producers receive no compensation for the benefits public goods confer on others, public goods are likely to be underproduced.

The idea expressed in the preceding paragraph may be represented formally as follows. The net social value V_g of a marginal unit of a public good is the sum of the net values v_i all members of a consuming population derive from that unit.

$$V_g = v_i + v_j + ... + v_n \qquad (7)$$

By definition, an additional unit of a public good can efficiently be produced when

$$V_g > \$0 \qquad (8)$$

Also by definition, an economically rational person will produce an additional unit of a good only when

$$v_i > \$0 \qquad (9)$$

Now suppose that two consumers, l and m, can produce a unit of a public good at a cost of $10 apiece, that no other consumer need bear any expense of production at all, and that each consumer, including l and m, would value an additional unit of the good at $8. In this event, $V_g > \$0$ for n > 2, which is to say that an extra unit of the good can efficiently be produced for a society of three or more consumers. Will l and m bear the expense of production? Not if they are economically rational, because the condition described in inequality (9) is not met. $v_i < \$0$ for both l and m even though $V_g > \$0$ for consumers as a group. The public good will not be produced even though its production would be efficient.

The logic underlying the production of information about law is essentially the same. Suppose V_o represents the aggregate net value the members of a society would derive if an additional judicial opinion were produced. As above, V_o is just the sum of the net values derived by individual consumers, so

$$V_o = v_i + v_j + ... + v_n \qquad (10)$$

The condition for the efficient production of an additional opinion is, then,

$$V_o > \$0 \qquad (11)$$

And the condition under which an economically rational person will bear the expense of taking a case to trial for the sake of producing an opinion is

$$v_i > \$0 \qquad (12)$$

Will all opinions that can be produced efficiently be produced in fact? Again, the answer is no. Suppose $V_o > \$0$. In that event, $v_i + v_j + ... + v_n > \$0$ as well. However, it does not follow that $v_i > \$0$ for each consumer individually. In the limit, $v_i < \$0$ could be true of every consumer but one. And in light of inequality (12), if the burden of paying for a lawsuit falls on a person for whom $v_i < \$0$, no lawsuit will be brought and no opinion will be produced.

Although the account of the logic of underproduction offered in the preceding paragraph is correct, it is too schematic to have much persuasive force. For that reason, I will flesh out the logic in greater detail.

The net social value of an opinion, V_o, is a function of many things. For example, it is a function of the quality of the reasoning an opinion contains, the jurisdiction of the issuing court, and the manner in which the opinion is made available for the public to read. An opinion allocating rights efficiently or justly may have greater social value than one that does not because the former may facilitate social and economic interactions more effectively than the latter. An opinion issued by an appellate court may have greater value than one issued by a trial court because the former may be more authoritative than the latter. An opinion published quickly and in an accessible form by an indexing service may have greater value than one published in an untimely and undigested manner by a government printing office because the former may be easier to find and use than the latter. These factors, and many others besides, affect the benefits opinions produce.

Obviously, the net social value of information about law is a function of the cost of producing such information as well. The most obvious costs are probably lawyers' fees and judges' salaries, but these are far from the only

costs that matter. "Judges' salaries and fringe benefits were ... only 9 per-
cent [of the federal judicial budget] in 1980," which ran about $606 mil-
lion.[34] The budget has since increased to about $1 billion and the percent-
age accounted for by judges' salaries appears to have declined. "[S]everal
off budget items should [also] be noted. Many federal judges ... employ
externs, who are law students working part-time for course credit given by
their schools. ... Some district [court] judges appoint private practitioners
(unpaid) to represent indigent civil litigants. ..."[35] And judges use special
masters, whose salaries are paid by the parties, as well.

A further cost of opinion writing is delay. Every time a judge pauses to
compose an opinion or to read an opinion a clerk or a staff attorney has
prepared, other pending matters are left to wait. As of 1983, a case filed in
a federal district court took 19 months to decide. The same case lasted 17.8
months in 1960. The waiting period in state courts in the United States is
thought to have increased by about 50% between 1954 and 1971.[36] It is difficult to assign a dollar value to the cost of delay, but delay is an important
cost all the same.

To complicate matters further, the *actual* social value of opinions is not
really the proper focus of study. To determine whether existing institutions
encourage disputants to sue at optimal rates, one must consider the *expected* net social value of the opinions lawsuits produce. One must consider the value of opinions *ex ante*—before they are actually written—because that is the point at which the decision to sue must be made. In other
words, an appropriate system of incentives will encourage litigants to sue
when the expected net social value of an opinion is positive, even though
the social value of the opinion actually produced may fail to cover its social cost.

To simplify the analysis—but not to oversimplify it, I hope—I will assume that the benefits and costs opinions generate vary mainly with the
outcome of a case, that is, with whether a plaintiff or a defendant prevails
at trial. This assumption is more reasonable than it first may seem. Some of
the costs and benefits opinions entail are small and can safely be ignored.
For example, the marginal cost per page of publishing and indexing opinions after they are written is fairly low. And some costs that vary with the
amount of time a judge spends on a case, for example, the cost of delay, can
be assumed to be constant at the margin without doing too much harm.

By contrast, the focus on the prevailing party seems warranted because
an opinion's social value may depend in large measure the nature of the
rights it assigns. Legal rights have value—they are things people care
about—and their value is in part a function of how they are arranged. For
example, it is a function of whether they are assigned to the individuals
who desire them most. If the identity of the prevailing party is generally a
signal of the economic value of the allocation of rights an opinion adopts—

and I shall assume it is—then a notation that records the way cases come down can serve as a rough but serviceable way of keeping track of the net social value opinions create.[37]

I will use the subscripts "$\backslash p$" and "$\backslash d$" to denote, respectively, a decision favoring a plaintiff and a decision favoring a defendant. For example, the variable "$v_{i\backslash p}$" represents the net value individual i derives from an opinion rendered in connection with a decision favoring a plaintiff, and the variable "$V_{o\backslash d}$" represents the aggregate net value a society of i-n individuals derives from an opinion favoring a defendant.

As stated above, an opinion can be produced efficiently when

$$V_o = v_i + v_j + \dots + v_n \tag{10}$$

We now know, however, that we must talk about the expected value of an opinion and that this value depends on whether a plaintiff or a defendant prevails at trial. Hence, we must rewrite equation (10) as

$$V_o = P_i v_{i\backslash p} + P_j v_{j\backslash p} + \dots +$$
$$P_n v_{n\backslash p} + (1 - P_i)v_{i\backslash d} + (1 - P_j)v_{j\backslash d} + \dots + (1 - P_j)v_{n\backslash d'} \tag{10'}$$

where $P_i v_{i\backslash p}$ represents i's estimate of the probability that the plaintiff will win times the net value i would derive from a pro-plaintiff opinion, and $(1 - P_i)v_{i\backslash d}$ represents i's estimate of the probability that the defendant will win times the net value i would derive from a pro-defendant opinion. The condition for the efficient production of an opinion is still

$$V_o > \$0 \tag{11}$$

And the condition under which an economically rational person will want to see an opinion produced is now:

$$v_i = P_i v_{i\backslash p} + (1 - P_i)v_{i\backslash d} > \$0 \tag{13}$$

Because few members of a society are involved in any given lawsuit, most can ignore litigation costs when calculating v_i, the net expected value an opinion entails. As far as the parties are concerned, however, litigation costs matter a great deal. For the plaintiff, $v_{p\backslash p}$ and $v_{p\backslash d}$ reflect the size of C, the cost of taking the case to court. The same is true of the defendant, who reduces $v_{d\backslash p}$ and $v_{d\backslash d}$ with every increase in C.

Thus, opinions may generate markedly assymetrical net gains across a population of consumers. Nonlitigants may profit greatly from the information an opinion provides, while litigants may enjoy little gain or even suffer a loss. For example, suppose a dispute arises and everyone in a society of 1000 members, including the participants, agrees that the likelihood of the plaintiff winning at trial, P_i, is .5. In this event, everyone must set $(1 - P_i)$, the probability that the defendant will win, at .5 as well. As before, C, the cost of taking the case to trial, is \$1000, S, the cost of settling out of court, is \$500, and J, the size of the judgment at stake, is \$10,000. Now suppose $v_{i\backslash p}$, the value of an opinion favoring the plaintiff, is \$1000 for each person, and $v_{i\backslash d}$, the value of an opinion favoring the defendant, is –\$250. In this event, the expected net gain to each nonlitigant is

$$v_i = .5(\$1000) + .5(-\$250) = \$375, \tag{12'}$$

and the expected gain to all nonlitigants as a group is \$374,250 (998 x \$375). The social cost of producing an opinion is \$2000—the parties' combined litigation costs—plus an amount R that reflects the cost of running the judiciary.[38] If R < \$372,250, V_o is positive and an opinion can efficiently be produced.

Unfortunately, regardless of the magnitude of R, the disputants will be inclined to settle. The condition for litigation is:

$$P_pJ + P_pv_{p\backslash p} + (1 - P_p)v_{p\backslash d} -$$
$$C + S > P_dJ - P_dv_{d\backslash p} - (1 - P_d)v_{d\backslash d} + C - S \tag{14}$$

This is just the condition for litigation stated in inequality (1) modified to reflect the value the litigants expect an opinion to produce. Plugging in the values stipulated above yields

$$.5(\$10,000) + .5(\$1,000) + .5(-\$250) - \$1000 + \$500 <$$
$$.5(\$10,000) - .5(\$1,000) - .5(-\$250) + \$1000 - \$500, \tag{14'}$$

or

$$\$4,875 < \$5,125,$$

which means the condition for litigation is not met. Thus, even if R were \$0, the disputants would refuse to take the case to court. They would settle and save \$250 in private litigation costs even though other consumers in their society would forfeit information with an expected value of more than \$300,000 as a result.

By rearranging the terms in inequality (14) we can restate the condition for litigation in a useful way. If the parties agree on the plaintiff's chance of success, then $P_p = P_d = P$ and the condition for litigation is:

$$Pv_{p\backslash p} + (1 - P)v_{p\backslash d} + Pv_{d\backslash p} + (1 - P)v_{p\backslash d} > 2(C - S) \tag{15}$$

In other words, the parties will sue only when the expected joint value of an opinion exceeds the amount they could jointly save by settling their dispute. Otherwise, they will decline to sue, whatever the cost to society may be.

Thus, litigants lack incentives to sue at optimal rates. Because they receive no reward for the external benefits information about law provides, they ignore those benefits when deciding whether to sue. As a result, too little information about law may be produced.

In anticipation of this objection, Landes and Posner suggest that the prospect of a shortage of information about law is avoided because litigants are paid to take cases to court. The payment comes in the form of free access to courts which, as we have seen, are expensive to run. In Landes and Posner's words, "[W]e subsidize litigation by making the taxpayers ... bear ... the costs of the judicial system ... on the theory that the taxpayers ... benefit from the forensic exertions of the actual litigants."[39] If Landes and Posner are right, litigants are compensated indirectly for the external benefits lawsuits provide and the prospect of an undersupply of information is reduced.[40]

Landes and Posner are right in saying that court time is underpriced. For example, plaintiffs who sue in federal courts in the United States pay very small filing fees, usually $60, and plaintiffs who proceed *in forma pauperis* pay no fees at all. By Posner's calculations, filing fees account for less than 2% of the federal judicial budget.[41]

Posner also proposes that the subsidy be reduced by about $1000 per case, notwithstanding the effect a user fee of that magnitude could have on the rate at which information about law is produced. He begins the argument for a stiff user fee by observing that "financially significant cases make good law" because litigants and judges invest larger amounts of resources in them than they do in cases where the stakes are small.[42] He then predicts that high-stakes lawsuits would be litigated in federal courts even if a filing fee of $1000 were imposed on plaintiffs across the board. Such a fee, in his words, "would tend to divert cases with small monetary stakes from the federal court system to more suitable dispute-resolution processes. ..."[43] The net effect, he suggests, would be a smaller federal caseload containing a larger percentage of high quality cases and an improvement in the quality of the information produced by the federal courts.[44]

In Posner's opinion, then, "the optimum subsidy" is smaller than the subsidy litigants who sue in federal courts currently receive.[45] In some sense this may be correct, but not in the sense that a smaller subsidy would motivate litigants to provide information about law—public goods—at optimal rates. Neither Posner's proposal nor the subsidy now in place can have that effect.

In the example discussed above, I assumed that the disputants paid no part of R, the public cost of running the courts. They paid only C, the private cost of taking a case to trial, and S, the somewhat smaller private cost of settling their dispute. The analysis, and the conclusion that a shortage of information could occur, would have been the same if I had instead assumed that the litigants paid R and were later reimbursed by the public. The litigants would still have refused to go to court because C would still have exceeded S. In other words, the parties would still have saved more by settling than they would have gained by going to court. A subsidy covering court costs alone leaves the possibility of an information shortage intact.

Obviously, if Posner's proposal were adopted, things would be worse. Litigants would find it economically rational to sue less often. They would settle cases in which the prospect of producing an opinion now draws them into court.

Posner's interest in user fees stems from his concern that the caseload crisis in the federal courts is out of hand. His concern is understandable. In 1963, 57,028 civil cases were filed in federal district courts. In 1983, the number of civil filings was 241,159, an increase of more than 400%. During the same period, the number of federal district court judges did not even double.[46] There is no doubt that federal judges, and possibly judges in other courts as well, are overworked.

The problem, however, is not that the current subsidy is too large. In some cases it is too small. Nor is the solution to reduce the subsidy across the board. Instead, the subsidy should vary in size with the value of the information lawsuits create. For example, complaints are often filed in federal courts solely for the purpose of having judges enter prearranged settlements in the form of consent decrees. In many such cases, the complaint and the proposed decree are filed the same day. Although litigants who use courts purely as forums for settling private disputes now receive a subsidy that is nearly complete, to my mind they should pay full price for the resources they consume. Private civil settlements produce no information for taxpayers to use. Therefore, taxpayers should not be asked to subsidize the settlement of private civil disputes.

It is, however, easier to say that subsidies should reflect the social value of lawsuits than it is to design an appropriate and workable system of fees. Perhaps the primary problem in designing such a system is that "the identification of [cases] that will be ... important precedent[s] may be difficult or impossible to make in advance. ..."[47] However, before concluding that "a general subsidy of litigation" is "more efficient than an attempt to subsidize" only cases that "contribute to the production of precedents,"[48] I would explore the possibility of subsidizing lawsuits ex post, after the results are in. When cases settle without producing opinions, as most cases do, I would have the litigants pay full price. When opinions are written, I would ask judges to assess the difficulty and potential value of the legal issues discussed, just as they now make such assessments when deciding whether to put opinions into print. A form could be used to simplify the task. Before all hope of bringing public and private interests into accord is lost, a system of subsidizing lawsuits ex post should be tried.

Conclusion

Lawsuits often provide information about legal norms for use by the public at large. They therefore help explain how people learn about law. But information about law is a public good that economically motivated individuals may refuse to supply at an optimal rate. They may prefer to settle cases that could more efficiently be decided in court. A policy of making courts available to litigants free of charge may improve things somewhat, but public and private interests can still diverge. If Posner's proposal of charging stiff users fees in all cases across the board were in effect, the prospect of an information shortage would probably be worse.

To say that litigants lack incentives to produce information at optimal rates is not, however, to prove that information is in fact in short supply. Only an empirical study can show that a shortage exists. All that can be said for now is that Landes and Posner's prediction that lawsuits will maintain an optimal supply of information about law lacks a basis in microeconomic theory and may therefore be unduly sanguine.

In two respects, then, the project begun in this essay is incomplete. Although I have explained and criticized Landes and Posner's account of the relationship between litigation, information, and uncertainty, I have neither shown that an information shortage exists nor designed a system of fees that would alleviate the problem without making the litigation crisis worse. Those are projects on which I hope to continue to work.

Notes

I wish to thank Ian Ayres, Mark Gergen, Lewis Kornhauser, Douglas Laycock, Richard Posner, Ed Strang, and Jay Westbrook for commenting on earlier drafts of this essay. The statistical analysis and computer simulation discussed in section 2 were prepared with assistance from Mary Bishop, Margaret Myers, Peter Smits, and Steven Skates. I appreciate their help very much.

This article continues work on the morality of compromises and settlements Jules Coleman and I began in "Justice in Settlements," 4 *Social Philosophy & Policy* 103 (1986). I thank Jules for his continuing help and advice. I composed this article in 1988, at David Braybrooke's invitation. I have not updated it since then.

1. See Landes and Posner, "Legal Precedent: A Theoretical and Empirical Analysis," 19 *Journal of Law & Economics* 249 (1976) (hereinafter "Legal Precedent"); Landes and Posner, "Adjudication as a Private Good", 8 *Journal of Legal Studies* 235 (1979) (hereinafter "Adjudication"); Posner, *Economic Analysis of Law* 2d 421-423 (1977);

Economic Analysis of Law 3d 511 (1986); Posner, *Federal Courts: Crisis and Reform* 9–10 (1985) (hereinafter *Federal Courts*); and Posner, *The Problems of Jurisprudence* pp. 358–359 (1990).

2. Landes and Posner, "Legal Precedent," p. 272.

3. Criticisms of Landes and Posner's account can be found in Coleman and Silver, "Justice In Settlements"; Owen Fiss, "Against Settlement," 93 *Yale Law Journal* 1073 (1984); and Carrie Menkel-Meadow, "For and Against Settlement: Uses and Abuses of the Mandatory Settlement Conference," 33 *U.C.L.A. Law Review* 485 (1985). Frank Easterbrook defends Landes and Posner in "Justice and Contract in Consent Judgments," *Univ. of Chicago Legal Forum* 19 (1987).

4. Posner, *Federal Courts*, Chapter 1.

5. For an example of the tendency of critics to mine Posner's work, see Ian Shapiro, "Richard Posner's Praxis," 48 *Ohio State Law Journal* 999 (1987). Shapiro leaves few stones, however small, unturned.

6. Posner, *Economic Analysis of Law* 2d, p. 435.

7. A particularly important objection to Landes and Posner's approach appears in Geoffrey Miller, "Some Agency Problems in Settlement," 16 *Journal of Legal Studies* 198 (1987). Miller shows that lawyers' and clients' incentives may differ and that this difference may affect their assessments of the attractiveness of settlements. Landes and Posner's simple exchange model assumes that lawyers and clients act as one. The model may therefore be incorrect.

8. Posner, *Economic Analysis of Law* 2d, p. 435.

9. Posner, *Economic Analysis of Law* 2d, pp. 435–436.

10. I assume the parties possess identical resources, are risk neutral, face the same stakes and costs, and do not expect to engage in litigation on the same issue again. I also make other assumptions found in *Economic Analysis of Law* 2d, p. 435.

11. The model does not predict where within the range of mutually beneficial outcomes a settlement will be reached. To derive that result, one would have to imbed a model of the bargaining process within the model of the decision to sue. At present, no suitable model of bargaining exists. See Miller, "Some Agency Problems in Settlement," p. 193. The model also assumes that all impediments to bargaining can be represented as costs. In other words, it assumes that bargaining is nonstrategic.

12. Posner, *Economic Analysis of Law*, p. 436.

13. Posner, *Federal Courts*, p. 54. See also "Adjudication," p. 252; and George Priest, "Selective Characteristics of Litigation," 9 *Journal of Legal Studies* 399, 405 (1980). The standard of review for findings of fact can be found in *Federal Rule of Civil Procedure* 52, which states that "[f]indings of fact ... shall not be set aside unless clearly erroneous, and due regard shall be given to the opportunity of the trial court to judge of the credibility of the witnesses."

14. Priest and Klein, "The Selection of Disputes for Litigation," 13 *Journal of Legal Studies* 1 (1984). Priest and Klein assume litigants know the law but are unsure how to apply the law to the facts.

15. Posner cites Priest and Klein's article with approval in *Economic Analysis of Law* 3d, p. 568.

16. Uncertainty receives far more attention than risk in discussions of the settlement process. See, for example, Priest and Klein, "The Selection of Disputes for

Litigation," p. 27, where the prospect that litigants may be risk-averse is dealt with in a single page. I will ignore attitudes toward risk as well, that is, I will assume that litigants are risk neutral in the analysis that follows.

17. The scale at the bottom of the curve, on which the level of negligence increases as one moves from left to right, was chosen for convenience. It is the scale of a standard normal curve. Each unit represents a distance of one standard deviation. Any linear transformation of this scale would produce results identical to those discussed below.

18. The concern here is with the magnitude of the error terms, not their signs.

19. My colleague Mark Gergen offered a host of reasons for questioning the realism of both the economic model of the decision to sue and Landes and Posner's account of the connection between uncertainty and litigation. I present some of his reasons here, and I thank him for all his advice.

20. Jules Coleman and I raise some objections to the economic analysis of settlement and litigation in "Justice in Settlements," p. 4.

21. Posner, *Federal Courts*, p. 10.

22. Landes and Posner's most complete statement of how the optimal production of precedents should be modeled can be found in "Legal Precedent," pp. 264–267.

23. Posner, *Federal Courts*, p. 122. On the practice of writing unpublished opinions, see George M. Weaver, "The Precedential Value of Unpublished Judicial Opinions," 39 *Mercer Law Review* 477 (1988); William L. Reynolds and William M. Richman, "An Evaluation of Limited Publication in the United States Courts of Appeals: The Price of Reform," 48 *University of Chicago Law Review* 573 (1981); and Daniel N. Hoffman, "Nonpublication of Federal Appellate Court Opinions," 6 *The Justice System Journal* 405 (1981).

24. Posner, *Federal Courts*, pp. 114, 125. On changes in the stock of precedents over time, see also "Legal Precedent," *passim*.

25. Landes and Posner, "Legal Precedent," p. 272.

26. Posner disagrees. He believes that federal judges are already overworked and that an increase in the burden of writing and publishing opinions would cause the quality of precedents to decline. See *Federal Courts*, p. 124. Even if Posner is right, however, his remarks show only that the presumption in favor of publishing opinions in all cases is now outweighed by the rising costs opinions entail. His remarks do not show that the presumption is incorrect.

27. Perhaps the most important procedural change affecting the rate at which information about law is produced is the license judges now have to encourage parties to settle out of court. For example, Federal Rule of Civil Procedure 16, which was amended in 1983, now encourages district court judges to hold conferences pretrial for the purpose of facilitating settlements. And both state and federal courts now use mandatory settlement procedures in cases where formerly they did not. See D. Marie Provine, "Managing Negotiated Justice: Settlement Procedures in the Courts," 12 *The Justice System Journal* 91 (1987); Frank G. Evans and Bruce Ramage, "Alternative Dispute Resolution Procedures at the Appellate Level," 51 *Texas Bar Journal* 3 (1988); and Annotation, "Validity and Effect of Local District Court Rules Providing for Use of Alternative Dispute Resolution Procedures as Pretrial Settlement Mechanisms," 86 *ALR Federal* 211 (1988). Versions of the argument that proce-

dural changes affect the rate at which information about law is produced appear in Fiss, "Against Settlement"; Coleman and Silver, "Justice In Settlements"; and Menkel-Meadow, "For and Against Settlement."

Easterbrook replies to the essays by Fiss and Coleman and Silver in "Justice and Contract in Consent Judgments." He writes that "[j]udges apparently believe that the existing supply of litigated cases offers more than enough opportunities to make or embellish legal rules." (p. 27). This response, which seems to say only that federal judges are overworked, misses the point entirely. Procedural changes alter judges' agendas. They remove some cases from the docket and bring others to the fore. For example, a constitutional amendment eliminating federal jurisdiction over abortion cases would prevent federal judges from ruling on the constitutionality of state abortion laws. And a statute denying attorneys' fees to prevailing plaintiffs would reduce the rate at which judges produce information about federal civil rights laws. Federal judges might still be overworked if these changes were made, and they might still think they have enough cases to decide. But if the flow of information about the constitutionality of abortion laws and the meaning of federal civil rights statutes is optimal now, it would be suboptimal after these changes were made.

28. The properties of public goods are described in many places. The classic treatment is Paul A. Samuelson, "The Pure Theory of Public Expenditure," 36 *Review of Economics and Statistics* 387 (1954). For more accessible discussions, see, Duncan Snidal, "Public Goods, Property Rights, and Political Organizations," 23 *International Studies Quarterly* 532 (1979); Russell Hardin, *Collective Action* (Baltimore: The Johns Hopkins University Press, 1982); Brian Barry and Russell Hardin, eds., *Rational Man and Irrational Society?* (Beverly Hills: Sage Publishers, 1982); and Robin W. Boadway and David E. Wildasin, *Public Sector Economics* (Boston: Little Brown, 2nd ed., 1984). My own contribution to the field can be found in Charles Silver, "Utilitarian Participation," 23 *Social Science Information* 701 (1984).

29. Posner, "Adjudication," p. 241. See also Landes and Posner, "Legal Precedent," pp. 263–267.

30. For a more thorough discussion of the concepts of jointness and nonexclusivity, see Snidal, "Public Goods, Property Rights, and Political Organizations," p. 28.

31. Boadway and Wildasin, *Public Sector Economcs*, pp. 28, 89.

32. Landes and Posner, "Legal Precedent," pp. 269–270.

33. Landes and Posner, "Legal Precedent," pp. 262–267 (discussing conditions for optimal provision of precedents).

34. Posner, *Federal Courts*. p. 28.

35. Posner, *Federal Courts*. p. 28.

36. Posner, *Federal Courts*. p. 86 n. 51, p. 96.

37. For the purposes of this discussion, I focus on the economic value of opinions only, and I use the words "economic value" to mean willingness to pay. I follow Landes and Posner in these two respects. However, I personally reject the view that only the economic value of opinions matters, and I also reject the idea that only the preferences of people with money count.

38. In the United States, litigants do not pay R. They pay only their attorneys' fees and expenses. The fixed costs of making courts available to litigants are de-

frayed with funds from the public fisc. For this reason, R has no effect on the incentives plaintiffs and defendants have to take cases to court.

39. Posner, *Federal Courts.* pp. 131–132.

40. Posner states this idea also in "Legal Precedent,"pp. 271–274; Landes and Posner, "Adjudication," pp. 241–242; *Economic Analysis of Law* 2d, p. 401; and *Federal Courts,* pp. 10, 131–132.

41. Posner, *Federal Courts.* p. 132 n.3.

42. Posner, *Federal Courts.* pp. 132–133.

43. Posner, *Federal Courts.* p. 132.

44. Posner, *Federal Courts.* p. 134.

45. Posner, *Federal Courts.* p. 132.

46. Posner, *Federal Courts.* Appendix B, Table B.3.

47. Posner, "Legal Precedent," p. 274.

48. Posner, "Legal Precedent," p. 274.

References

Cooter, R., and Kornhauser, L.A. 1980. "Can Litigation Improve the Law Without the Help of Judges?" *Journal of Legal Studies* 9: 139–163.

Elliott, E.D. 1984. "Holmes and Evolution: Legal Process as Artificial Intelligence," *Journal of Legal Studies* 13: 113–46.

Goodman, J.C. 1978. "An Economic Theory of the Evolution of the Common Law," *Journal of Legal Studies* 7: 393–406.

Kornhauser, L.A. 1989. "An Economic Perspective on Stare Decisis," *Chicago-Kent Law Review* 65: 63–92.

Kornhauser, L.A. 1992. "Modelling Collegial Courts I," *International Review of Law and Economics,* 12: 169–185.

Kornhauser, L.A., and Sager, L.G. 1986. "Unpacking the Court," *Yale Law Journal* 96: 82–117.

Landes, W.M., and Posner, R.A. 1976. "Legal Precedent: A Theoretical and Empircal Analysis," *Journal of Law and Economics* 19: 249–307.

Landes, W.M., and Posner, R.A. 1979. "Adjudication as a Private Good," *Journal of Legal Studies* 8: 235–84.

Priest, G.L. 1977. "The Common Law Process and the Selection of Efficient Rules," *Journal of Legal Studies* 6: 65–82.

Rubin, P.H. 1977. "Why is the Common Law Efficient?" *Journal of Legal Studies,* 6: 51–63.

11

Notes on the Logic of Legal Change

Lewis A. Kornhauser

Commenting on Silver's paper, Kornhauser points out that (for all that it is concerned with changes in rules) it shifts to a very different perspective on legal change from the one found in Bonfield's contribution and (it might be added) in the other contributions that have been classified here as adopting an issue-processing perspective. Silver's perspective is the perspective of economists.

Legal institutions, unlike many social phenomena, present a reasonably well-defined and discrete setting in which to study the history of social rules. Despite their apparent simplicity, however, the processes of legal change are in themselves maddeningly complex. I shall largely restrict my remarks to general comments about one narrow aspect of legal change: common law litigation. An indication of some of the complexities that beset the study of legal rules and legal evolution, however, will, I hope, not only set my more specific examples in context but also suggest similar difficulties in the study of change in less formalized social settings.

I begin with two distinctions. First, the mechanisms of legal change may differ among the different "sources" of law: legislature, administrative agency, and court. Both the causes and justifications of legislatively induced change may differ from those of administratively or judicially induced change. Second, the formal nature of legal institutions implies that legal rules are publicly announced. Consequently, a much clearer gap between the announcement (or promulgation) of a legal rule and the social behavior of those subject to it appears. Someone violates every legal rule, and some legal rules, from parking regulations to narcotics bans, are systematically violated. When we ask whether the legal rule has changed, about whose behavior are we concerned? Those of the lawmakers, so that the announcement of a new rule manifests a legal change? Or those subject to the law, in which case a change in the legal rule must be accompanied by some (dramatic) change in behavior?[1]

Matters are in fact more complicated than this simple distinction between lawmakers and law subjects suggests. First, various individuals are neither law makers nor mere law subjects. Enforcement officials such as police and prosecutors may choose to enforce a legal rule selectively or not at all. Our evaluation of this selective enforcement depends on our evaluation of the motives of the officials and the process (or criteria) of selection.

Second, the assertion "society generally follows (or generally disobeys) legal norm A" contains several ambiguities. On one reading, the assertion simply states that social behavior generally conforms to that required by the norm. On a second reading, the assertion contends that the legal norm is a *reason* for the conforming behavior (or, in the case of general disobedience, the reason for the norm has been weighed and rejected). Attempts to measure compliance to legal norms illustrate this tension. If I say that the narcotics laws are widely disobeyed, it need not be the case that most (or indeed many) people take narcotics. More graphically, consider the criminal statutes proscribing burglary. These are "often" disobeyed though no immediate measure of frequency (relative to opportunity) of disobedience presents itself. Our sense is that most individuals do not eschew burglary *because* of the law. Many decisions are made because of individual tastes or individual circumstances that the law leaves "unchanged" at the margin. Behavior would not alter for most people if a legal rule altered.

The difficulties caused by the distance between actual social behaviors and the content of legal rules also arise, I think, in the study of other, less formal rules. In this essay, however, I restrict my attention to changes in the announced common law legal rules.

Two broad categories of theories of the evolution of the common law exist. Two papers presented here illustrate each of these categories. Professor Bonfield has emphasized how our interpretations of the evolution of legal doctrine depends upon the decision-maker's understanding of the nature of law. Every jurisprudential theory of adjudication contains within it some theory of evolution of the common law. These theories explain the change in the common law in terms of the practice and intention of common law judges. By contrast, Professor Silver has focussed on the actions and intentions of the litigants rather than the judges. The law evolves, on this account, because of economic (or perhaps social) pressures rather than because of the intentions of the judges or the normative content of the legal rules. I discuss each class of theory in turn.

Jurisprudential Models of the Logic of Legal Change

Adjudication in the United States has a complex structure. First, controversies "arrive" in the system at the instance of the aggrieved parties rather than at the instance of the judge. Similarly, the parties determine, within broad constraints set up by the legal system, the characterization of their own controversy. Third, an adjudication has two parts: a finding of facts and a declaration of law. These two facets of adjudication have very different features. The initial decision of the finder of fact is subject to little review; thus each court of first instance has broad power to find facts as it chooses. Declarations of law, on the other hand, may be reviewed by higher courts. As a single court sits at the apex of each court system, the announcement of legal norms is, to some extent, centralized. Fourth, the federal system of the U.S. legal system in part runs counter to the tendency towards centralization. Fifth, many announcements of legal norms are made by panels of judges rather than single judges.[1] Sixth, not only do judges decide only those controversies brought to them by litigants, the judges announce, in the decision of each controversy, only those legal rules necessary for the resolution of *that* specific controversy. This practice ensures that the law develops "incrementally." For example, in a contract dispute, the controversy may require only that the court announce (or "clarify") the legal rule governing mitigation of damages by the promisee. Two factors mitigate this tendency towards incrementalism. In general, judges strive to render the law "coherent" which entails more than that the law impose consistent legal obligations.[2] A decision would then try to attend to interrelated rules governing what constitutes breach and the measure of general and special damages. Further, courts often issue "dicta" or statements that do not have the binding effects of law but indicate a court's views on how related issues should be decided.

Other legal practices re-enforce this tendency towards incremental change in legal rules. In common law adjudication, courts resolve controversies through reliance on or reference to prior decisions. This procedure, commonly termed "precedent," consists of a variety of complex practices that determine the extent to which the decision in the case before the court is determined by the prior decisions of that court (or, in hierarchical systems, of that court, higher courts, and "neighboring" courts). Essential to this practice, of course, is some procedure that determines the legal rule announced in the prior decisions.

"Natural-selection" theories of the common law focus on the first two aspects of adjudication: the determinants of which controversies arrive at the court and how the litigants choose to formulate those controversies. Jurisprudential theories of adjudication have concentrated on the last aspect of the process: articulation and criticism of the practice of precedent. This jurisprudential discussion has been embedded in a particularly simple vision of the structure of adjudication. The jurisprudential theories generally assume a single judge sitting on the sole court of an isolated jurisdiction. Occasionally, the judge has infinite life and thus decides every controversy in the jurisdiction; in other instances, the judge has finite life and decides all those controversies that arise in some given time period. Consequently, she must confront both the problem of interpreting the decisions of judges who preceded her and of constraining the interpretation of her own decisions by judges who follow her.

Three different types of explanation of legal change are consistent with this vision of the solitary judge who constructs a unitary (or coherent) body of law. First, the world in which the judge acts may change over time. Consequently, the legal rules that furthered her unchanging normative goals must be adapted to the new conditions. Various actual decisions apparently offer this justification for changes in legal doctrine. In his announcement of the implied warranty of habitability (of rental housing), for example, Judge Skelly Wright in part relied on his claim that the conditions of urban housing differed so dramatically from the conditions of agricultural life in which the rules governing tenancy developed that the rules required modification.[3]

Second, legal change may occur because, though the world in which the judges acts has remained stable, her normative goals may have altered. Again, this justification of change often appears in actual legal decisions. Arguably, the twentieth century evolution from negligence to strict liability in tort law reflects a shift in judicial understanding of the moral grounds of responsibility for one's conduct. Such a shift in understanding would have required a change in the legal rules even if the world governed by the law had not changed at all.

The third theory of legal change consonant with jurisprudential theories of adjudication sees legal change as independent not only of the social world but also as "independent" of the aims of the judges. It regards legal practice as the major determinant of legal change. "Practice" here refers to precedent and the "canons" of legal reasoning. "Independence" is perhaps too strong a term to characterize the asserted importance of legal practice in directing legal change. Much legal practice might be described as a decentralized method of defining social aims and goals in a world rife with ambiguity and conflict.[4]

Superficially, the first two theories of legal change have the most plausibility but this plausibility rests in large part on the simple structure of the legal system in which the theories are embedded. If the legal system consists of a single judge, acting alone, then her intentions and beliefs clearly should animate any legal change. In actual legal systems, however, the multiplicity of judges will rarely have nearly convergent, let alone identical, intentions and beliefs. Further, the structure of fact-finding in common law systems is unlikely to reduce disagreement in belief. As noted earlier, controversy-specific facts are not subject to review or any other form of centralized control. More importantly, controversy-specific facts often differ from policy-relevant facts. Judge Wright, in the implied warranty case referred to above, concluded that the world had changed not on the basis of any factual inquiry but solely on his own perception of the social world. The movement from agrarian society to an urban one could hardly escape notice but many less dramatic changes will either go unremarked or will be perceived differently by different judges.

Similarly, the unity of intention so evident in a single-judge system appears less likely in actual legal systems. The pyramidal structure of most court systems does offer the possibility of resolving conflicts among judicial goals. At the apex of the system, however, sits a panel of judges rather than a single judge. The aggregation of the goals of this panel does not necessarily lead to a coherent set of aims.[5] The "openness" of any common law system to other common law systems also militates against the dominance of a single set of intentions. In the United States, forty-nine states, the District of Columbia, and the United States have independent common-law legal structures; each influences the development of the others.[6]

Indeed, the social rules that constitute legal practice itself arguably serve as a major factor in unifying the diverse aims of a multiplicity of judges into a coherent legal system. This function of legal practice justifies the attention that jurisprudes have devoted to the study of legal reasoning. Any fair assessment of the fruits of that study, however, could only marvel at its failure to provide a clear account of changes in the announced legal norms. The inadequacy of the jurisprudential account of change in part explains the emergence of evolutionary theories of common law change.

"Natural-Selection" or Evolutionary Models of the Common Law

"Natural-Selection" or evolutionary models of the common law focus not on the actions and decisions of judges but on those of litigants.[7] Given the structure of common law adjudication, three litigant-related phenomena are relevant: (1) the social process that engenders disputes; (2) the social process that determines which disputes get brought to court for resolution; and (3) given that a dispute is before a court, the process that determines how each litigant will prosecute her case. Each of these processes is quite complex. The diversity of the aims and motives of actual litigants further complicates efforts to untangle and understand these processes.

Actual litigants may be motivated by ideological, moral, or other commitments, spite, or self-interest. In the models discussed below, self-interest, quite narrowly defined, serves as the sole motivation of agents in each of the three social processes. Agents are assumed to be economically rational; that is, each has a well-defined preference which she resolutely and with perfect foresight pursues. The agents of the models therefore clearly have motives and aims that diverge from the motives and aims of the judges within the system. Such a divergence of aims between the litigants and the judges will persist under virtually any assumption of the motives and aims of the litigants or any assumption of the motives and aims of judges. The same legal result is unlikely to further the aims of both self-interested judges and self-interested litigants, let alone the aims of public-spirited judges and self-interested litigants. Similarly, the ideological or moral commitments of the litigants are unlikely to conform to those of the judges.

This divergence in aims of judges and litigants lies at the center of evolutionary models. If the social processes that spawn litigation are somehow random or neutral in the sense that there is no systematic bias in the nature of the cases brought to judges to decide, the judicial process alone would drive the development of the law. If, on the other hand, the processes that produce litigation are biased in some way, that bias might still be apparent in the *outcomes* of the legal process; legal change would be driven, at least in part, by factors outside the judicial process.

A clearer understanding of evolutionary theories of the common law requires a bit more structure. Consider some behavior that might be governed by n distinct legal rules. A particular accident type, for example, might be subject to n distinct standards of care (including strict liability for which the standard of care is infinite). Suppose we may rank these rules according to some criterion or characteristic; we may then "name" them such that rule i ranks above rule j if and only if i is greater than j. In the economic models of evolution, the ranking criterion is generally a measure of efficiency of the legal rule. In the example, each rule would be identified by the standard of care it enforced. The measure of "efficiency" might be the sum of accident prevention costs and expected accident losses (or the sum of net benefits from the accident-generating activities less the sum of accident prevention costs and expected accident losses). Other measures of social desirability might also be used; in the standard of care example, the accident rate might serve as a measure of social desirability.

Evolutionary models of the common law distinguish between the judicial process and the legal process. The judicial process refers to how judges determine the movement of the law. In the context of the n-rule example, consider the following representation of the judicial process. Suppose the rule i prevails in the system. Given that rule i is litigated (in a "neutral" fashion to be elaborated below), the judicial process determines the probability p_{ij} that rule j will be announced. For each rule i, n different announcements are possible; the judicial process may thus be represented by an nxn matrix that defines a Markov process with stationary transition probabilities. In a Markov process, only the current state, and not the "history" that led to that state, plays a role in determining the movement of the system. Representing the judicial process as a Markov process therefore underplays the role of precedent in the judicial system.[8] The Markov assumption, however, does present the most favorable environment for the claim that non-judicial factors drive, at least in part, the legal process.

The legal process is more complex; it integrates the "pressures" for change controlled by the litigants with the judicial process. If one models each of the three social processes within litigant control as affecting the probabilities that rule j will prevail in period t+1 given that rule i prevailed in period t, one may also represent the legal process as a Markov process, though one different from that representing the judicial process.

Under suitable assumptions, the matrix representing the judicial process can in turn be represented by a unique stationary vector z, the element z_i of which is the percentage of time the judicial process announces rule i.[9] That is, one should imagine that in each time period t, the court announces a new legal rule, with the probability that rule j will be announced in time t determined by the probabilities p_{ij} of change from the rule i that prevailed in period $t - 1$. z_i represents the percentage of times rule i is announced by the court. Similarly, the matrix representing the legal process can in turn be represented by a unique stationary vector x, the element x_i of which is the percentage of time rule i prevails in the legal process. For a rule to "prevail" during a period t in the legal process means that either the court announces rule i in period t or that rule i was announced in some prior period T and no dispute was litigated between T and t. To say that non-judicial factors drive the legal process, then, is to say that x differs from z. Ideally, one would like to claim more, that x differs from z in some systematic fashion.

As noted earlier, three different social processes might drive the system away from the resting point of the judicial process. Two of these might be modeled as "differential litigation." If rule i prevailed, for example, more disputes might be generated than if rule j prevailed. Alternatively, the same number of disputes might arise under each rule, but, under rule i, the disputes might be more likely to end up in court than under rule j. Rubin (1977), Priest (1977), and Cooter and Kornhauser (1980) offer models of differential litigation. Rubin and Priest had each claimed that economically inefficient rules were more likely to be litigated than efficient rules and that, consequently, efficient rules would prevail more often in the legal process as a whole than they would in the judicial process alone.[10] Call this claim conjecture 1. Cooter and Kornhauser place conjecture 1 in the mathematical framework outlined here (and more extensively in the appendix). They then offer a theorem that suggests either that conjecture 1 is false or that a second, related conjecture might be false. Imagine two legal processes A and B which share a judicial process but differ in the rates which various rules are litigated. Suppose that in process A inefficient rules are litigated more often than they are in process B. Conjecture 2 then claims that efficient rules should prevail more often in process A than in process B.[11] The appendix to this paper gives a counterexample to conjecture 2. The third social process that might push the legal process away from the stationary state of the judicial process is that which determines how agents manage their litigations. At the outset of the discussion of jurisprudential theories of change, it was noted that how litigants chose to formulate the issues posed by their case might affect its resolution. Goodman (1978) modelled this process as one of differential investment. He claimed that those advocating a change from an inefficient rule to an efficient one would invest more in the litigation than those seeking to sustain the inefficient rule. Consequently, he contended, the efficient rule would prevail more often than the inefficient one and more often than it would prevail if litigant investment were neutral, i.e., the amount expended were independent of the rule advocated.[12]

The claim that efficient rules are "naturally selected" by the litigation process has two distinct parts. First, one must establish that in fact inefficient rules are litigated more frequently than efficient ones (or that litigants invest more to establish an efficient rule than they invest to establish an inefficient one). Second, one must prove that such a bias in litigation rates (or investment in litigation) in fact leads to the selection of efficient rules by the legal system.

The claim that inefficient rules are litigated more frequently than efficient rules reduces, to an economist at least, to the claim that either disputes are more likely to arise under inefficient rules or that disputes that arise under inefficient rules are more likely to be litigated than ones that arise under efficient rules. Neither part of the disjunction seems obviously true. That agents face excessive costs under an inefficient rule does not necessarily imply that disputes over their obligations are more likely. In any case, to my knowledge, no one has asserted more disputes arise under inefficient rules than efficient ones.

Both Rubin and Priest have claimed that, given a dispute has arisen, inefficient rules are more likely to be litigated than efficient ones and Charles Silver has addressed this aspect of the evolutionary claim in his contribution to this volume.[13] This claim in turn reduces to a claim about the choice faced by disputants between settlement out-of-court and litigation, specifically, that the rate of settlement should fall with a decrease in efficiency of the rule (or an increase in the social surplus to be gained from a change in the legal rule). Indeed, in the model of the settlement/litigation choice that Silver offers,[14] inefficient and efficient rules differ only in the amount of surplus that is possibly extractable from them. That is, the efficiency of the prevailing rule should not affect either (self-interested) party's beliefs about her likelihood of prevailing.

The relative efficiency of the rule does, however, affect the stakes. A change to an efficient legal rule would produce some joint savings but it may also reallocate the burdens. If the parties can negotiate around the rule (unlike in Silver's indemnity example), then the savings available through settlement will be identical to those available from litigation. If the parties cannot realize all their savings through settlement, then "total" social welfare might be increased by litigation. Moreover, at least *one* party will have an incentive to litigate. If the change in the legal rule, however, also redistributes the burden, the party that would lose from the redistribution has an incentive to oppose the change and to settle.

The first step in the evolutionary claim, that the rate of litigation should increase as the inefficiency of the rule increases, thus seems problematic. It develops that the second step, that the bias in litigation rates "selects" efficient rules, also presents difficulties. In the simple worlds considered in these early models, this claim of the "natural selection" of efficient rules was, indeed, true. Their models, however, had two unrealistic assumptions. First, Rubin assumed that efficient rules were never litigated. Consequently, once the judicial process announced an efficient rule, the legal process maintained it. Contrary to Rubin's assumption, however, individual litigants may have an economic incentive to litigate efficient rules. The individual litigant, after all, cares about the distribution of wealth. She might prefer a distributionally favorable but inefficient rule to a prevailing, efficient rule. Alternatively, there may be more than one efficient rule, each distributionally favoring a different party.[15]

Second, Rubin (and Goodman)[16] assumed that the court could choose only between two rules. In this circumstance, one can easily demonstrate that the overall legal process will be more efficient than the judicial process if and only if the efficient rule is litigated less often than the inefficient one.[17] In most circumstances, however, judges have more than two options before them. In the accident context, for example, they must choose not only a pattern of liability (as between negligence with contributory negligence and strict liability with dual contributory negligence) but some standard of care. When more than two legal rules exist, the condition that inefficient rules be litigated more frequently than efficient ones may not be sufficient to insure that the results of the legal process are more efficient than those that the pure judicial process would yield; conjecture 1 thus remains an open question.

In Appendix One, it is shown that for judicial processes that exhibit sufficient "neutrality," the Rubin/Priest claim is true. The required "neutrality" implies that, given that rule i prevails, the probability that the court adopts a different rule j is identical to the probability it adopts a different rule k. The probability of changing the rule may depend on the rule that prevails.

Concluding Remarks

The discussion of the previous two sections suggests that we lack any comprehensive or convincing theory of the evolution of announced legal rules. Our lack of understanding may simply reflect the complexity of the problem and the relatively little effort that has been devoted at least to evolutionary theories of the common law. On the other hand, the lack of progress may suggest that different legal rules change for different reasons, that we can learn little from the bare characterization of legal rule used in the economic models. It may be that a richer formal description of a legal rule may suffice to advance our understanding and it may be that the processes of legal change depend on the content of the legal rule as well.

One should recall the caveat of the introduction that understanding the evolution of announced legal rules leaves unexplained changes in behavior. In jurisprudential models, this gap is evident as judicial decisions may pay little attention to how individuals will adjust their behavior to the legal rules.[18] Evolutionary theories of the common law present a more complex picture. Individual behavior, not judicial behavior, drives legal change in these models but one ought to distinguish between the primary behavior affected by the legal rule and dispute-related behavior that arises when something goes wrong. Phrased somewhat differently, would a litigant whose view of the appropriate legal rule prevailed adopt behaviors that complied with that legal rule?

Notes

Copyright 1988 Lewis A. Kornhauser.

These comments were prepared for the Murphy Institute Conference on the Logic of Social Change in April, 1988. David Braybrooke, Julie Nelson, Richard Revesz, and Charles Silver provided helpful comments on an early draft. I am responsible for remaining errors. Kornhauser (1989, 1992a, 1992b, and forthcoming) are subsequent attempts to address some of the issues raised in this essay.

1. On this issue, see Kornhauser and Sager (1986, 1993) and Kornhauser (1992a, 1992b).

2. Coherence is discussed in Kornhauser and Sager (1986, 1993) and Kornhauser (1992b).

3. *Javins v. First National Realty Corp.*, 428 F.2d 1071 (D.C. Cir. 1970). In *Javins*, the lessees of an apartment in Washington, D.C. appealed from an order of eviction based on non-payment of rent. In their defense, they had sought to present evidence that the apartment did not meet the standards imposed on all housing units by the D.C. housing code. The trial court had barred this defense on the basis of the common law rule that the lessor of real property has no obligation to repair unless she explicitly covenants to do so in the written lease. This legal rule illustrated a long common law tradition that treats contracts for real property differently than contracts for goods or services. Judge Wright reversed; as one ground of his judgment, he held that the law of contract, rather than the law of property, should govern the rights and obligations of the parties to a lease for urban real property.

4. Kornhauser (1989) suggests a fourth reason for change in the legal rule: the judge may have acquired information about the world. Kornhauser (1992a) sketches

how the arrival of cases from litigants might couple with the logic of judicial decision to yield "autonomous" or, at least, path dependent evolution of the law.

5. This issue is discussed at greater length in Kornhauser and Sager (1986, 1993).

6. Louisiana follows the civil law rather than common law tradition. One should also note that each of the 12 federal appellate circuits may differ in legal regime as there is no rule of intercircuit *stare decisis*.

7. In the legal literature, the term "evolutionary models" is used in a more general sense; it may include mechanisms that rely predominantly on judicial action to explain change. Oliver Wendell Holmes, for example, is said to have had an evolutionary model of legal change. "Evolutionary" for Holmes seemed to indicate "nondirective"; that is, the process of legal change, though the result of the decisions of individual judges (and of nothing else) lay beyond the control of each individual judge. See Elliott (1984). The more restrictive sense of "evolutionary model" emerged with the economic models of "natural selection" of efficient rules introduced by Rubin (1977) and Priest (1977).

8. One aspect of precedent can be captured in a Markov process. Given that the system is in state i, one may assume that the probability that rule i will be announced, given a litigation, might be higher than the probability that any other rule would be announced. To the extent that the rule of *stare decisis* merely says that the prevailing rule should in general be followed, the Markov assumption captures it. On the other hand, the Markov assumption does not permit a rule to become "entrenched"; that is, the probability that rule i will be affirmed does not change with the number of times it has been previously affirmed.

9. Cooter and Kornhauser (1980) outline the conditions on the judicial process necessary for the existence of a unique stationary vector.

10. In fact Rubin argued that the legal process would achieve and maintain the efficient rule. This result depended critically on the claim that the efficient rule was an absorbing state of the process; i.e., that an efficient rule would never be litigated. In many legal contexts, two legal rules, each with different distributional consequences, are efficient; one would thus expect one party to have an incentive to litigate even when some efficient legal rule prevailed. For some efficient rule always to prevail would then require that, upon hearing a challenge to an efficient rule, the judicial process would announce an inefficient rule with probability zero. Such an assumption assumes a judicial bias for efficiency. Thus, once one recognizes that good reasons for litigant challenges to efficient rules exist, one must reformulate Rubin's claim to the weaker one articulated in the text.

11. Cooter and Kornhauser in fact do not formulate conjecture 2. They offer a theorem which gives sufficient conditions for one legal process A to be "more efficient" than a second legal process B. Taking B to be the judicial process alone and A the overall legal process derived from B and differential litigation, one finds that A and B do not satisfy the conditions of the theorem. It is not clear what one should conclude from this observation.

12. Goodman's model assumes that the judge must choose one of two rules. The model does not extend in an obvious way to circumstances in which the judge faces more than two choices of the legal rule. One must assume that the relative investments of the parties affect the distribution according to which the system will be changed. Once one specifies these distributions and the rule for determining relative investments, one can place Goodman's model in the Markov framework developed by Cooter and Kornhauser.

13. Silver investigates this question with a different goal in mind. He challenges the claim of Landes and Posner that common law adjudication produces the appropriate (or efficient) level of uncertainty of the legal "rules." In fact, the uncertainty in Landes' and Posner's formalism may be of the outcomes of disputes or of the content of the legal norm. Their interpretation of the formalism suggests that they are concerned about the content of the legal norm. Under this interpretation, I have difficulty understanding the Landes/Posner claim largely because I am not sure what uncertainty in a legal rule entails. On one reading, it means that the rule might be either A or B, each of which is precise and clear, but we are unsure which one, in fact, prevails. Alternatively, a legal rule might be uncertain in the sense that under given conditions more than one outcome is admissible; judges have "discretion" to decide. In this latter sense, the socially desirable level of uncertainty in a legal rule should depend on the content of a legal rule. Consider two precise rules A and B with A being very inefficient and B efficient. Let A' and B' be "uncertain" (or blurred) versions of A and B respectively. If discretion under A' means that more efficient outcomes sometimes prevail than would prevail under A, then surely we prefer A' to A.

14. In Silver's model, bargains break down *only* because each party overestimates her prospects for success. This limitation in causes of breakdown is a consequence of the assumptions of the model. For instance, in his model, each party knows the reservation bid or offer of her opponent. In models with asymmetric information, however, bargaining breakdowns will occur naturally in equilibrium even if both parties have accurate estimates of their prospects of success. In these models, a party knows her own reservation bid but does not know the reservation offer of her opponent.

15. Economic models of accident law offer an illustration of this situation with efficient negligence rules being "dual" in a distributional sense to efficient strict liability rules.

16. It is not clear how to generalize Goodman's model to worlds in which more than two rules are possible. In Goodman's model, given litigation, each party invests in the litigation proportionally to the amount she will gain. If judges choose only between the rules advocated by the parties, there is no guarantee that one of the parties will advocate an efficient rule. If judges may choose a rule advocated by neither party, then one must explain how the differential investments of the parties affect the probability of adopting any given rule. An explanation of this sort will generate a model similar to that explored in Cooter and Kornhauser (and in the appendix to this note).

17. See Proposition 1 of Appendix 1.

18. On the other hand, a judicial practice which directed judges to consider the effects of their decisions on behavior would introduce a link between announced legal rules and changes in legal behavior.

References

Cooter, R., and Kornhauser, L. A. 1980. "Can Litigation Improve the Law Without the Help of Judges?" *Journal of Legal Studies* 9: 139–163.

Elliott, E. D. 1984. "Holmes and Evolution: Legal Process as Artificial Intelligence," *Journal of Legal Studies* 13: 113–146.

Goodman, J. C. 1978. "An Economic Theory of the Evolution of the Common Law," *Journal of Legal Studies* 7: 393–406.

Kornhauser, L. A. 1989. "An Economic Perspective on Stare Decisis," *Chicago-Kent Law Review* 65: 63–92.

Kornhauser, L. A. 1992a. "Modeling Collegial Courts I: Path Dependence," *International Review of Law and Economics* 12: 169–185.

Kornhauser, L. A. 1992b. "Modeling Collegial Courts II: Legal Doctrine," *Journal of Law, Economics, and Organization* 8: 441–470.

Kornhauser, L. A. (Forthcoming). "Adjudication by a Resource-constrained Team: Hierarchy and Precedent in a Court System," *Southern California Law Review*.

Kornhauser, L. A., and Sager, L.G. 1986. "Unpacking the Court," *Yale Law Journal* 96: 82–117.

Kornhauser, L. A., and Sager, L.G. 1993. "The One and the Many: Adjudication in Collegial Courts," *California Law Review* 81: 1–59.

Landes, W. M., and Posner, R.A. 1976. "Legal Precedent: A Theoretical and Empirical Analysis," *Journal of Law and Economics* 19: 249–307.

Landes, W. M., and Posner, R.A. 1979. "Adjudication as a Private Good," *Journal of Legal Studies* 8: pp. 235–84.

Priest, G. L. 1977. "The Common Law Process and the Selection of Efficient Rules," *Journal of Legal Studies* 6: pp. 65–82.

Rubin, P. H. 1977. "Why is the Common Law Efficient?" *Journal of Legal Studies*, 6: pp. 51–63.

Silver, C. 1996. "Do We Know Enough About Social Norms?", this volume.

PART THREE

The Economists' Approach to the Origin of Rules and to Changes in Them

Comment on Reconciling the Philosophers' Approach to Rules with the Economists'

David Braybrooke

In a brief intervention, Braybrooke says something to reconcile the issue-processing perspective of logicians, philosophers, and others (including most legal scholars as well as anthropologists and sociologists) with the economists' perspective, illustrated in application by Silver; but becoming even more basic theoretically in the pieces by North, Kornhauser, Heiner, and Schofield about to come.

Silver, as Kornhauser has pointed out, takes an approach to changes in rules characteristic of economists rather than the approach, more common in legal studies and more common with philosophers and social scientists, that focuses on what I have called "issue-processing." However, this shift to economics in the discussion of changes in rules does not go so far as economists and some philosophers have gone in taking an economic approach to the origin and conception of rules. These writers, represented in this volume by North, Kornhauser, Heiner, and Schofield[1] treat rules as least cost solutions to problems about transaction costs or as solutions to game-theoretical problems. Uncertainty colors both sorts of problems. How do people cope with uncertainty, especially uncertainty about the behavior of others? They will do better one by one, Heiner shows, by adopting rules for their own conduct; they will do better collectively, if they can count on the others to be guided by known rules. Schofield agrees, but shows that chaos may still lie in wait for collective rules, in particular the rules for collective decision, and especially if these are taken, as has been the case in formal studies until lately, as rules for aggregating preferences rather than beliefs.

There is a sense in which this approach is not so general as the one taken commonly by philosophers. Their approach, though it is not incompatible with the economists' approach in particular cases, leaves open the question whether any given rule is a rational solution to an economic problem, or even (if it is a personal rule) a rational device for coping with uncertainty. We should not lightly assume that all social rules are solutions to economic problems, or rationally justified at all in other ways. Children do not learn received rules as solutions to economic problems. They learn them from the insistence of those in authority over them and conform—perhaps perfectly—without in many cases beginning at any time in their lives to consider the rules as such solutions. This opens up all sorts of room for rules to be present without rational justification—which they may have lost if they once had it, or indeed they may never have had. In the economic perspective, it may be suggested that sooner or later, because of their costs, such rules will not be maintained, but that is at best an empirical hypothesis. It is an hypothesis that must allow for a good deal of difficulty—amid the confusion of social events—in detecting the costs that might suggest lack of justification. (Why should this rule be singled out as too costly to offset the benefits conferred, when the costs can at first sight be attributed to a variety of other causes?) It must also allow for a good deal of delay in taking the costs, once detected, to be conclusive against justification (consider, e.g., the rules of religious observance).

Yet undeniably rules—settled social rules or settled personal ones—do reduce uncertainty about what the people who conform to them are going to do; and given this basic point, the suggestion that some rules originate just to reduce uncertainty is eminently worth following up, as the results of doing so confirm. The theory of games itself was developed especially to deal with uncertainty arising for personal choice from the interactions of given persons with others. Solutions have been easier to come by for two person games than for games with more than two players; but some n-person games have solutions that have been identified with conventions binding on all participants. These may be treated, depending on which in an array of definitions of "rule" like the one set forth by Kornhauser is chosen, as rules themselves or as rules-in-the-making, fixed as rules proper by becoming associated with corrective measures (blockings) in their teaching or maintenance even if provisions for punishment are not added as well. We have on the one hand David Lewis's theory of conventions, which treats them as solutions to games of coordination in which everyone wins and no one has any temptation to defect.[2] We have on the other hand a good understanding of n-person games of the form of (repeated) Prisoner's Dilemma or of the form of the Assurance Game, and know what sorts of rules have to be adopted to solve them or escape them.[3] Rules that serve in these connections have been held to be the most basic social rules, indispensable for bringing rational—non-tuistic—agents into a social order by contract and indispensable for maintaining a social order once established. Examples have to do with respect for one another's security of life and limb; respect for private property; respect for contractual obligations arising in particular transactions.

Clearly these examples identify some familiar members of the set of settled social rules. But if the generalized economic approach to rules captures through game theory some personal rules for coping with uncertainty, the generalized approach embraces, without needing game theory to do so, some rules for personal choice with any amount of information, including full information; and these can easily be related to some familiar settled social rules. There are such rules prescribing prudence, providence, even rational choice—rules that by guiding the choices of individual persons lead them each to adopt corresponding rules for personal choice. They work with certainty; but they have a role to play in uncertainty, too. Heiner would say that rational agents adopt prudential rules for personal choice suited to coping with the uncertainty that they face; but this is compatible with granting established social rules for prudence and providence a leading or at least suggestive part. Further social rules may be looked upon by economists as least-cost solutions to problems about transaction costs raised by changes in technology (North). Thus, throughout the range of the economists' treatment of rules, examples, and important examples, of settled social rules can be produced; and their character, in regard at least to the net benefits that they confer upon the people who adhere to them, plays a crucial part in the problems raised and the solutions arrived at. Again, I am assimilating to the work of economists the work of decision-theorists and of people other than economists taking a game-theoretical view of rules.

Notes

1. Some philosophers who have taken the economists' approach include David P. Gauthier, *The Logic of Leviathan* (Oxford: The Clarendon Press, 1969); Edna Ullman-Margalit, *The Emergence of Norms* (Oxford: The Clarendon Press, 1977); Jean Hampton, *Hobbes and the Social Contract Tradition* (Cambridge: Cambridge University Press, 1986); Gregory S. Kavka, *Hobbesian Moral and Political Theory* (Princeton: Princeton University Press, 1986). See also an issue of *Ethics* devoted to the study of norms, Vol. 100, No. 4, July 1990.

2. David K. Lewis, *Convention: a Philosophical Study* (Cambridge, Mass.: Harvard University Press, 1969).

3. See, for instance, in addition to Ullman-Margalit and the other writers cited above, Russell Hardin, "Collective Action as an Agreeable n-Prisoners' Dilemma," *Behavior Science*, Vol. 16, 1971, pp. 472–481; and for the Assurance Game, Amartya Sen, "Isolation, Assurance, and the Social Rate of Discount," *Quarterly Journal of Economics*, Vol. 80, 1967, pp. 112–124.

12

Institutional Change: A Framework of Analysis

Douglass C. North

North is an outstanding figure in the economists' approach to the history of rules and changes in rules, though he believes, as he makes clear in the work that outlines the basis of his thinking (Structure and Change in Economic History [New York: W. W. Norton & Co., 1981]), that "ideology" (in part, the rationalization of institutions and the rules that give form to them) in large part escapes economic analysis. Economics—neoclassical economics—can explain via the free-rider problem why as so frequently happens people do not organize to advance their interests even when large numbers of people would benefit from such organization; but it is in the direction of ideological controversies over the justice of rules that historians must look for the explanation of those large-number organized efforts that do occur. Moreover, in the sphere of issues amenable to economic explanation, North holds that neo-classical models assuming smooth adjustments in supply and demand must often give way to models that give chief weight to transaction costs and to people's efforts to reduce them. The rules that give form to institutions may be intended to be least-cost solutions for people seeking to protect and increase their revenues; but they have more often than not been at best least-cost solutions for a subclass of the population (the rulers of a given state) and even then successful only to a degree in reducing transaction costs. Nevertheless, it is shifts in perceived opportunities to seize benefits while reducing such costs that time and again account for changes in rules, including in time changes in the most fundamental ones.

A theory of institutional change is essential for further progress in the social sciences in general and economics in particular. Essential because neo-classical theory (and other theories in the social scientist's toolbag) at present cannot satisfactorily account for the very diverse performance of societies and economies both at a moment of time and over time. The explanations derived from neo-classical theory are not satisfactory because, while the models may account for most of the differences in performance between economies on the basis of differential investment in education, savings rates, etc., they do not account for why economies would fail to

"

undertake the appropriate activities *if they had a high payoff*.[1] Institutions determine the payoffs. While the fundamental neo-classical assumption of scarcity and hence competition has been robust (and is basic to this analysis), the assumption of a frictionless exchange process has led economic theory astray. Institutions are the structure that humans impose on human interaction and therefore define the incentives that (together with the other constraints (budget, technology, etc.) determine the choices that individuals make that shape the performance of societies and economies over time.

In the following pages, I sketch out a framework for analyzing institutions. This framework builds on the economic theory of choice subject to constraints. However it incorporates new assumptions about both the constraints that individuals face and the process by which they make choices within those constraints. Among the traditional neoclassical assumptions that are relaxed are those of costless exchange, perfect information, and unlimited cognitive capabilities. Too many gaps still remain in our understanding of this new approach to call it a theory. What I do provide are a set of definitions, principles, and a structure which provide much of the scaffolding necessary to develop a theory of institutional change.

Institutions and Organizations: Definitions and Descriptions

Institutions consist of formal rules, informal constraints (norms of behavior, conventions, and self imposed codes of conduct) and the enforcement characteristics of both. The degree to which there is an identity between the objectives of the institutional constraints and the choices individuals make in that institutional setting depends on the effectiveness of enforcement. Enforcement is carried out by the first party (self imposed codes of conduct), by the second party (retaliation), and/or by a third party (societal sanctions or coercive enforcement by the state). Institutions affect economic performance by determining (together with the technology employed) transaction and transformation (production) costs.

If institutions are the rules of the game, organizations are the players. They are groups of individuals engaged in purposive activity. The constraints imposed by the institutional framework (together with the other constraints) define the opportunity set and therefore the kind of organizations that will come into existence. Given its objective function—profit maximization, winning elections, regulating businesses, educating students—the organization which may be a firm, a political party, a regulatory agency, a school or college, will engage in acquiring skills and knowledge that will enhance its survival possibilities in the context of ubiquitous scarcity and hence competition. The kinds of skills and knowledge that will pay off will be a function of the incentive structure inherent in the institutional matrix. If the highest rates of return in a society are to be made from piracy, then organizations will invest in knowledge and skills that will make them better pirates; if organizations realize the highest payoffs by increasing productivity then they will invest in skills and knowledge to achieve that objective. Organizations may not only directly invest in acquiring skills and knowledge but indirectly (via the political process) induce public investment in those kinds of knowledge that they believe will enhance their survival prospects.

The new (or neo) institutional economics has produced a substantial literature dealing with institutions and organizations. The property rights literature (Alchian, 1965, Demsetz, 1967), for example, analyzes the implications of institutions and organizations for performance, but in most of it the formation and evolution of institutions and organizations remain exogenous to the analysis. Oliver Williamson (1975, 1985) treating the institutional framework as exogenous, explores the transaction and transformation costs of various organizational forms. My objective (North, 1990, as well as here) is to put forth an explanation of institutional (and organizational) change that is endogenous, an essential step in my view to further progress in economic history and economic development.

Institutional Change: Agents, Sources, Process, Direction

The agent of change is the entrepreneur, the decisionmaker(s) in organizations. The subjective perceptions (mental models) of entrepreneurs determine the choices they make.

The sources of change are the opportunities perceived by entrepreneurs. They stem from either external changes in the environment or the acquisition of learning and skills and their incorporation in the mental constructs of the actors. Changes in relative prices have been the most commonly observed external sources of institutional change in history, but changes in taste have also been important. The acquisition of learning and skills will lead to the construction of new mental models by entrepreneurs to decipher the environment; in turn the models will alter perceived relative prices of potential choices. In fact it is usually some mixture of external change and internal learning that triggers the choices that lead to institutional change.

Deliberate institutional change will come about therefore as a result of the demands of entrepreneurs in the context of the perceived costs of altering the institutional framework at various margins. The entrepreneur will assess the gains to be derived from recontracting within the existing institutional framework compared to the gains from devoting resources to altering that framework. Bargaining strength and the incidence of transaction costs are not the same in the polity as in the economy, otherwise it would not be worthwhile for groups to shift the issues to the political arena.

Thus entrepreneurs who perceive themselves and their organizations as relative (or absolute) losers in economic exchange as a consequence of the existing structure of relative prices can turn to the political process to right their perceived wrongs by altering that relative price structure. In any case it is the perceptions of the entrepreneur—correct or incorrect—that are the sources of action.

Changes in the formal rules may come about as a result of legislative changes such as the passage of a new statute, of judicial changes stemming from court decisions that alter the common law, of regulatory rule changes enacted by regulatory agencies, and of constitutional rule changes that alter the rules by which other rules are made.

Changes in informal constraints—norms, conventions, or personal standards of honesty, for example—have the same originating sources of change as do changes in formal rules; but they occur gradually and sometimes quite subconsciously as individuals evolve alternative patterns of behavior consistent with their newly perceived evaluation of costs and benefits.

The process of change is overwhelmingly incremental (although I shall deal with revolutionary change below). The reason is that the economies of scope, the complementarities, and the network externalities that arise from a given institutional matrix of formal rules, informal constraints, and enforcement characteristics will typically bias costs and benefits in favor of choices consistent with the existing framework. The larger the number of rule changes, ceteris paribus the greater the number of losers and hence opposition. Therefore, except in the case of gridlock (described below), institutional change will occur at those margins considered most pliable in the context of the bargaining power of interested parties. The incremental change may come from a change in the rules via statute or legal change. For informal constraints there may be a very gradual withering away of an accepted norm or social convention or the gradual adoption of a new one as the nature of the political, social, or economic exchange gradually changes.

The direction of change is determined by path dependence. The political and economic organizations that have come into existence in consequence of the institutional matrix typically have a stake in perpetuating the existing framework. The complementarities, economies of scope, and network externalities mentioned above bias change in favor of the interests of the existing organizations. Both the interests of the existing organizations that produce path dependence and the mental models of the actors—the entrepreneurs—that produce ideologies "rationalize" the existing institutional matrix and therefore bias the perception of the actors in favor of policies conceived to be in the interests of existing organizations.

Both external sources of change and unanticipated consequences of their policies may weaken the power of existing organizations, strengthen or give rise to organizations with different interests, and change the path.

The critical actor(s) in such situations will be political entrepreneurs whose degrees of freedom will increase in such situations and, on the basis of their perception of the issues, give them the ability to induce the growth of organizations with different interests (or strengthen existing ones).

Revolutionary change occurs as a result of gridlock arising from a lack of mediating institutions that enable conflicting parties to reach compromises that capture some of the gains from potential trades. The key to the existence of such mediating political (and economic) institutions is not only formal rules and organizations but also informal constraints that can foster dialogue between conflicting parties. The inability to achieve compromise solutions may also reflect limited degrees of freedom of the entrepreneurs to bargain and still maintain the loyalty of their constituent groups. Thus the real choice set of the conflicting parties may have no intersection, so that even though there are potentially large gains from resolving disagreements, the combination of the limited bargaining freedom of the entrepreneurs and a lack of facilitating institutions makes it impossible.

However revolutionary change is never as revolutionary as its rhetoric would have us believe. It is not just that the power of ideological rhetoric fades as the mental models of the constituents confront their utopian ideals with the harsh realities of post revolutionary existence. Formal rules may change over night, but informal constraints do not. Inconsistency between the formal rules and the informal constraints (which may be the result of deep-seated cultural inheritance because they have traditionally resolved basic exchange problems) results in tensions which typically get resolved by some restructuring of the overall constraints—in both directions—to produce a new equilibrium that is far less revolutionary than the rhetoric.

The Framework Illustrated

An extended sketch from American economic history illustrates the way in which institutions, organizations, and the mental models of the actors interact to produce institutional change.

The basic institutional framework of the American colonies that had been carried over from England provided a hospitable environment for economic growth. The incentive structure not only encouraged decentralized and local political autonomy but also provided low cost economic transacting through fee simple ownership of land (with some early exceptions in proprietary colonies) and secure property rights. The organizations that arose to take advantage of the resultant opportunities—colonial assemblies, plantations, merchant houses, shipping firms, family farms—produced a thriving colonial economy. But the entire colonial period was one of a long learning process—discovering staple exports (tobacco, fish, rice, indigo), developing markets (West Indies, South Europe); improving productivity (substituting slaves for indentured servants on tobacco plantations, reducing turn-around time in shipping). In brief, the learning resulted in reducing transaction or transformation costs or in increasing revenues which resulted in improving the efficiency of the colonial economy.

While planters, merchants, shippers, and farmers could and did make modest changes in the institutional framework as their perceived needs changed, they were basically limited by their colonial status—not perceived as a serious burden as long as the threat of French and Indian intervention was present. With the elimination of that threat with the French and Indian War (1755–1763), the colonists increasingly perceived their interests as divergent from Britain and its colonial policies. The American Revolution was sparked not only by changes in the institutions such as the Quebec Act (closing off western lands to settlement by American colonists) and the very moderate taxes imposed on the colonists—which produced a violent reaction, but also by the intellectual tradition from Hobbes to Locke that shaped the mental models of the actors. The British never anticipated that the taxes imposed on the colonists would produce such a violent reaction and the colonists for their part were wrong in their perception that British policy after 1763 would destroy the colonial economy (after all Canada did very well staying within the Empire). It was the perceptions of the colonists in the context of the intellectual traditions of the times that guided Samuel Adams, Thomas Paine, Thomas Jefferson, George Washington, and others in their policies.

The post revolutionary Northwest Ordinance and Constitution codified, elaborated, and modified colonial institutions in the light of contemporary issues (and the bargaining strength of the players). But despite the Revolution, the basic institutional framework of formal rules (including contracts enacted before the war) and informal cultural norms was maintained and continued the incentives for a thriving economy. Productivity increase came not only from high pay-off to the acquisition of productive skills and knowledge by economic organizations and from the encouragement of technological change (such as by patent law), but also from induced investment through the polity in public education, land grant colleges, agricultural experiment stations, etc. As organizations evolved to take advantage of opportunities they became more productive (Chandler, 1977) and gradually they also altered the institutional framework. The judicial and political framework (the Marshall Court decisions, the Fourteenth Amendment) and the structure of property rights were altered or modified (Munn vs. Illinois), but so too were many norms of behavior and other informal constraints altered (reflected in changing attitudes towards slavery and blacks, and the role of women in society, and temperance, for example).

The price paid for this rapid economic growth was partly inherent in adaptively efficient institutions. The system wiped out losers—farmers that went bust on the frontier, shipping firms that failed as the U.S. lost its comparative advantage in shipping and laborers that suffered unemployment and declining wages from immigrant competition in the 1850s. It was also partly a consequence of institutions that exploited individuals and groups—Indians and slaves, and not infrequently immigrants, workers, and farmers—to the benefit of those with superior bargaining power.

The political framework resulted in the losers having, albeit imperfect, access to remedies for their perceived source of misfortune—remedies that also altered the institutional framework. Perceived sources consisted of immediately observed grievances filtered through ongoing intellectual currents and ideologies of the actors. The late nineteenth century farmers could frequently observe price discrimination by the railroad or grain elevator, but the Populist Party platform reflected broad ideological views encompassing the perceived burden of the gold standard and widespread monopoly, as well as the pernicious consequences of bankers. Whatever the underlying sources of the farmers' plight that produced discontent, farmers' perceptions mattered and changed the political and economic institutional framework.

Nor was it just the farmers' perceptions that mattered. So did the subjective models of the other actors or organizations able to influence outcomes as a result of the institutional matrix. Whether the Supreme Court understood the implications of *Munn v. Illinois* (commonly regarded as a milestone in the growth of federal government regulation) and the many other court decisions that were gradually altering the legal framework depended on the degree to which the information feedback on the consequences of existing laws was accurate and hence gave true models. True or false, the models the judiciary acted upon were incrementally altering the judicial framework.

As with all institutional frameworks, the rules were a mixed bag of those that those that promoted increased productivity and those that encouraged monopoly, income redistribution, and inefficient resource allocation; but the former have overwhelmingly dominated the institutional framework and produced a path dependent pattern of economic growth that has persisted for more than three centuries. To illustrate this path dependent process I turn from this overarching story to a more detailed examination of one facet of this story—land policy—that will put more meat on the analytical bones of this framework.

The Northwest Ordinance of 1787 was the third in a series of enactments passed by the Continental Congress in the 1780s to establish an overall policy for the disposal of the vast public lands. The Ordinance is brief. It provided for rules of inheritance and fee simple ownership of land, set up

the basic structure of territorial governments, and provided the mechanisms by which territories gradually became self-governing. Additionally,
it made provision for when a territory would be admitted as a state. Then
there was a series of Articles of Compact, in effect a bill of rights for the
territories. There were additional provisions about good faith to the Indians, free navigation on the Mississippi and St. Lawrence rivers, public debt,
land disposal, and the number of states that could be divided up within
the Northwest Territory; and finally there was a provision prohibiting slavery in the territories (although the return of runaway slaves was specified).

These provisions can be directly traced to the English and colonial background; many of them including much of the bill of rights were explicit
provisions of the colonial charters (Hughes, 1987). The impetus for the
Ordinance was relative price changes stemming from the financial crisis of
the new nation and states as they emerged from the Revolution combined
with the necessity of developing policies to administer the vast territories
that had been acquired as a result of the peace treaty following independence. Contoversial implications for the current and future distribution of
political power and (not unrelated) the slavery issue (North and Rutten,
1987) shaped specific provisions.

The agents of change (and their organizations) were the Reverend
Manassah Cutler (and the Ohio and Scioto Companies) who asked Congress to provide a settled plan of self-government for the proposed settlers
of the huge blocks of land Congress had granted to those companies—
thereby inducing Congress to establish the committee that wrote the Ordinance; and Nathan Dane and Rufus King (representatives from Massachusetts and members of the committee), who wrote many of the Ordinance's
provisions and specifically the one barring slavery in the Northwest Territory (Hughes, 1987).

The downstream consequences of the Ordinance were continually being shaped by the relative price changes that reflected the rising implicit
rents resulting from the rising value of land together with the government
sale prices and weak enforcement policies. The consequent rapid settlement was in turn altering the political balance of power. Territories became
states with different interests than the older states, and their agendas incrementally shaped later public land policies. Claims clubs emerged to
thwart competitive bidding (for land that the squatters had settled upon);
squatters finally got a general preemption act (giving them first claim on
the land they had settled upon); the minimum size of units for sale was
reduced, and eventually the Homestead Act passed (giving land away free).

Some of the consequences may have been unanticipated. The prohibition of slavery in the new territories, for example, induced a large proportion of settlers to come from New England; they brought with them attitudes that were distinctly different from settlers of other regions and from

immigrants. They were more literate, a lower proportion were tenants, and they possessed greater real estate wealth (Atack and Bateman, 1987). Their attitude played a major role in early investment in public education and in other public policies that were in distinct contrast to those that evolved in territories south of the Ohio River where slavery was permitted.

Overall the history of land policy is only intelligible as a continuously unfolding story of incremental change but one in which the initial path stamped out by the three great land ordinances of the 1780s was decisive in shaping the long run path. That is, the fundamental features of the three ordinances, which provided for low cost political and economic transacting, structured the political and economic framework of the territories and led to rapid economic growth, settlement, and integration into the U.S. economy. Even downstream public policies that produced inefficient consequences such as the Homestead Act, which imposed inefficient size restrictions on initial land holdings, were mitigated by the low costs of transacting which led to subsequent consolidations and efficient size units of use.

The Implications of an Institutional Framework

Information processing by the actors as a result of the costliness of transacting underlies the formation of institutions. At issue are both the meaning of rationality and the characteristics of transacting that prevent the actors from achieving the joint maximization result of the zero transaction cost model.

The instrumental rationality postulate of neo-classical theory assumes that the actors possess information necessary to evaluate alternatives correctly and in consequence make choices that will achieve the desired ends. In fact such a postulate implicitly assumes the existence of particular sets of institutions and costless information. If institutions play a purely passive role so that they do not constrain the choices of the players and the players are in possession of the information necessary to make correct choices, then the instrumental rationality postulate is the correct building block. If, on the other hand, the players are incompletely informed, devise subjective models as guides to choices, and can only very imperfectly correct their models with information feedback, then a procedural rationality postulate is the essential building block to theorizing. Such a postulate not only can account for the incomplete and imperfect markets that characterize much of the present and the past world, but also leads the researcher to the key issue of just what it is that makes markets imperfect—the cost of transacting.

The cost of transacting arises because information is costly and asymmetrically held by the parties to exchange. In consequence, any way that the players develop institutions to structure human interaction results in some degree of imperfection of the markets. In effect the incentive consequences of institutions provide mixed signals to the participants, so that even in those cases where the institutional framework is more conducive to capturing the gains from trade than was an earlier institutional framework, there will be incentives to cheat, free ride, and so forth that will contribute to market imperfections. The success stories of economic history describe institutional innovations that have lowered the costs of transacting and permitted capturing more of the gains from trade and hence permitted expansion of markets. But such innovations, for the most part, have not created the conditions necessary for the efficient markets of the neoclassical model. The polity specifies and enforces the property rights of the economic marketplace, and the characteristics of the political market are the essential key to understanding the imperfections of markets.

Just as the efficiency of an economic market can be measured by the degree to which the competitive structure via arbitrage and efficient information feedback mimics or approximates the conditions of a zero transaction cost framework, so a political market is efficient to the degree that constituents accurately evaluate the policies pursued by competing candidates in terms of the net effect on their well being; enact only legislation (or regulation) that maximizes the aggregate income of the affected parties to the exchange, and by compensating those adversely affected insure that no party is injured by an action.

To achieve such results constituents and legislators would need to possess true models that allowed them to accurately evaluate the gains and losses of alternative policies, legislators would vote their constituents' interests—that is, the vote of each legislator would be weighted by the net gains or losses of the constituents—and losers would be compensated such as to make the exchange worthwhile to them—all at a transaction cost that still resulted in the highest net aggregate gain.

I do not wish to imply that the political process in democracies does not sometimes approach such a nirvana outcome, just as economic markets sometimes approximate the zero transaction cost model implicit in much economic theory. But such instances are rare and exceptional. Voter ignorance, incomplete information, and in consequence the prevalence of ideological stereotypes as the underpinnings of the subjective models individuals develop to explain their environment and make choices result in political markets that can and do perpetuate unproductive institutions and consequent organizations.[2]

The implications for economic theory of the foregoing analysis of institutions and imperfect (or procedural) rationality are:

1. Economic (and political) models are specific to particular constellations of institutional constraints that vary radically both through time and

cross-sectionally in different economies. The models are institution-specific and in many cases highly sensitive to altered institutional constraints.

Even more important, the specific institutional constraints dictate the margins at which organizations operate and hence make intelligible the interplay between the rules of the game and the behavior of the actors. If organizations devote their efforts to unproductive activity, the institutional constraints have provided the incentive structure for such activity. Third world countries are poor because the institutional constraints define a set of payoffs to political/economic activity that do not encourage productive activity. Socialist economies are beginning to learn the hard lesson that the underlying institutional framework is the source of the current poor performance and are attempting to grapple with ways to restructure the institutional framework to redirect incentives that in turn will direct organizations along productivity increasing paths. And as for the first world, we not only need to appreciate the importance of the overall institutional framework that has been responsible for the growth of the economy, but to be self conscious about the consequences of the marginal changes that are continually occurring. We have long been aware that taxes, regulations, judicial decisions, and statute laws shape the policies of organizations, but such awareness has not led economic theory to modeling the political/economic process that produces these results.

2. A self-conscious incorporation of institutions will force social scientists in general and economists in particular to question the behavioral assumptions that underlie their disciplines and, in consequence, to explore much more systematically than we have done so far the implications of the costly and imperfect processing of information for the consequent behavior of the actors. Social scientists *have* incorporated the costliness of information in their models but have not (for the most part) come to grips with the subjective mental constructs by which individuals process information and arrive at conclusions that shape their choices.

3. Ideas and ideologies matter, and institutions play a major role in determining just how much they matter. Ideas and ideologies shape the mental constructs that individuals use to interpret the world around them and make choices. Moreover, by structuring the interaction of human beings in certain ways, formal institutions deliberately or accidentally lower the price of acting on one's ideas and therefore increase the role of mental constructs and ideological stereotypes in choices. Voting systems, lifetime tenure for judges, indeed the institutional framework of hierarchies in general all provide a setting that alters the price one pays for expressing and acting on one's ideas, convictions, dogmas, or insights.

4. The polity and the economy are inextricably linked in any understanding of the performance of an economy and therefore we must develop a true political economy discipline. A set of institutional constraints

and consequent organizations defines the exchange relationships between the two and therefore determines the way a political/economic system works. Not only do polities specify and enforce property rights that shape the basic incentive structure of an economy; in the modern world the share of gross national product going through government and the ubiquitous and ever changing regulations imposed by it are the keys to economic performance.

Toward a Theory of Institutional Change

Let me conclude by summing up the key features of this analytical framework of institutional change.

1. The continuous interaction between institutions and organizations in the economic setting of scarcity and hence competition is the key to institutional change.

2. Competition forces organizations to continually invest in knowledge to survive.

3. The institutional framework dictates the kind of knowledge perceived to have the maximum pay-off.

4. The mental constructs of the players, given the complexity of the environment, the limited information feedback on the consequences of actions, and the inherited cultural conditioning of the players, determine perceptions.

5. The economies of scope, complementarities, and network externalities of an institutional matrix make institutional change overwhelmingly incremental and path dependent.

Notes

This essay draws from and builds upon a recent book by the author entitled, *Institutions, Institutional Change and Economic Performance*, (Cambridge: Cambridge University Press, 1990). I would like to thank members of the Washington University workshop in economic history and particularly Art Denzau, Brad Hansen, and Andrew Rutten for their comments and suggestions. I would also like to thank Elisabeth Case for editing this essay. [The paper that North read at the Murphy Institute Conference had been promised for publication elsewhere. He and the *Journal of Economics and Business* have given permission to include instead a recent paper giving a general view of his approach to changes in rules and institutions, "Towards a Theory of Institutional Change," Issue 4, 1991, pp. 3–11. Copyright by *Economics and Business*, now *The Quarterly Review of Economics and Business*. —Ed.]

1. An excellent survey of the new neo-classical growth literature is to be found in "A Contribution to the Empirics of Economic Growth," by G. Mankiw, D. Romer, and D. Weil (NBER Working Paper No. 3541).

2. See the author's "A Transaction Cost Theory of Politics," *Journal of Theoretical Politics*, Vol. 2, No. 4, 1990, pp. 355–367, for an elaboration of this argument.

References

Alchian, Armen. 1965. "Some Economics of Property Rights," *Il Politico*, 30, 4:816–29. Reprinted in A. Alchian. 1977. *Economic Forces At Work*. Indianapolis: Liberty Press.

Atack, Jeremy, and Fred Bateman. 1987. "Yankee Farming and Settlement in the Old Northwest: A Comparative Analysis," in Klingaman and Vedder: 77–102.

Chandler, Alfred D. 1977. *The Visible Hand: The Managerial Revolution in American Business*. Cambridge, Mass.: Harvard University Press.

Demsetz, Harold. 1967. "Toward a Theory of Property Rights," *American Economic Review*, 57: 347–359.

Hughes, J.R.T. 1987. "The Great Land Ordinances," in Klingaman and Vedder: 1–18.

Klingaman, D. C., and R. A. Vedder, (eds.). 1987. *Essays on the Economy of the Old Northwest*. Athens: Ohio University Press.

Mankiw, Gregory, David Romer, and David Weil. 1991. "A Contribution to the Empirics of Economic Growth," NBER Working Paper No. 3541. Cambridge, Mass.: National Bureau of Economic Research.

North, Douglass C. 1990. *Institutions, Institutional Change and Economic Performance*. Cambridge: Cambridge University Press.

North, Douglass C. and Andrew Rutten. 1987. "The Northwest Ordinance in Historical Perspective," in Klingaman and Vedder: 19–35.

Williamson, Oliver. 1978. *Markets and Hierarchies: Analysis and Antitrust Implications*. New York: Free Press.

Williamson, Oliver. 1987. *The Economic Institutions of Capitalism: Firms, Markets, Relational Contracting*. New York: Free Press.

13

Conceptions of Social Rule

Lewis A. Kornhauser

Now comes the chapter by Kornhauser that begins with the distinction of three senses of "rule" anticipated early in the book as a point of departure for the book as a whole and then for departure immediately into the explication and application of "rule" in the third of Kornhauser's senses—the sense appropriate to the issue-processing perspective. In his paper, Kornhauser moves on from the distinction to treat rules as devices created to seize game-theoretical opportunities for benefits from social cooperation; and argues that this sort of treatment should be extended to many more cases than hitherto have been brought under it.

Studies of the social world investigate a wide range of phenomena that are termed "social rules," that have social rules as constituent parts, or in explanations of which "social rules" play an important role. We study laws, institutions, customs, games, rituals, and ceremonies. Each of these phenomena may be subject to different social constraints and rules of change. Their study may require distinguishing among different senses of the term "social rule." In section 1, I organize discussion around three conceptions of social rule that commonly appear in everyday (or, at least, "social science") use: (1) social rule as a regularity of behavior; (2) social rule as *convention;* and (3) social rule as a norm (or as a special type of authoritative reason for action). In section 2, I examine the technical notion of equilibrium which underlies the understanding of social rule as convention. A convention identifies which equilibrium of a coordination game parties will play. Many social situations, however, can be modelled by games that have multiple equilibria though they are not coordination games. I argue that this conception of a social rule as convention should be extended beyond the conventions of coordination games to this common knowledge of which of several equilibria of a game will be played. This characterization of a social rule also sharpens the issues of their role in social explanation. In section 3, I offer a few additional comments on the conception of social rule as authoritative reason for action.

Regularities, Conventions, and Norms

In some descriptions or explanations of social behavior, "social rule" refers simply to a regularity of behavior among members of some group. In some community, for example, most individuals might habitually go to the movies on Saturday night. This behavior is regular in two senses. Each individual acts in a similar fashion; that is, the behavior of the community members converges. Second, each individual's behavior is persistent or repetitive. One would not, for example, consider a one-time coincidence of behavior as a social rule.

To explain this regularity of behavior one first accounts for each individual's choice and then seeks to identify some cause of the regularity. To an economist, an individual's preferences in conjunction with the environment in which she chooses determine her behavior. An explanation of the social rule of "Saturday night at the movies" would then refer to each individual's preferences among activities during leisure, the prices of the various activities, and the structure of work and family obligations and of leisure time for each individual in the community. The parallel behavior then results from some similarity among preferences and the similarity in the time structure confronting each individual.

A regularity in behavior might change (or dissolve) for a variety of reasons. Individual preferences might diverge. Prices might change. New options might arise. Or the environment in which individuals acted might change. Some individuals, for example, might abandon Saturday night at the movies because they develop a preference for physical exercise, bridge, or sleep. Alternatively, film prices might rise or cable television (or home video cassette recorders) might become available. Possibly, some people might have their work schedules altered.

In its second common usage, "social rule" refers to a practice that has stronger features than merely persistence and convergence of behavior. David Lewis, for example, spoke of conventions in which the persistent, convergent behavior is supplemented by four other features: (a) the convention identifies one of several equilibria of a coordination game; (b) parties to the convention share the belief that other parties to the convention will adhere to it (and they share beliefs about the beliefs about behavior of parties to the convention); (c) each individual i prefers adherence to (over violation of) the convention given that everyone else adheres to it; and (d) each individual other than i prefers that i adheres to the convention (given that everyone else adheres to it). This last condition identifies the equilibrium as a "coordination equilibrium" in which no party to the convention would have been better off had any other individual acted differently.[1] "Convention" in this technical sense draws on another common usage of the term "convention" as agreement. The requirement of shared belief tracks the common law notion that contract requires a meeting of the minds while the third and fourth conditions allow the inference of consent to the arrangement. Condition (c) suggests that an agent i would consent to adhere to the convention because adherence advances her interest; condition (d) suggests that other agents would consent to i's adherence to the convention, because i's adherence advances *their* interests.

In a coordination game, the interests of the players are (largely) coincident. Each player can do well only if the other players do well also. The matrix in Figure 13.1 represents the structure of a simple, two-person coordination game. Each player wishes to match the strategy of the other player; if they succeed, each does better than if they fail. This feature of coincidence of interest reappears in condition (d). In a pure coordination game, every equilibrium will satisfy condition (d).

Figure 13.1   Game 1: Simple Coordination Game

	L	R
L	1, 1	0, 0
R	0, 0	2, 2

Condition (c) characterizes an equilibrium. According to condition (c), each agent is individually rational; she pursues her own self-interest. Any equilibrium should satisfy at least condition (c) which requires that, in equilibrium, no individual can unilaterally improve her own payoff.

The notion of consent embodied in Lewis' definition is therefore stronger than the notion of equilibrium which requires only that condition (c) be met. On the other hand, condition (d) is insufficient to insure that the parties will achieve a Pareto optimum. In the game represented in Figure 13.1, for example, both (L, L) and (R, R) satisfy conditions (c) and (d) although only (R, R) is Pareto optimal.

A coordination game would be of little strategic (or other) interest, if it had only a single equilibrium; common knowledge of the "rationality" of the other players would then suffice to identify for each player her sole equilibrium strategy as her choice. When multiple equilibria exist, however, (game-theoretically) sophisticated agents cannot identify their optimum strategy solely from examination of the structure of the game. Which equilibrium prevails will depend on the specific beliefs that the agents have; all must have not only common knowledge of the game structure but also common knowledge of the equilibrium that all aim at. Condition (b) emphasizes this aspect of "conventionality." Thus, in the social situation model by Figure 13.1, two different conventions are possible. If Row believes that Column will play L and that Column believes that Row will play L and if

Column believes that Row will play L and that Row believes that Column will play L, then (L, L) is the convention.[2] If, however, Row and Column have common knowledge that the other will play R, then (R, R) is the convention.

Though often applied to social arrangements, few practices strictly meet the requirements of a social rule as convention. Two common examples come close to complete conformance to the definition. The convention "drive on the right side of the road" describes more than mere parallel behavior; it relies on common knowledge that such a convention exists and that each individual prefers to drive with traffic rather than against it. Moreover, all drivers prefer that each of them adheres to the convention. Analogously, the "institution" of money has a large "conventional" element. That certain pictures of George Washington serve as a medium of exchange in the United States depends on the common knowledge that each party to the convention will accept such pictures in exchange for real goods and services and that each party prefers a monetary to a barter economy. Even in these examples, however, one can imagine circumstances in which the short term interest of one party dictates violation of the convention. When eastbound traffic is snarled and westbound traffic very light, an individual with strong reason to hurry might prefer to breach the convention "drive on the right side of the road." In times of hyperinflation, an individual would prefer that others adhere to the convention and accept money in exchange for goods though she would rather accept only barter in her transactions.

Other "conventions" present more complex issues. Language is conventional in the sense that speakers share beliefs about syntax and semantics in general but need not share beliefs in every particular. Language works very well with such diffuse commonality of beliefs; indeed too rigid a requirement of agreement on meanings might prevent the language from adapting to changes in social structure, social needs, or social understanding. Dialects (and "new" languages), on the other hand, may perhaps evolve from too little agreement on meanings.

The third and strongest sense of "social rule" elaborates the notion of authoritative force of a strategy that emerges from the reflection on Nash equilibria. Consider H.L.A. Hart's example of a rule: "The male head is to be bared on entering a church."[3] While the parties to the social norm share an attitude towards the social rule, they do not necessarily share the "conventional" belief that other members of the society will conform their behavior to the rule. Shared beliefs in a convention dictate that individuals acting in their own self-interest will behave conventionally. In Hart's example, adherence to the norm need not be in the self-interest of the individual; the rule itself serves as a *reason for action* (or a basis for criticism of those who fail to comply) distinct from self-interest. A social rule as norm thus implies that the rule has some *authority* distinct from its incentive (or dis-incentive) properties.[4]

At times, however, both a convention and normative authority dictate identical conduct. In some instances, legal enactment confers normative authority on a social rule as a convention. Individuals might choose to drive on the right not only because the society has adopted that convention but also because that convention has been enacted into law and each has an obligation to obey that law. In other instances, the convention might acquire some normative authority even without legal enactment. Others might come to criticize those who sporadically breach the convention for having acted wrongly.

The "social" aspect of norms also contains some ambiguity. It might refer to a regularity in behavior of the community. Or it might refer to the ground or scope of the rule's authority. Some understandings of morality, for example, consider moral norms to be "objective," that is, to be universally applicable, regardless of the beliefs of the moral agents. On other accounts, however, moral norms are socially constructed; they have force within a community but not without it. Hart's "bare the male head in church," for example, might be a universal, divinely inspired norm or it might be a socially constructed norm.[5]

As an individual may have many reasons for action, the existence of a social rule in the normative sense does not necessarily imply any social regularities of behavior.[6] Each individual may be cognizant of and attentive to the norm but its force may be insufficient to overcome other reasons for action that dictate non-conformance with the normative requirements. Conversely, social behavior convergent with that required by a norm does not necessarily imply that the community holds the norm. None of the actors may have considered the norm a reason for adopting the behavior required by it. Each may have chosen to act out of self-interest and the uniformity of behavior results from the co-incidence of their self-interests.[7]

Legal norms present a stark instance of the entanglement of different conceptions of social rule. An individual might conform to a criminal prohibition because she considers its embodiment in a legal norm as an authoritative reason to conform. Or she might conform because she believes another authoritative norm, such as a moral one, requires the same behavior. On the other hand, she might conform for prudential reasons, which themselves might have two sources. The sanction for violation of the legal norm might raise the cost of the conduct sufficiently to induce her compliance. Or, the prohibited conduct might be undesirable even in the absence of the legal sanction. Thus, while one may easily determine the content of and changes in announced legal norms, it may prove difficult to determine to what extent these announced norms govern social behaviors.

Social Rules as Equilibria of Games

Both the conception of social rule as persistent, regular behavior and of social rule as convention apparently identify the social rule with some concept of equilibrium. In the former case, the behavior is the result of each individual's separate decision processes. To an economist, each individual would choose her optimal action given her preferences and environment. This coincidence of decisions of many individuals might then be described as an equilibrium in the sense that each individual decision, being individually optimal, is in "equilibrium."

The idea of convention draws more explicitly on game-theoretic notions of equilibrium. To understand clearly what the conception of social rule as convention includes requires clarity about the structure of game theory. Game-theoretic models assume that the players have common knowledge of three elements: (i) the rules of the game which identify the sequence of moves, the options open to each player at each move, the information structure of the game, and the payoffs; (ii) the utility functions of all players (that is, how each player evaluates her payoffs); and (iii) the rationality of the other players.[8]

Given common knowledge of these three elements of the strategic situation, each player can determine the equilibria of the game. Here "equilibrium" means "Nash equilibrium" or, condition (c) in the characterization of convention given above. That is, the players' strategies are in equilibrium (in the sense of Nash) if and only if each player prefers to play her equilibrium strategy given that all other players have adopted their equilibrium strategies. If the game has only one equilibrium, game theory offers unequivocal advice to each player: adopt the sole equilibrium strategy. If multiple equilibria exist, then each player may still face a perplexing choice of strategy.

Two classifications of equilibria of a given game may illuminate the difficulty. Consider a two-person game.[9] Suppose that (x, y) and (x',y') are equilibria of this game. Then equilibria are *interchangeable* if and only if (x,y') and (x',y) are also equilibria. Two equilibria are *equivalent* if and only if the payoffs to all parties are identical. If all equilibria are equivalent and interchangeable, then players face no difficulty at all. If each chooses one of her equilibrium strategies, then all receive their unique equilibrium payoffs. Coordination games (and hence conventions) have non-interchangeable equilibria.

If equilibria are either non-interchangeable or non-equivalent, then the players must rely on some extra-game-theoretic information to select out the equilibrium they should play. In the absence of such information, the players face a difficulty in choice. If the equilibria are equivalent, but non-interchangeable, then failure to agree on the equilibrium at which the group should arrive may result in a non-equilibrium outcome. Consider the game represented in normal form by Figure 13.2.[10]

(A, a) and (C, c) are the sole equilibria (in pure strategies) of this game. They are equivalent (as the payoffs to each player are identical in each equilibrium) but not interchangeable as neither (A, c) nor (C, a) is an equilibrium.

Figure 13.2   Game 2: Equivalent but Non-Interchangeable Equilibria

	a	b	c
A	5, 4	7, 2	1, 3
B	3, 5	0, 0	2, 5
C	4, 2	7, 3	5, 4

Game 2 meets all the criteria of a coordination game except criterion (d). Regardless of which equilibrium strategy A or C that Row plays, it is not best for him that Column play her equilibrium strategy a; Row would prefer that Column play b. Similarly, Column, playing either of her equilibrium strategies a or c, would prefer that Row play B rather than the relevant equilibrium strategy. In a coordination game, as, for example in the game of Figure 13.1, each player prefers that her opponent play the corresponding equilibrium strategy.

In game 2, however, both Row and Column would benefit from common knowledge about which equilibrium (A, a) or (C, c) they should play. As each is rational and knows she faces a rational opponent, each expects to play an equilibrium strategy. Thus, each wishes to coordinate her choice of strategy with her opponent's choice; that is, they wish to identify the equilibrium that they will play. This common knowledge condition identifies the social rule in conventions; it, rather than condition (d), seems essential to the notion of social rule.

Consider now the game represented by the payoff matrix of Figure 13.3. There are four interchangeable but non-equivalent equilibria that result from Row playing either A or C and Column playing either a or c. Clearly, (A, a) is best for both parties but it is not clear how the parties can arrive at that choice, particularly if they must play the game only once. Suppose that they had common knowledge that, in their society, parties confronted with game 3 played (C, c).

Neither Row nor Column has any self-interested reason unilaterally to deviate from the "social rule" (C, c). Of course neither has any self-interested reason to adhere to it. A unilateral deviation by either party leaves the payoff to the deviator unchanged; deviation only raises the payoff to the other party. In a situation of repeated play,[11] however, a foresighted

Figure 13.3   Game 3: Non-Equivalent but Interchangeable Equilibria

	a	b	c
A	5, 4	2, 1	2, 4
B	3, 3	0, 0	0, 4
C	5, 3	3, 2	2, 3

player might see some reason to deviate from (C, c). Row, for example, could, without cost to himself, bestow a benefit on Column by switching to A and he might believe that the benefit bestowed on Column would encourage her to reciprocate by switching to her strategy a. If (C, c) persisted, one might argue that the common knowledge of (C, c) as the social rule weighed against self-interest as a reason for action.

This argument for the force of the social rule in games with non-equivalent but interchangeable equilibria, however, relies on the intuitive lack of appeal of (C, c) as an equilibrium. Both players do worse in (C, c) than in (A, a); neither suffers from a unilateral change in her strategy. Aiming at (A, a) does not threaten social stability because of the interchangeability of the equilibria. Most social structures probably lack this fluidity; social stability depends more critically on each individual's strategic choices and hence resemble the game in Figure 13.2, perhaps with non-equivalent, non-interchangeable equilibria,[12] rather than that in Figure 13.3.

To identify a social rule with a particular equilibrium in a game thus apparently gives little explanatory force to the social rule.[13] The behavioral assumptions underlying the equilibrium concept carry most of the explanatory force. Thus, the particular notion of individual rationality embodied in the concept of Nash equilibrium "explains" the choice of some equilibria of each of the games 1 through 4. The additional assumption of common knowledge of which equilibrium is to be played provides the rest of the explanation for the play of a specific equilibrium. Interest, then, should focus not so much on the "social rule" but on the mechanism that fosters or achieves common knowledge of which of the multiple equilibria should be played.

Of course, when we speak of social rules, we have in mind persistent behaviors in recurrent situations. This suggests that repeated games provide the appropriate framework in which to model social rules. Repeated games have a more complex structure than the underlying game which is repeated. That is, the equilibrium of a repeated game may include periods in which some non-equilibrium outcome of the one-shot game prevails. These non-equilibrium payoffs are supported by punishment strategies (that in equilibrium are never invoked). When the repeated game has multiple equilibria, which is likely, one might identify social rules with these more complex equilibria.[14] The repeated game context, however, has not altered at all the account of a social rule; the social rule identifies which of several equilibria will be played.

Social Rules as Reasons for Action

Social rules as regularities of behavior may offer an observer of the society a useful characterization of behavior in that society but such social rules do not provide members of the society with any reasons for action. As the discussion of section 2 suggested, social rules, when identified with particular equilibria of games, do indeed constitute part of each agent's reason for action. The common knowledge that agents of this society played a specific equilibrium (coupled with the rationality assumption), gave each player reason to play her corresponding equilibrium strategy. The social rule as common knowledge of specific equilibrium play, however, does not serve as a norm of behavior. Self-interest coupled with the beliefs derived from common knowledge dictate that each actor adopt the relevant equilibrium strategy. The social rule itself is not authoritative in the sense that it provides a reason for action distinct from the agent's self-interest.

In some instances, the social rule seems to have authority because which social rule prevails has great consequences. In the game in Figure 13.4, for example, two equilibria, (A, a) and (C, c) are possible. Row and Column have directly conflicting preferences over these two equilibria. Row would prefer a social rule that identified (A, a) as the equilibrium; Column would prefer a social rule that identified (C, c). Which social rule prevails therefore has dramatic distributional consequences for the society. Yet, the social rule, even in game 4, carries no more authority than the self-interest of the players which dictates to each that she adhere to the social rule. Given the rationality of all players and the common knowledge provided by the social rule that a specific set of equilibrium strategies will be adopted by the other player, each player fares best by adopting the identified equilibrium strategy.

The stumbling block to integrating authoritative reasons for action into the game theoretic conception of social rule apparently lies in the narrow conception of rationality embedded in the game theoretic conception of social rule. Rational action, in this model, depends only on the (first-order) desires and beliefs of the agents. These desires are best understood as prefer-

Figure 13.4   Game 4: Non-Equivalent and Non-Interchangeable Equilibria

	a	b	c
A	5, 4	2, 1	1, 3
B	3, 3	0, 0	0, 4
C	4, 2	3, 2	2, 5

ences over uncertain prospects (or lotteries). As the beliefs themselves are embedded in the prospects over which the agent has preferences,[15] a simple belief cannot afford a reason for action that would prevail over the agent's own desires. To introduce an authoritative reason for action into this model requires either that one complicates the structure of preferences in some way or that one alters the role that beliefs play in the agent's decision process.

One alternative would distance the content of the social rule from the structure of a specific game. Instead, one might view the social rule as governing some class of games identifiable by some easily recognizable, recurrent features of a social situation. Players learn from their history what behavior to expect from others in recurrent situations. To the extent that the players identify these situations by features independent of the payoff structures, then they may persist in playing non-optimal (even non-equilibrium) outcomes as the payoff structures shift slowly over time.

The discrepancy between social rule understood as common knowledge that society has adopted a particular equilibrium and our more naive notions might be put as follows. The features of a social situation that identify it as one subject to a specific social rule may be compatible with more than one game form. Consider, for example, the rule "drive on the right." This rule applies to all driving situations even though these situations differ in their payoff structures. The payoff structures might differ because of the density of traffic (and hence the probability of an accident should someone breach the convention). Or the payoff structures might differ because the purposes of the drivers may vary. Someone rushing to the hospital with a critically ill relative in the car faces a greater cost to delay than someone who will merely be late to a baseball game. Many of the game forms "covered" by the social rule may have that rule as an equilibrium. In others, self-interest might dictate that one or more players deviate from the actions prescribed by the social rule. The social rule now appears to operate in part like a rule-of-thumb: in circumstances in which the social rule applies, it is generally (but not always) good for each person to adhere to the social rule.

A rule-of-thumb, however, hardly qualifies as a norm. That an agent has deviated from a rule-of-thumb hardly constitutes a serious criticism of that agent's action. In this context, especially, reasons for deviation—the particular payoffs faced by the agent in the particular circumstances—from the rule will be the agent's private information. In the absence of knowledge of the actual game the agent faced, a criticism based on the range of games she might have played carries little weight. Conversely, knowledge of the actual game suggests that the agent's behavior should be evaluated in terms of the actual decision problem she encountered.

Alteration of the agent's preference structure presents even more formidable difficulties as it seems difficult to avoid abandoning well-developed theories of rational decision. One might simply include among an agent's preferences a desire to comply with social rules. This ad-hoc tactic has several consequences. First, it requires that compliance or deviation from the social rule constitute part of the description of the payoff to each player. This requirement in turn suggests that one could no longer identify a social rule with a particular equilibrium of a game. Rather, the rule would be identified with a particular strategy of a player. Playing this strategy would raise a player's valuation of her payoffs regardless of the choices of the other party. Consider for example the game in Figure 13.5 which modifies the simple coordination game of Figure 13.1.

The numbers in each cell represent Row's and Column's valuations of the outcomes. Assume that the social rule dictates "L" for each party who

Figure 13.5   Game 5: Modified Coordination Game

	L	R
L	1 + a, 1 + a	a, 0
R	0, a	2, 2

values compliance with the rule at a. If a is large enough, then (L, L) would be the only equilibrium.

A social rule in game 5 would offer an "authoritative" reason for action simply by sufficiently altering each player's valuation of the payoffs. In other circumstances, the social rule might transform a non-equilibrium outcome to an equilibrium by a similar change of the valuation of the payoffs to the strategies identified by the social rule. On this account, social rules operate exactly like any incentive (or punishment): they "affect" (or contribute to) the total "price" paid by an actor for adopting a particular strategy. More importantly, social rules, on this interpretation, are (in part) constitutive of the game individuals face. An explanation of social rules would then require us to study the larger game in which parties choose the rules of their social interactions.

Concluding Remarks

Two implicit questions have underlain the discussion. First, can some feature of game-theoretic models be interpreted as "social rules?" The identification of such a feature would illustrate the role that social rules play in explanations of social phenomena. Second, to what extent can economic and game theoretic models explain the evolution and persistence of social rules themselves?

Not surprisingly, the discussion suggested a positive answer to the first question for social rules understood as convention. Lewis's idea of convention, after all, was closely tied to the theory of games at the outset; it is not surprising then to identify social rules with a process of equilibrium selection in certain classes of games. This identification provides a straightforward conception of the role of social rules in social explanation. Unfortunately, theories of equilibrium selection remain crude at best. Invoking the term "social rule" renames a significant gap in our knowledge rather than advancing the knowledge itself.

The discussion of social rules as authoritative reasons for action was inconclusive on both questions. Social rules in this sense are constitutive of the game theoretic model of a social phenomenon; they define (in part) the outcomes that result from plays of the game. To answer the first question, then, we must begin with a conception of the bare social situation and construct a theory of how social rules transform this bare situation into the rule-governed one.

Notes

Copyright 1988, Lewis A. Kornhauser.

These comments were prepared for the Murphy Institute Conference on the Logic of Social Change in April 1988. I have benefited from discussions with Lawrence Sager and Jeffrey Gordon. They and David Braybrooke commented on an earlier draft. I am responsible for the remaining errors and obscurities. On a number of points, my views have changed.

1. David Lewis, *Convention* (Cambridge, Mass: Harvard University Press, 1969).

2. Common knowledge in fact requires that each party's nth order beliefs about the other's (n – 1)st order beliefs for every n be mutually consistent and confirming.

3. H.L.A. Hart, *The Concept of Law* (Oxford: Clarendon Press, 1961), p. 54.

4. This aspect of a norm is not captured by the usual economist's tactic to account for norms in a model. One assumes that the agent has a preference for norm compliance generally or for the specific behavior required by the norm. The agent may then rank any action in terms of its overall consequences, including satisfaction of her taste for compliance. Non-compliance generates a "cost" in terms of lower preference satisfaction.

On this account of "normative force," normative change must be explained by changes either in the intensity of other preferences or in the preference for compliance itself. Further, this formulation does not adequately capture the complexity of the deliberation process that most people seem to engage in when confronted with conflicting demands of self-interest and "duty."

Professor North (see preceding chapter) essentially adopts this "taste for norm compliance" stratagem in his discussion of institutional change. The stratagem may offer insight into the problems of developing economies but I think it offers little aid in understanding how social rules themselves evolve.

Professor Baigent, by contrast, offers a more complex account (see Appendix 2, below) of the agent's "psychology" that allows norms to play a more subtle role in her decision process.

5. In this example, "socially constructed" has two senses. The act of baring one's head in church has *meaning* that derives from the social context, indeed, from the existence of the norm. Failure to bare one's head in church may thus make a statement about religion or the community. "Socially constructed" has a narrower sense as well. It refers to the fact that the norm arises out of social practice. Hence the obligation is specific to the community which engages in the practice.

6. Some distinction exists between norms that are formally promulgated and those that are emergent from practice. In the case of an emergent norm, a wide discrepancy between actual and required behavior would imply that the community recognizes the norm as a basis for criticism of virtually all actions but that almost no one attends to that criticism. The norm would then seem to offer reason to criticize others but little reason to heed identical criticism. This structure seems unstable.

In the case of formal norms, a wider discrepancy between actual and required behavior may be more possible. It may reflect a discrepancy between the group that enunciates the formal norm and the community to which it applies.

7. George Akerlof presents an interesting model of caste in which everyone adheres to the rules governing exchange among castes even though no one "values" or otherwise grants authority to the caste system. "The Economics of Caste and of the Rat Race and Other Woeful Tales," *Quarterly Journal of Economics*, Vol. 90, 1976, pp. 599–617, reprinted in *An Economic Theorist's Book of Tales* (Cambridge: Cambridge University Press, 1984).

8. In games of incomplete information, a player may not know the utility function of some other players. In this case, she knows the distribution of types of players she may be facing.

9. In the text, I consider only equilibria in pure strategies. To identify social rules with mixed strategy equilibria makes little sense as it would be difficult to verify adherence to or deviation from the social rule.

10. The first number in each cell of the matrix is the payoff to Row; the second number the payoff to Column.

11. Technically, repeating the game in Figure 13.3 creates a new, different game which would have a richer set of equilibria. (C, c) played in every period, however, would remain an equilibrium of the repeated game.

12. That is, most social phenomena are probably neither pure coordination games nor have interchangeable equilibria. They have a structure like the game in Figure 13.4 (which is presented in section 3) in which (A, a) and (C, c) are the sole (nonequivalent) equilibria.

13. It might be clearer to identify the social rule with the common knowledge of which equilibrium will be played rather than with the equilibrium itself. One should distinguish, however, the equilibrium from the equilibrium outcomes. Two equivalent equilibria are different (as at least one player must play distinct strategies) though the outcomes are identical.

14. On strategies of this type see J. P. Benoit and V. Krishna, "Finitely Repeated Games," *Econometrica*, Vol. 53, 1985, pp. 889–904.

15. This clause conceals many complexities and ambiguities. In classical game theory, the agents have preferences over objective lotteries, i.e., lotteries in which objective probabilities govern the likelihood of each possible outcome. The agents

then have common knowledge of these probabilities and of the structure of the game they play. If the game has multiple equilibria, common knowledge as to which equilibrium strategies other players will adopt serves to specify more precisely the lottery that each player faces. The agent's preferences then dictate the outcome.

14

The Origin of Rules in Uncertainty

Ronald A. Heiner

In a certain sense Heiner pushes the question of what difference rules make deeper than Kornhauser. With Heiner what is at stake is not just missed opportunities for gains from solving game-theoretical problems about cooperation (important as these are), but the very possibility of dealing as rational persons with uncertainty. Modulating from the discussion of regularities to the discussion of rules proper, he argues that it is only by acting regularly, as by appropriate rules, that agents can realize this possibility. The focus of his argument to begin with is upon rules that agents adopt for themselves; but the argument expands to embrace social rules adopted by groups of agents; and it will frequently be the case that the rules that agents adopt for their personal conduct will be rules that their society has presented them with.

The Difficulties Besetting Optimization

Standard choice theory tries to explain behavior by matching the "competence" of an agent with the "difficulty" in selecting most preferred alternatives. It assumes for the purpose of theoretical explanation that there is no gap between an agent's competence and the difficulty of the decision problem to be solved (hereafter called a "C-D gap"). On the other hand, the presence of a C-D gap will introduce uncertainty in selecting most preferred alternatives, which will tend to produce errors and surprises. Such mistakes are by their nature unpredictable and erratic. Yet, it is only the systematic elements of behavior that we can hope to scientifically explain and predict. Thus, in order to theoretically isolate the systematic tendencies in behavior, we must exclude a C-D gap, no matter how implausible or unrealistic this might be.

This perspective has been a dominant factor in loyalty to traditional optimizing concepts. Nevertheless, I believe it is mistaken, and that essentially the opposite view is true. To see why, think of the above argument as an empirical hypothesis about the effect of "irrationality"; namely, that the additional uncertainty from a larger C-D gap will generate more errors and surprises, thus producing more irregularity and noise in behavior. There are numerous complicating factors about how to test this hypothesis, especially how to measure a person's C-D gap. We can avoid these problems by broadening our horizon to consider an interspecies comparison between humans and other animals. Here it is clear without detailed argument that the average C-D gap of other animals is larger than that of humans. Yet when we observe nonhuman species, the overwhelming qualitative impression is not one of greater irregularity, but instead of greater rigidity and inflexibility of behavior. Pattern is not more difficult but rather easier to notice in animals than in humans.

The qualitative difference between humans and other animals is obviously not new to us, having long ago been given the capsulized description of "instinct." Still, I do not believe that we have recognized the significance of this general pattern for evaluating and constructing theoretical models of behavior. This pattern is telling us that it is not the absence of a C-D gap, but rather its presence which conditions regularity in behavior.

Why should this be the case? Think of an omniscient agent with literally no uncertainty in identifying the most preferred action under any conceivable condition, regardless of the complexity of the environment which he encounters. Intuitively, such an agent would benefit from maximum flexibility to use all potential information or to adjust to all environmental conditions, no matter how rare or subtle those conditions might be. But what if there is uncertainty because agents are unable to decipher all of the complexity of the environment (i.e., there is uncertainty due to a C-D gap)? Will allowing complete flexibility still benefit the agents? For example, if we could somehow "loosen up" the behavior of an organism without affecting its perceptual abilities, would it compete more effectively for food or mating partners than before?

I believe the general answer to this question is negative: that when genuine uncertainty exists, allowing greater flexibility to react to more information or administer a more complex repertoire of actions will not necessarily enhance an agent's performance. Even if we confine our attention to human behavior, we can find evidence for this proposition, especially in highly competitive situations with noticeable elements of complexity relative to human information processing and other perceptual abilities.

For example, in sequential replication games of the basic prisoner's dilemma, round robin competition identified the simplest strategy (the tit for tat strategy) as dominant over all of the others (submitted by persons in economics, mathematics, psychology, political science, and sociology).[1] Moreover, the worst performance came from the strategy that specified the most "sophisticated" learning and probability adjustment process to guide its behavior.[2] Another example is the publishing history of strategies to win at blackjack. Earlier books emphasized sophisticated card-counting, bet-variation methods (see especially Edward Thorpe's book, *Beat the Dealer*).[3] However, while no one has challenged the mathematical validity of these earlier more complex methods, their actual use resulted in worse performance by most persons attempting to use them (which generated sizable unexpected profits to the casinos).[4] As a result, later books have steadily evolved toward more rigidly structured methods (for example, two recent books are *No Need to Count* and *Winning Casino Blackjack for the Non-Counter*).[5]

Consider also Rubic's cube. There are over 43 trillion possible initial positions from which to unscramble the cube. Minimizing the number of moves to solve the cube would require an extremely complex pattern of adjustment from one particular scrambled position to another. Yet, if mistakes are made in trying to select a short cut, the cube will remain un-scrambled indefinitely. Consequently, cube experts have developed rigidly structured solving procedures that employ a small repertoire of solving patterns to unscramble the cube. These procedures follow a predetermined hierarchical sequence that is largely independent of the initial scrambled position.[6] However, they almost always require a much longer sequence of moves than the minimum number needed to unscramble the cube. Thus, they are not an approximation to the enormously complex behavior that would be exhibited by an omniscient agent who could immediately select the shortest sequence for each scrambled position. Note also that the information needed to behave in this fashion (present in the initially scrambled patterns on the face of the cube) is costless to observe and instantly available; one need only look at the cube while unscrambling it.

Finally, consider the research of Herbert Simon over a number of years,[7] which has shown that decision makers in a variety of contexts (including both individual and organizational behavior) systematically restrict the use and acquisition of information compared to that potentially available. For example, Simon's idea of "satisficing" represents a feedback mechanism between an internal target variable (called the "aspiration level") and the scope of information evaluated to implement that target. Over time, the feedback process will both guide and discipline the use of information and the resulting behavioral complexity that will evolve within a person or organization. Other learning, cognitive processes, and decision algorithms can be similarly interpreted.

The above examples suggest that allowing flexibility to react to infor-mation or to select actions will not necessarily improve performance if there is uncertainty about how to use that information or about when to select particular actions. Thus, an agent's overall performance may actually be improved by restricting flexibility to use information or to choose particu-lar actions.

How Uncertainty Generates Flexibility-Constrained Behavior

The argument to this point has suggested that uncertainty due to a C-D gap may generate flexibility-constrained behavior. The next step is to characterize more precisely how such uncertainty might produce this result. To do so, a simple "reliability condition" is developed that specifies when to allow or prohibit flexibility to select potential actions or to use information that might prompt particular actions to be chosen.

Two major classes of variables determine the uncertainty resulting from a C-D gap. The first are environmental variables (denoted by $\mathbf{e}$) which determine the complexity of the decision problem to be solved by an agent (including the complexity of environmental situations potentially encountered; the relative likelihood of these situations; and the stability of the relationships that determine possible situations and their relative likelihood). The second are perceptual variables (denoted by $\mathbf{p}$) which characterize an agent's competence in deciphering relationships between its behavior and the environment.[8] Thus, the $\mathbf{p}$ and $\mathbf{e}$ variables determine the "gap" between competence and difficulty, the (C-D gap) which produces uncertainty about how to use information in selecting potential actions. In general, there is greater uncertainty as either an agent's perceptual abilities become less reliable or the environment becomes more complex.

Now consider a conceptual experiment about an agent initially limited to a fixed repertoire of actions, and ask whether allowing flexibility to select an additional action will improve the agent's performance. Under certain conditions, the new action will be more preferred than the other actions in the agent's repertoire (the "right " time to select the action), but otherwise it will be less preferred than one of those actions (the "wrong" time to select the action). Depending on the likelihood of different situations produced by the environment, the probability of the right or wrong time to select the action are written as $\pi(\mathbf{e})$ and $1 - \pi(\mathbf{e})$, respectively.

Because of uncertainty, the agent will not necessarily select the new action when it is the right time to do so. The conditional probability of selecting the action when it is actually the right time is written $r(U)$, where the likelihood of so doing depends on the structure of uncertainty, $U = u(\mathbf{p},\mathbf{e})$. When this happens, the resulting gain in performance (compared to staying within the initial repertoire) is written $g(\mathbf{e})$, which depends on how the environment affects the consequences from different actions. Similarly, the conditional probability of selecting the new action when it is actually the wrong time is written $w(U)$, with consequent loss in performance of $l(\mathbf{e})$.

In the special case of no uncertainty, the new action would always be selected at the right time and never at the wrong time, so that $r = 1$ and $w = 0$. In general, however, the presence of uncertainty will imply $r < 1$ and $w > 0$.

We can intuitively measure the *reliability* of selecting a new action by the ratio r/w, which represents the chance of "correctly" selecting the action at the right time relative to the chance of "mistakenly" selecting it at the wrong time. Greater uncertainty will both reduce the chance of correct selections and increase the chance of mistaken selections, thus causing the ratio r/w to drop (i.e., greater uncertainty reduces the reliability of selecting the new action).

Note also that $r(U)$ and $w(U)$ are not assumed to be known to an agent. The reason is that uncertainty produces mistakes about distinguishing the right from the wrong conditions to select an action, which distinction is necessary to determine the conditional probabilities of choosing an action under these two sets of conditions. For the same reason, the probability of the right situation to select an action, $\pi(e)$, may also be unknown to an agent. Thus, it is not assumed that an agent can tell whether a mistake has been made; nor are we necessarily dealing with situations where an agent consciously decides when to select an action. Rather, the more general issue is whether some process—conscious or not—will cause (or prevent) an "alertness" or "sensitivity" to information that might prompt selection of an action. For example, when will a person develop an alertness to potential information about whether to choose a particular action, or whether to modify a previous behavior pattern; or when will instinctive mechanisms in an organism precondition a sensitivity to certain environmental stimuli, while simultaneously blocking alertness to other potential stimuli?

Now, with the above components, we can formulate an answer to the question posed earlier: When is the selection of a new action sufficiently reliable for an agent to benefit from allowing flexibility to select that action?

To answer this question we must determine whether the gains $g(e)$ from selecting the action under the right conditions (when it is actually more preferred) will cumulate faster than the losses $l(e)$ from selecting it under the wrong conditions (when it is actually less preferred). Thus, combine the above elements in the following way. Right conditions occur with probability $\pi(e)$, which are correctly recognized with probability $r(U)$; so that the expected gain from allowing flexibility to select another action is $g(e)r(U)\pi(e)$. Similarly, the expected loss conditional on allowing the action to be selected is $l(e)w(U)(1 - \pi(e))$. Accordingly, gains will cumulate faster than losses if $g(e)r(U)\pi(e) > l(e)w(U)(1 - \pi(e))$. Hence, simple rearrangement yields the following Reliability Condition:

$$\frac{r(U)}{w(U)} > \frac{l(e)}{g(e)} \times \frac{1 - \pi(e)}{\pi(e)}$$

The left-hand side of the inequality is a reliability ratio, $r(U)/w(U)$, which measures the probability of "correctly" responding under that right circumstances relative to the probability of "mistakenly" responding under the wrong circumstances. The right-hand side of the inequality represents a minimum lower bound or tolerance limit (hereafter denoted simply by $T(e) = l(e)/g(e) \times (1 - \pi(e))/\pi(e))$, which a reliability ratio must satisfy. That is, $T(e)$ determines how likely the chance of selecting an action under the right conditions must be, compared to the chance of selecting it under the wrong conditions, before allowing flexibility to select that action will improve performance.

We can intuitively interpret the ratio $r(U)/w(U)$ as the "actual" reliability of selecting an action, in comparison to the minimum "required" reliability specified by the tolerance limit, $T(e)$. The components of the Reliability Condition summarize a potentially complex set of relationships between an agent's repertoire and the structure of the environment. Nevertheless, these relationships boil down to a conceptually simple answer about when to allow flexibility to select an additional action: *do so if the actual reliability in selecting the action exceeds the minimum required reliability necessary to improve performance.* Stated in its simplest notational form, this answer amounts to the condition, $r/w > T$.

The question which motivated this answer was phrased in terms of adding a new action to an agent's repertoire. However, once the Reliability Condition has been obtained we can also apply it to a range of further issues about when to allow or ignore particular actions. For example, it can be applied to dropping actions from a repertoire; namely, retain only those actions which satisfy $r/w > T$ compared to ignoring them.

We can also think of the Reliability Condition as solving a "decision" problem in which an agent determines what information it will allow to influence its behavior; or alternatively, as a "design" problem in engineering the appropriate information sensitivity of an agent. For each possible action, the Reliability Condition must be satisfied before allowing potential information to prompt its selection. Those actions that can be guided with sufficient reliability are permitted; those that cannot are eliminated. In this way, an agent's outward behavior is determined by its response pattern to potential information.

Two General Implications

Now that we have the Reliability Condition, its implications in two basic areas are briefly discussed.

Uncertainty Generates Rules Which Are Adapted Only to Likely or Recurrent Situations

Note a simple but important feature of the tolerance limit. For any given l/g ratio, the likelihood of wrong to right conditions $(1 - \pi)/\pi$, increases for smaller π; so that T also rises as the probability of right circumstances π decreases (see Figure 14.1). *Thus, an agent must be more reliable in selecting an action if the right situations for exhibiting it are less likely. Moreover, the required reliability quickly accelerates to infinity as the likelihood of right situations drops to zero.* Thus, for a given structure of uncertainty, U = u(**p**, **e**), which determines the reliability of selecting a particular action (i.e., which determines the ratio $r(U)/w(U)$), the Reliability Condition will be violated for sufficiently small but positive, $\pi(\mathbf{e}) > 0$. (See Figure 14.1.)

Figure 14.1

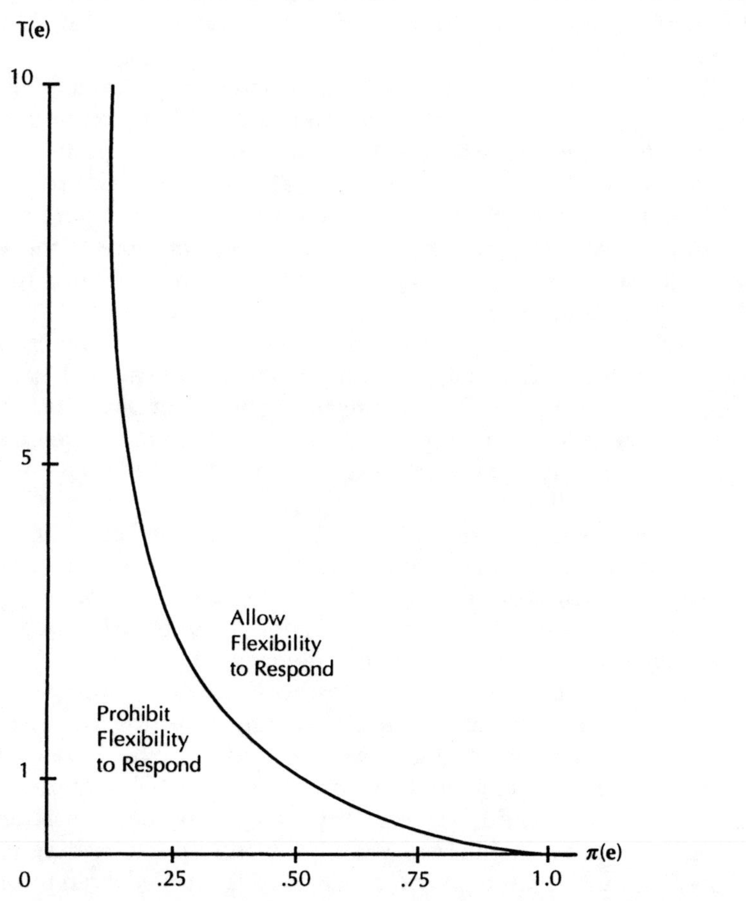

Note: The curve shows how the tolerance limit *T(e)* changes for a constant *l(e)/g(e)* ratio (in this case *l/g* = 1) as the probability of right conditions π varies. Note how quickly *T* begins to rise as π drops below .25. The curve represents a boundary of minimum reliability that must be satisfied (i.e., *r/w* > *T*) before responding to information will enhance an agent's performance.

This intuitively means that to satisfy the Reliability Condition, an agent must ignore actions which are appropriate for only "rare" or "unusual" situations. Conversely, an agent's repertoire must be limited to actions which are adapted only to relatively likely or "recurrent" situations. Thus, a general characteristic of such a repertoire is that it excludes actions which will in fact enhance performance under certain conditions, even thought those conditions occur with positive probability, $\pi(\mathbf{e}) > 0$. We thus have a formal characterization of the pervasive association of both human and animal behavior with various connotations of "rule-governed" behavior, such as instinct, habits, routines, rules of thumb, administrative procedures, customs, norms, and so forth. All of these phrases refer to some type of rigidity or inflexibility in adjusting to different situations as a universal qualitative feature of behavior.

Therefore, since behavior patterns which satisfy the Reliability Condition must have this property, we will call them *behavioral rules* or simply *rules*. Note that we have been able to derive the basic rigidity feature which justifies attributing to such behavior patterns the idea of rules. This contrasts sharply with the typical procedure of using the language of rules (often with the intent of suggesting certain connotations to the reader), yet without really justifying from a more basic theoretical structure why such terminology is appropriate.

If we use the jargon of standard economics, rule-governed behavior means that an agent must ignore actions which are actually preferred under certain conditions. Thus, the resulting behavior patterns are *not* an approximation to maximizing so as to always chose most preferred alternatives (i.e., behaving "as if" an agent could successfully maximize with no C-D gap).

In general, rules restrict behavior to only a limited repertoire of actions. Such restrictions do not assume an awareness of all the potential actions or information which are thereby implicitly ignored. Thus, no explicit decision about what potential actions to ignore is necessarily involved.

An agent need only be capable of determining when to select particular actions from a limited range of allowable alternatives. To do so does not require an ability to understand why the resulting behavior patterns evolved. This is obviously the case for animals, where we do not expect them to have an "intellectual awareness" of why they are programmed to exhibit certain behavior patterns. Yet even for humans, the general characteristic will be an inability to articulate a full understanding of why particular behavior patterns have arisen. This is implied even though human behavior is much more flexible than that of other species, and even though conscious mental processes are involved in most human behavior patterns.

As a simple example involving human behavior, consider the solving methods for Rubic's cube mentioned above in Section 1. The environment represents all of the different scrambled positions or "situations" which might eventuate on the face of the cube, of which there are over 43 trillion. If each situation is produced by a simple random draw from the set of possible situations, the probability π of the right situation (the appropriate scrambled position) arising for any particular solving sequence is extremely low. Assuming the l/g ratio (resulting from unscrambling the cube in greater or lesser time or number of moves) is not close to zero, the required reliability for selecting each of these sequences will also be very high. Without this ability, the repertoire of solving patterns must be severely restricted in order to satisfy the Reliability Condition, and structured so that their use is largely independent of particular scrambled positions (i.e., they are adapted only to the recurrent features of the environment).

Greater Uncertainty Will Cause
Rule-Governed Behavior to Be More Predictable

What is the effect of *greater* uncertainty on rule-governed behavior? In general, greater uncertainty (from either less reliable perceptual abilities or a more unpredictable environment) will both reduce the chance of recognizing the right situation to select an action, and increase the chance of not recognizing the wrong situation for selecting it. That is, greater uncertainty will both reduce $r(U)$ and increase $w(U)$, so that the reliability ratios, $r(U)/w(U)$, of particular actions will drop.

As these ratios drop, some of them may no longer exceed their respective tolerance limits, resulting in violations of the Reliability Condition. More violations will occur as uncertainty becomes more pervasive. Thus, greater uncertainty will cause behavioral rules to be more restrictive in eliminating particular actions or response patterns to potential information. This will further constrain behavior to simpler, less sophisticated patterns which are easier for an external observer to recognize and predict. Therefore, *greater uncertainty will cause rule-governed behavior to exhibit increasingly predictable regularities, so that uncertainty becomes the basic source of predictable behavior.*

This is the most important implication of my analysis, one that has far-reaching implications across a diverse range of fields. It also has important implications for how we have been trying to model behavior. It implies that genuine uncertainty, far from being unanalyzable or irrelevant to understanding behavior, is the very source of the empirical regularities that we have sought to explain by excluding such uncertainty. This means that the conceptual basis for most of our existing models is seriously flawed.

A major symptom of this has been the dominant tendency to model more complex decision problems by implicitly upgrading the competence of the agent to handle that complexity (so that traditional optimizing concepts can be used). For example, the number of decision alternatives or competing agents is increased, or complex probabilistic contingencies are introduced, or repercussions from future events are permitted, etc. Over the years this has resulted in the characterization of increasingly sophisticated "optimal" behavior strategies, with little fruit in understanding observed behavior.

This trend is typified by recent Bayesian models of optimal risk behavior, which are synonymous with sophisticated continually updated response to new information. Some examples are optimal "search" models that specify various sequential strategies for job search, price or quality information, etc. Yet, they bypass the issue that overrides everything else: when to permit any search given the uncertainty in detecting whether the positive gains from efficient search strategies will outweigh the required search costs, especially when a diverse range of search opportunities might eventuate, and the timing of these future opportunities is also unknown.

The Evolution of Social Institutions

Social Institutions Evolve Because of Uncertainty

Neoclassical decision and general equilibrium models are typically without any explicit institutional structure, and have thus tended to direct attention away from questions about the evolution of particular forms of market organization and other social institutions. In contrast, the Reliability Condition naturally suggests the systematic importance of such institutions to determine the scope and complexity of exchange relationships, and other social interactions involving cultural norms, customs, and aggressive behavior.

In this regard, it is noteworthy that Schotter's recent book on the theory of institutions defines them in a manner immediately implied by the Reliability Condition: "A social institution is a regularity in social behavior that ... specifies behavior in specific recurrent situations, and is either self-policed or policed by some external authority."[9]

Thus, evolved institutions are social rule-mechanisms for dealing with recurrent situations faced by agents in different societies. That is, institutions are regularities in the interaction between agents that arise because of uncertainty in deciphering the complex interdependencies created by these interactions. I will return to this topic below and consider the evolution of legal and exchange institutions.

A persistent theme in human literature illustrates a closely related issue that has been largely ignored by traditional choice theory; namely, the attempt of individuals to constrain or bind the flexibility of their actions. A famous example in *The Odyssey* describes Ulysses trying to prevent himself from responding to the allurement of certain sirens: "but you must bind me hard and fast, so that I cannot stir from the spot where you shall stand me ... and if I beg you to release me, you must tighten and add to my bonds."

Consider the theory of justice advanced by John Rawls.[10] Underlying his whole analysis is the recognition that if individuals have reliable information about their own future circumstances (will they be smart or resourceful, or have special educational opportunities, or own highly valued property, etc.), they will respond to such information in the way they view the social policies and institutions that would affect their particular situations. This will produce a wide diversity of opinions about how to formulate and apply normative principles. Hence, in order to produce a highly uniform consensus or regularity in social judgements, Rawls introduced a pervasive uncertainty into the conceptual problem in the form of a "veil of ignorance." Such a procedure virtually eliminates reliable information (even in probabilistic form) about any particular individual's specific future circumstances that might eventuate depending on what principles are mutually agreed to by the whole group. With a sufficient structure of uncertainty, individual judgements might be constrained to possibly a single, universally accepted principle of justice to guide social policy.

The important point is that the source of such a universal consensus is uncertainty in using potential information about when to deviate from these regularities.

Evolution of Property Rights, Trading, and Market Structure

Let me sketch a scenario about the evolution of an exchange system. Suppose initially that the reliable range of flexibility of agent's behavioral rules is more than sufficient to handle the complexity of the social environment (say in the primitive beginnings of human society). As a result, agent interactions evolve into more complex relationships in which the consequences from each agent's individual behavior depend on the actions of more and more other agents. In addition, the behavior of these other agents will become increasingly remote to the local experience of each agent as the network of social interdependencies broadens. Consequently, uncertainty in determining the consequences from selecting particular actions will successively increase for each agent in the society.

At some point, the evolution of more complex social interdependence will stop, unless social structures also evolve that reduce the scope of nonlocal information that individual agents must know to reliably forecast the consequences of their own behavior. (In more precise terms, the scope of information over which agents can reliably interpret successively narrows as the social environment becomes more complex.)

In general, further evolution toward social interdependence will require institutions that permit agents to know about successively smaller fractions of the larger social environment. That is, *institutions must evolve which enable each agent in the society to know less and less about the behavior of other agents and about the complex interdependencies generated by their interaction.*

One of the basic ways of accomplishing this is to divide up the decision authority to use resources so that only particular agents (or small groups of agents) have the right to control their use. With such a right-to-control institution, individual agents no longer have to know how other agents might use their "privately owned" resources. A whole range of factors that are within an agent's local experience can now be used to determine the consequences of particular use decisions. Two of the more important possibilities are decisions about whether to consume or delay the use of a resource, and about whether to transfer the right-to-control resources to other agents. Obtaining the right to control itself becomes valuable, given that only local information is now required to control the use of a resource.

In more basic terms, the question is whether agents will be willing to cooperate with each other through increasingly complex interdependencies that have the potential—if properly coordinated—to increase average output per agent. As the society becomes more complex, agents will cooperate only in ways that enable them to use increasingly local information to detect whether they will individually benefit. That is, they will exhibit a "propensity to cooperate" only in situations where increasingly local experience indicates a benefit—even if such restriction cuts off a whole range of benefits that might result from more subtly interconnected forms of cooperation. A major way of satisfying this restrictive criteria is to cooperate only in situations where agents immediately reciprocate the cooperative actions of each other, such that each perceives a net benefit based on his own self-evaluation of the forsaken and received items.

This form of reciprocation enables agents to decide based on immediately local experience about the results from cooperating. Thus, their tendency to cooperate in such situations will be relatively great compared to myriad other possibilities that would require the reliable use of more nonlocal information to avoid mistakes. (In more precise terms, we can show that the probability of agents cooperating in such situations will be much higher than for other forms of cooperation.) This limited tendency to cooperate can itself be regarded as a behavioral regularity, one that Adam Smith recognized as the "propensity to truck or barter." Notice also that such a propensity depends on a structure of property rights that enables agents' self-evaluation to determine the use of resources without knowing the behavior of other agents.

The above discussion is only a brief illustration of a large number of implications about legal and market institutions. These institutions will evolve so as to provide predictable opportunity for mutual reciprocation situations; and so as to reduce the scope and complexity of information that must be reliably interpreted for agents to benefit from these situations. For example, a few implications include: a restriction to more centralized market organization and to financial instruments that enable agents to avoid knowing the particular circumstances, attributes, and identity of potential reciprocators and the items reciprocated; a severe restriction of futures markets and auction markets to certain strategic locations within a larger network of inventory markets structured so as to reduce price fluctuations; and ownership structures that enable agents to avoid detecting whether continued reciprocation will be maintained, especially when this is necessary for particular reciprocators to realize longer term benefits or to prevent certain losses.[11] The essential factor in all of these institutional regularities is uncertainty in deciphering the complexity of the social environment.[12]

Finally, let me mention another key feature about the possibility of coordination failures. A complex cooperative system must somehow limit the occurrence of serious coordination failures. Nevertheless, its very complexity can evolve only to the extent that it enables agents to benefit without deciphering more than a tiny fraction of its overall structure. As a result, a complex system cannot prevent coordination failures that would require agents to understand a sizeable fraction of its complexity in order to avert them.

Conclusion

I have argued that uncertainty is the basic source of predictable behavior, and also the main conditioning factor of evolutionary process through which such behavior evolves. Uncertainty exists because agents cannot decipher all of the complexity of the decision problems they face, which literally prevents them from selecting most preferred alternatives. Consequently, the flexibility of behavior to react to information is constrained to smaller behavioral repertoires that can be reliably administered. Numerous deviations from the resulting behavior patterns are actually superior in certain situations, but they are still ignored because of uncertainty about when to deviate from these regularities.

In contrast, standard economics analyzes the special case of no uncertainty in selecting most preferred options. This way of understanding behavior forces the determinants of uncertainty into the residual "error term" between observed behavior and the more systematic patterns claimed to result from optimization. I am thus suggesting a reversal of the explanation assumed in standard economics: the factors that standard theory places in the error term are in fact what is producing behavioral regularities, while optimizing will tend to produce sophisticated deviations from these patterns. Hence, the observed regularities that economics has tried to explain on the basis of optimization would disappear if agents could actually maximize.

Another basic conclusion is that appropriately structured behavioral rules will not necessarily arise. Rather, they will evolve to the extent that selection processes quickly eliminate poorly administered behavior. This will more likely occur when agents are involved in highly competitive interactions that themselves indirectly result from scarcity. However, if weak selection processes are present, relatively vulnerable or dysfunctional behavior may evolve.

One area of major normative significance is the development of human social institutions; in particular, political institutions that have the opportunity to influence the outcomes generated by exchange competition. This is especially important if human agents are able to foresee numerous potential cases where the cooperative results of exchange institutions could be improved, but without being able to reliably administer the additional complexity necessary to realize those improvements.

Think of this issue in terms of the Reliability Condition. People may be able to identify government actions where situations exist in which a society will benefit (i.e., the probability of right circumstances π for selecting these actions is positive). Nevertheless, they may be unable to administer these actions with sufficient reliability to benefit the society by adding them to the government's repertoire of authorized activities (i.e., $r/w < T$ even though $\pi > 0$). If this is the case, the society will benefit by appropriately limiting the scope and complexity of government behavior.

But how is such limitation to arise? It is here that we enter the area of "constitutionalism," defined broadly as the design of rule-mechanisms to restrict the flexibility of government to react to whatever influences might prompt it to engage in vulnerable activities. The writing of seventeenth- and eighteenth-century political philosophers and statesmen were primarily concerned with these issues. Out of their efforts came a number of features incorporated in the United States Constitution, such as the separation of powers mechanism.

On a wider scale, the history of civilization can be organized around a theme of groping for social rule-mechanisms. Nevertheless, the understanding of such mechanisms is only in its rudimentary beginnings; and in the last hundred years, the general trend has been away from these topics—especially for analysts trained in mainstream economic theory. The reason is that mainstream theories have systematically directed attention away from the study of processes that limit flexibility to choose potentially preferred actions. A refocusing of research on such processes—with the appropriate analytical framework to guide us—may have practical consequences for the viability of existing institutions.

Notes

Excerpted from an article, "The Origin of Predictable Behavior," *American Economic Review*, Vol. 73, 1983, pp. 560–595. Reprinted with the permission of the American Economic Association. Posing the problem in terms of a gap in an agent's decision competence relative to the difficulty of a decision problem was suggested to me by Axel Leijonhufvud.

1. For a description of the tournament and its results see Robert Axelrod, "Effective Choice in the Prisoner's Dilemma." *Journal of Conflict Resolution*, Vol. 24, 1980, pp. 3–25. The top strategies were all variants of the simple tit for tat strategy, but none were able to beat the basic strategy (in particular, see pp. 8 and 18). When a second round of the tournament was run, tit for tat still won even though numerous more complex strategies were submitted (see Axelrod, "More Effective Choice in the Prisoner's Dilemma," *Journal of Conflict Resolution*, Vol. 24, 1980, pp. 379–403). For recent analysis of this issue, see David Kreps et al., "Rational Cooperation in the Finitely Repeated Prisoner's Dilemma," *Journal of Economic Theory*, Vol. 27, 1982, pp. 245–252.

2. Axelrod describes the worst of the submitted strategies in the first round:

This rule has a probablilty of cooperating *P*, which is initially 30% and is updated every 10 moves. *P* is adjusted if the other player seems random, very cooperative, or very uncooperative. *P* is also adjusted after move 130 if the rule has a lower score than the other player. Unfortunately, the complex process of adjustment frequently left the probablility of cooperation in the 30% to 70% range, and therefore the rule appeared random to many other players ("Effective Choice," p. 24).

3. Thorpe, Edward (New York: Vintage Books, 1962).

4. For example, see Richard A. Canfield, *Blackjack: Your Way to Riches* (Secaucus: Lyle Stuart, Inc., 1979), pp. 19, 37–38, 144–150.

5. Leon B. Dubey, Jr, *No Need to Count: A Practical Approach to Casino Blackjack* (San Diego: A.S. Barnes & Co., 1980); Avery D. Cardoza, *Winning Casino Blackjack for the Noncounter* (Santa Cruz: Cardoza School of Blackjack, 1981).

6. In following a typical set of instructions, one selects a side of the cube and begins by placing either its corner or its edge pieces in their proper positions; next, one places in sequence the pieces in the middle section; finally, one repositions the pieces on the remaining opposite side of the cube. See Czes Kosniowski, *Conquer That Cube* (Cambridge: Cambridge University Press, 1981).

7. "A Behavioral Theory of Rational Choice." *Quarterly Journal of Economics*, Vol. 69, 1955, pp. 99–118. See also, for example, Simon's articles, "From Substantive to Procedural Rationality," in S. Latsis, ed., *Method and Appraisal in Economics* (Cambridge: Cambridge University Press, 1976), pp. 129–148; and "On How to Decide What to Do," *Bell Journal of Economics*, Vol. 9, 1978, pp. 494–507.

8. In economics, the **p** variables might describe mistaken perceptions about what is more preferred, information processing errors, unreliable probability information, etc.; while the **e** variables describe the complexity and volatility of both present and future exchange, legal and political conditions. In biology, **p** might refer to the sensory and cognitive mechanisms of an organism, and **e** to the structure and sta-

bility of ecological relationships involving competition for food or mating partners.

9. Andrew Schotter, *The Economic Theory of Social Institutions* (New York: Cambridge University Press, 1981).

10. John Rawls, *A Theory of Justice* (Cambridge, Mass.: Harvard University Press,
1971).

11. The reliability model can be used both to predict the likelihood of opportu-
nistic behavior (discontinuing reciprocation), and how the likelihood of such behavior affects the required reliability of various kinds of contractual arrangements.
In many cases, the only solution is to structure ownership of assets in a way that
eliminates having to detect when to engage in certain contracts. This will produce
a stable regularity in contractual and market ownership patterns, which are also
studied under the rubric of "transaction costs."

12. Standard choice theory concentrates exclusively on the potential gains from
trade (via Edgeworth exchange boxes, etc.), rather than on the effect of uncertain-
ties created in trying to realize that potential. Consequently, we now have an elaborate general equilibrium theory of exchange which is devoid of the very institutional regularities necessary for complex exchange economies to evolve in the first
place.

15

Rules, Equilibrium, Beliefs, and Social Mathematics

Norman Schofield

Shared rules are not just aids to rational behavior on the part of individual agents, taken individually. They are crucial to achieving in the market or in other social institutions results more stable and more acceptable than chaos. For the market to reach equilibrium, for example, agents must abide by a rule of acting nontuistically; if the costs of a public good are to be allocated fairly under a cooperative scheme, agents must abide by a rule of ignoring temptations to defect. Democracy depends on certain rules for collective decision: Schofield shows that they are not sufficient safeguards against chaos if they are understood as rules for aggregating preferences, though prospects are less alarming if they are understood as rules for aggregating beliefs.

Mathematics, Mechanics, and Structural Stability

Mathematics is an internally consistent, formal language with no *necessary* empirical content. However, abstract components of this language have proved to be the only way by which to structure aspects of empirical reality (for example Lie groups in Quantum mechanics, non-Euclidean geometries in relativity theory, etc.) This mapping property of mathematics is surprising and two meta-theoretical hypotheses have been put forward in the past to account for it. One, the "language of God" hypothesis, is that the deep structure of the universe is in fact mathematical, so we are justified in using the metaphor that God is a mathematician. The second hypothesis is that evolution has hard-wired human beings so that our internal deep structure corresponds, in some as yet unfathomable fashion, with the deep structure of reality, and that mathematics is the natural mapping between these deep structures. Both these hypotheses imply that we discover mathematical structures rather than invent them. Although the hypotheses are extreme, they do give us reason to believe that the discipline of mathematics is both internally consistent and aesthetically appealing.

Many practising mathematicians would agree with one or other of the two hypotheses. Some of the greatest mathematicians/scientists, (I am thinking of Newton, Poincaré, and Einstein) might also have argued that reality itself, in its deep structure, is internally consistent and beautiful. A further point: the deep structure is also extremely interesting in that the mathematical forms that best describe it become more complex but more "elegant" the deeper one goes into the structure. Consider the supreme subtlety of the structures that are revealed in pursuing the unified theory of gravitation, of electromagnetism, and of weak and strong nuclear forces.

Mechanics is the branch of applied mathematics concerned with the interaction of matter at the macro-level. Its formal structure is described by Newton's (1642–1727) laws of motion and the inverse square law. Most scientific research up to the end of the nineteenth century was concerned with the elaboration of the principles of mechanics. (Chemistry, of course, developed different principles and it was not until the twentieth century that chemistry and physics have become integrated.) In fact it was only with Maxwell's derivation of the laws of electromagnetism (in 1864) that the second great family of physical relationships could be formally constructed. Even given the empirical utility of mechanics there was one area of profound theoretical difficulty which I want to emphasize. Although the inverse square law provided the theoretical basis for the empirics on the solar system (Copernicus 1473–1543; Tycho Brahe 1546–1601; Johannes Kepler 1571–1630), it was evident by the late eighteenth century that there was a potentially serious problem with the formal model of the planetary system. That is, even though a model could be provided of a single planet orbiting a sun, it was unclear whether a family of orbiting planets would be "structurally stable." In other words would the perturbations induced in each orbit by other planets cause the orbital computations to diverge? Laplace in his great work on celestial mechanics (published between 1799 and 1825) argued that the solar system was indeed structurally stable. The theoretical question was whether the orbital equations, including perturbation terms, were convergent. This question was different from the actual problem of empirical prediction; instead it referred to the problem of theoretical computability of the orbits. The mathematics available to Laplace were insufficient to answer the question. Henri Poincaré (1854–1912) attempted to prove structural stability in his treatise of 1890, but it became apparent that there was an error in his proof. Indeed it was possible for the solar system to be structurally unstable. If this were in fact so, then it would be impossible, in principle, to compute planetary orbits far into the future. Poincaré's work shows a profound interconnection between the purely theoretical analysis of non-linear differential equations and real world applications in the study of the solar system. Indeed Poincaré's work led to the development of the abstract mathematics of differential topology.

The point I wish to make is that although the fundamental law of motion (or physical rule) was well understood, the application of the theory could have been impossible, or at least technically intractable. As it happens the solar system is essentially structurally stable[1] so it is possible (as even the ancients knew) to predict eclipses, tides, etc. However the solar system does incorporate unstable dynamical components, including a number of asteroid orbits. More general dynamical systems can be structurally unstable, even chaotic.[2] Although the laws of motion may be well understood, it may be impossible in principle to predict events within a chaotic dynamical system.

Before proceeding it is necessary to be clearer about the meaning of structural stability and chaos. Let R stand for the set of all dynamical systems on a space W. Suppose further that there is a metric d on R. Given a particular dynamical system X in R, an e-perturbation of X is any dynamical system Y, say, such that $d(X, Y) < e$. Thus Y may be obtained from X by slightly modifying the parameters that describe X. One way of describing X is in terms of its phase portrait, that is the representation of the orbits, or laws of motion, describing X. Two dynamical systems, X and Y, are equivalent if there is a smooth transformation from one phase portrait to the other. In this case we write $X \equiv Y$. If X and Y are equivalent then essentially they describe the same system. A system X is *structurally stable* if there is some e > 0 such that, for any Y with $d(X, Y) < e$, then $X \equiv Y$. To illustrate with the solar system, if indeed the dynamical system, X, used to describe the solar system is structurally stable and as long as the errors, e, are sufficiently small, then X and the true system Y will have identical phase portraits. On the other hand X is *structurally unstable* if for any e > 0 there exists Y with $d(X, Y) < e$ such that X and Y are not equivalent.

Initially it was conjectured that structural stability is *generic*. Essentially this means that any dynamical system could be approximated by one that was structurally stable. (More abstractly a generic property is one that holds true for an open and dense set of systems.) Although structural stability was shown to be generic when W was two dimensional[3] the conjecture was shown to be false in higher dimensions. In particular, Smale's construction of a particular "chaotic" system, X, implied that in any neighborhood of X there were countably many non-equivalent dynamical systems. Because some error, e, always occurs in describing a system, it is impossible, in principle, to describe, even in qualitative terms, the nature of the phase portrait of X. Thus the chaotic system, X, exhibits an extreme form of sensitivity of specification.

As Kauffman[4] has recently put it:

One implication of the occurrence or non-occurrence of structural stability is that, in structurally stable systems, smooth walks in parameter space lead to mostly smooth changes in dynamical behavior. ... By contrast, chaotic systems, which are not structurally stable, adapt on uncorrelated landscapes. Very small changes in the parameters pass through many interlaced bifurcation surfaces and so change the behavior of the system dramatically.

Since the 1960s there has been increasing interest in exploring the possibility that complex "adaptive" systems can be found at the border between the structurally stable and chaotic systems.[5] If we let R_S and R_C stand for structurally stable and chaotic systems, respectively, then this "evolutionary principle" suggests that an "optimal" adaptive form is described by a dynamical system on R, itself leading to some system neither in R_S nor in R_C, but to one which is "on the edge of chaos."

To try to give an illustration of this possiblity, consider the dynamical system of evolving life on this planet. This is unimaginably complex, but it is clearly coupled to the behavior of the solar system, which I shall call X. As I have suggested, X is almost structurally stable, but may contain unstable, or chaotic, components. On occasion, these chaotic components may affect the earth itself. For example, the onset and behavior of the ice ages over the last 100,000 years would appear to have chaotic characteristics, and there may be a relationship between these climatic variations and the recent rapid evolution of human intelligence.[6] To extrapolate from this, it appears plausible that life could not have evolved on this planet were the solar system completely chaotic. However the limited chaotic phenomena within the solar system very possibly have contributed to the astonishing variety of life on earth. To speculate even more, the mass extinctions, and thus the very structure of evolution,[7] may be determined by chaotic features within the solar system.

In the last few years, the ideas of chaos and complexity have become quite well known, even in economics.[8] In this chapter I wish to discuss these notions in the context of the political economy, that is in the area of interaction of the polity and the economy, and to speculate on how these ideas can help understand complex social systems.

We may take it that such systems operate as they do because the agents belonging to them conform to certain rules (and expect other agents to conform likewise). That is not in itself enough to exclude degeneration, maybe rapid degeneration, into chaos. However, if the rules directly governing collective choice are treated by all concerned as rules under which beliefs rather than preferences are aggregated the situation in this respect becomes less alarming.

Social Mathematics

It is hardly surprising that the fundamental ideas of social mathematics, of modeling the political economy, developed in the century after Newton's

Philosophiae Naturalis Principia Mathematica (the first edition of which was published in 1687). These early masterpieces include Adam Smith's *Theory of Moral Sentiments* and *Wealth of Nations,*[9] Condorcet's *Essai sur l'application de l'analyse à la probabilité des voix*[10] as well as the *Federalist Papers* (1786–1787).[11] I shall use Condorcet's term Social Mathematic(s) for the formal examination of human behavior, intending to mean that economic, political, and social phenomena are the subjects of analysis. I also refer to the Federalist Papers since I shall argue that the writings of Hamilton, Jay, and Madison were concerned not only with practical questions of political design, but also with fundamental, theoretical aspects of decisionmaking.

Smith's brilliant analysis leads directly to modern neo-classical economics, the theory and analysis of human incentives in the particular context of fixed resources, private economic goods, given technology and exchange. The fundamental result in this field is the existence of a *price equilibrium:* an outcome and price vector where supply and demand are equated, with the property that the allocation of resources is Pareto optimal.[12] The existence of equilibrium depends on the assumption that individuals treat prices as exogenous and that they maximize their utility or preference on their budget sets.

The generalization of this model to a more abstract context is the subject matter of game theory. Individuals are assumed to have compact strategy sets and well-defined (continuous, quasi-concave) utilities. Under certain assumptions on individuals' "best-response" functions, there will exist an outcome called a "Nash equilibrium." This whole research area focuses on *individual* behavior which is "optimal" with respect to the individual's *preferences.* I shall identify this field as the *Nash* research program, to distinguish it from three other related, but distinct, research programs (see Table 15.1).

Table 15.1 Four Research Programs in Social Mathematics

	Individual	Collective
Preferences	Nash	Arrow
Beliefs	Aumann	Condorcet

Although it is known that the market aggregates preferences efficiently (under appropriate conditions), it is less clear that the market can aggregate information or beliefs efficiently. Suppose each agent has private data and uses these to compute the *a priori* probability of some event. If these priors are then encoded in a statistic (a price vector, for example) and there is a common knowledge foundation which allows the agents to infer information from changes in the price vector, then the final posterior probabilities of the agents will converge.[13] The study of processes such as those which aggregate *individual beliefs* I shall term the *Aumann* research program. Note that whereas a Nash equilibrium is a way to identify a *compromise* in a decision problem, the common posterior probability or *belief* mentioned above can be viewed as an *agreement*. We can identify this agreement as a *belief* equilibrium, and note that on matters of judgement or belief it is possible that agents will agree when they share information, as long as conflicting preferences do not contaminate the process of decision-making. It is obvious enough that modern markets in foreign exchange, commodity futures, etc., more closely resemble procedures of belief aggregation than preference aggregation. That is, traders do not necessarily value currencies or futures in terms of their use, but in terms of the agents' beliefs about the likely market valuations of these assets. I shall return later to the question of "optimality" of belief equilibria in such markets. For the moment it is worth emphasizing Arrow's[14] observation on the common knowledge foundation of the belief aggregation theorem: It is important that each agent be able to make inferences from changes in the price statistic so as to estimate the nature of the information held by others. To do so, each individual has to have knowledge about other agents' internal modelling characteristics including the rules that they intend to follow; that is how other agents' beliefs and actions, including their undertaking to conform to rules themselves are affected by their observations. While the virtue of markets lies in their ability to decentralize decision making, the efficient functioning of "belief" markets may necessitate extreme computation on the part of every individual. While the classical case against planned economies is the "calculation" argument,[15] it may be that the efficiency of decentralized markets is dependent on an identical, but individual-based, calculation argument.

Although the neo-classical equilibrium result demonstrates Pareto optimality, it is restricted to the case of "private" preferences. The work by Arrow[16] and Black[17] may be regarded as attempts to extend the equilibrium result to the more general context of public goods. Arrow was concerned with the existence of an aggregation procedure that could combine individual preferences so as to give a social preference that could be represented by a social utility function. Since it is unreasonable to put *a priori* restrictions on individual preferences for public goods, Arrow assumed that preferences were unrestricted. Using this, he showed that the only social utility function that satisfied the Pareto condition was dictatorship.

Black's previously referred to book, *Committees and Elections*, was specifically restricted to the case of voting and examined the possibility of an unbeaten outcome under majority rule. In the case that the set of alternatives, *W*, is an interval (a compact, one-dimensional set) and each individual has single-peaked (or convex) preferences, then there is an equilibrium (called a majority motion by Black). Suppose, however, that there are two dimensions of public policy (say economic and social liberalism versus conservatism) and three individuals, then "the conditions that must be satisfied before there can be any majority motion are highly restrictive. The frequency of occurrence as a fraction of the total number of cases possible..., is infinitesimally small or 'practically zero.'"[18] We would say, today, that the majority rule equilibrium (or core) is generically empty. Black's inference has been generalized and shown to be valid for any voting rule.[19] That is if D is an arbitrary voting rule with no vetoer, then there is an integer $w(D)$ which classifies D in the following sense: If the dimension of the space, W, is at least $w(D)$, then the core of the rule is generically empty.[20] One way to understand this theorem is in the following way: Let $F : W \rightarrow W$ be the "win" correspondence, defined by y in $F(x)$ iff there is a winning coalition (under the rule D) which prefers y to x. Clearly F is parametrized by the preferences of the members of the society. Suppose now that there exists some point x_0 in W where $F(x_0)$ does *not* belong to a half-space H at x_0 (a half space H at x_0 is an open set in W such that $(y - x_0) . v > 0$ for some y in W and all v in H). Then it can be shown that there is a voting cycle near x_0, namely a sequence of points $x_1, ..., x_r$ with x_{i+1} in $F(x_i)$ for $i = 0, ..., r-1$ yet x_0 in $F(x_r)$. Thus voting can lead from x_0 back to x_0. Moreover, when the dimension of W exceeds $w(D)$, this condition is generically satisfied at nearly every point in W. In particular for almost any pair of points (x_0, y_0), there exists a voting trajectory from x_0 to y_0. This result was termed the Chaos Voting Theorem because of the analogue with chaos in discrete deterministic systems. To see the connection, let $f : W \rightarrow W$ be a change of state function mapping x_t to $x_{t+1} = f(x_t)$. Li and Yorke[21] defined f to be chaotic if there is an open set S in W such that for any x, y in S then a sufficient number of iterations of f can lead from x to y (i.e., $y = f^k(x)$ for some k). Another way of interpreting this is that the system f is sensitive to initial conditions: thus for $M > 0$ and $e > 0$, there exists some integer k such that $||x_0 - x_1|| < e$, yet $||f^k(x_0) - f^k(x_1)|| > M$, where $||\ ||$ is the norm on W. The Chaos Voting theorem suggested that any actual voting procedure could be chaotic in the sense used by Li and Yorke.[22]

The work by both Arrow and Black was directed at modelling rules of *preference* aggregation based not upon individual behavior but in terms of coalitional or collective actions. To distinguish this work from that of the Nash Program, I shall refer to this endeavor as the *Arrow* program.

In contrast to the research on collective preference aggregation, much work has been devoted recently to developing Condorcet's original ideas on collective *belief* aggregation. Part of the work presented in Condorcet's *Essai* concerned what is now known as the *Jury Theorem*. Consider a binary choice problem where there are two possible choices, say $i = 0$ and $j = 1$. For the actual jury problem the choices allowed by the rules are obviously innocence and guilt, and it is evident that in such a case one of the choices is true and the other false. Without loss of generality we may suppose $j = 1$ is actually true. Suppose that each juror *(k)* is described by a random variable x_k (where $x_k = 0$ means k votes for innocence). Then the probability $Pr(x_k = 1)$ $= P_{jk}$ is the probability that juror k chooses the true option. Suppose that a jury of size n uses majority rule. Let us write p_j for the probability that a majority votes for $j = 1$. It is now possible to obtain a connection between p_j, the probability that the jury chooses the truth, and the juror probabilities, $\{P_{jk} : k = 1, ..., n\}$. Condorcet essentially argued that as long as $P_{jk} > 1/2$ (for each k), and the voters' choices are (statistically) independent, then p_j approaches 1 as n approaches ∞. As McLean and Hewitt[23] have recently observed in their discussion of Condorcet's work, the theorem is to be regarded as a result on the aggregation of *judgements* (or beliefs) and not preferences. Even Black, who reintroduced Condorcet's work to modern audiences, appeared unaware of this distinction, since he observed that the phrase "'the probability of the correctness of a voter's opinion' seems to be without definite meaning."[24] In a jury, it is evident that one can indeed assign meaning to the probability P_{jk}. The theorem has recently been extended in a number of directions. Instead of assuming that $P_{jk} > 1/2$ for each juror, let P_j be the average (or expected vote for j). Boland[25] has shown that as long as $\{x_k\}$ are statistically independent, and if $P_j > 1/2 + 1/(2n)$, then $p_j > P_j$, for any n, and $p_j \to 1$ as $n \to \infty$. In other words, the jury is superior to "an average voter" in determining the truth, and the jury is an "efficient" method of truth seeking as it becomes large in size.

To interpret this theorem, we may suppose that each juror's behavior is determined by private information. Then majoritarian decisionmaking is an efficient method of information or belief aggregation, under the assumption of voter independence. It should be noted that this theorem implictly assumes a symmetry in the costs associated with the two kinds of errors (freeing a guilty defendant and imprisoning an innocent person). To reduce the probability of imprisoning someone innocent, it becomes optimal to use a unanimity rule, etc.[26]

On the basis of his analysis, Condorcet argued for the virtues of the rules defining a uni-cameral representative republic, based on a method of hierarchical decisonmaking. That is, he believed that representatives would exercise their judgement and be less swayed by the passions (or preferences) than would the mass of voters. Condorcet himself was active in politics during the years preceding his death in 1794, as president of the French Legislative Assembly in 1792, as a member of the National Convention of 1792, and as the architect of the "Girondin Constitution" proposed in February 1793. This proposal was defeated by the Jacobins. In March 1794 Condorcet was declared an outlaw, was imprisoned, and died at the end of the month.[27] For all the tragedy of his life, Condorcet may have had a significant impact on the development of the American Constitution. It is known that Jefferson and Condorcet were close friends in Paris in 1786.[28] Although McLean and Urken[29] doubt that Jefferson or Madison closely read Condorcet's *Essai*, there are two different possibilities that follow from the *Essai*. In trying to extend the Jury Theorem to more than two alternatives, Condorcet stumbled on the possibility of voting cycles. McGrath[30] contends that Madison's bicameralism is consistent with an attempt to control cyclical majorities. Indeed much of the formal theory of neo-institutionalism has been directed at showing how the cross vetoes that will occur in a system with President, Senate, and House can nullify voting cycles.[31] Personally I believe Madison was more influenced by the balance that he judged occurred in Britain between the Monarch, the House of Commons, and the House of Lords.

However, the *Federalist X* by *"Publius"* (alias Madison) on November 22, 1787, gives a very clear Condorcetian argument. Madison discusses the dangers of factions, where by faction he means "a number of citizens, whether amounting to a majority or minority of the whole, who are united and activated by some common impulse of passion, or of interest, adverse to the rights of other citizens, or the permanent and aggregate interests of the community."[32]

I read the last phrase as referring to the Rousseauian General Will, that is, a choice that "in truth" will benefit all.

Madison goes on to argue that a Democracy (by which he means a non-representative direct democracy) will always be subject to the mischiefs of faction: "Such Democracies have ever been spectacles of turbulence and contention. ..."[33] On the contrary "A Republic, by which I mean a Government in which the scheme of representation takes place, opens a different prospect ..." and "will present ... a greater probability of a fit choice." Finally:

> The other point of difference is, the greater number of citizens and extent of territory which may be brought within the compass of a Republican, than of a Democratic Government; and it is this circumstance principally which renders factious combinations less to be dreaded in the former, than in the latter.[34]

To understand Madison's point on the connection between size and optimality, I think it plausible that he believed that number and extent would increase heterogeneity. We can infer that this would reduce the average correlation among the voters' judgements. Even if voter's choices are not statistically independent, weak average pairwise correlations in choice can be compatible with the Condorcet Jury Theorem, and thus with the "optimality of belief aggregation."[35] Indeed Madison's argument would imply that no permanent faction of substantial size would ever be capable of maintaining itself for long.[36]

In a sense the Condorcetian-Madisonian argument, putting the rules for collective decision into a very different context, gives a very different view of political competition from that suggested by the Arrovian research program. To see this, suppose that two candidates, i and j, adopt policy positions x and y, and the typical voter, k, votes for j with probability $P_{jk}(x, y)$. Models of "probabilistic voting" by Enelow and Hinich, and Coughlin,[37] etc. envisage each candidate adopting policies designed to maximize their own expected vote (namely $P_j(x, y)$ for j and $P_i(x, y)$ for i). Under certain conditions (including voter independence) there exists a Nash equilibrium (x^*, y^*), generally where the candidates adopt the same position. If we view this model as a method of belief aggregation, then from our previous interpretation, this Nash equilibrium would be that choice which maximizes the probability of being the best social outcome (given the distribution of private information). Such a result is clearly important but obviously at odds with the predictions of chaos from the preference-based models.

Having pointed out the very different predictions (whether of chaos or equilibrium) in these four research programs, I shall attempt, in the next section, to provide a synthesis.

Chaos or Equilibrium?

As we saw in the first section, by the late 1960s it was understood that smooth or dynamical systems could be chaotic. More importantly, within the class of all dynamical systems, R, the subclass of chaotic systems R_C was open. Particular chaotic systems, such as the three-body gravitation system[38] or the Lorenz "strange attractor"[39] have become well known.

Although, in the social sciences, the formal possibility of chaos was proved first for voting models within the Arrow research program, later work showed that disorder of some kind was inherent in many of the models within the Nash research program. For example, while economic theory demonstrated the existence of a price equilibrium, it was soon realized that the equilibrium could be highly unstable.[40] More importantly the so-called Sonnenschein,[41] Mantel,[42] and Debreu[43] (or SMD) theorem showed that the map from economic systems to demand, and thus to price adjustment processes, is onto. This implies that the price adjustment mechanism can, in principle, be as chaotic as one could desire.[44] Saari[45] has since shown that almost any aggregation procedure (whether decision theoretic, statistical, rank ordering, etc.) is susceptible to a form of chaos (namely "anything can happen").

Chaos has even been turning up in game theory. One of the central concerns of the Nash program has been to model behavior by rational agents responding to other agents whom they know to be rational but whose characteristics they do not fully know. In a sense this has resulted in the combination of the Nash and Aumann programs, since for such a theory it is necessary to model both the preferences and beliefs of the agents. In games of incomplete information the "folk theorem"[46] again suggests that "anything can happen." Recent work on modelling how rational agents learn about their opponents in such games indicates that these systems are either chaotic[47] or face a Godelian "incompleteness" problem.[48] I shall return to the incompleteness problem later. For the moment it is worth emphasizing that all attempts to model the conventions and institutions that govern human behavior depend to some degree on common knowledge foundations. For example, in problems of social cooperation a key feature is the belief that each agent has about the attachment to rules and the likely behavior (and thus the beliefs) of other agents. Whether the process of learning and adaptation leads to cooperation (or war) may turn on subtleties of the initial conditions.

A recent paper by Nyarko[49] has attempted to model such a preference-belief game. Each agent, i, is described by an action space W_i and belief space B_i, where B_i describes i's beliefs about the preferences and beliefs of others. The collective action-belief space is $W \times B = \Pi(W_i \times B_i)$ and the "best response" induced by agents' behavior is a function $f : W \times B \to W_i \times B_i$. Nyarko shows that if f is a contraction mapping (domains become smaller under f), then reiteration of the game will eventually result in an "equilibrium" where beliefs are unchanging and are compatible with the actions of the individual. On the other hand it is possible for f to be chaotic: that is for almost any pair of collective actions, x, y and any path c from x to y, there exists some initial collective belief b, such that reiteration of f from the initial state (x, b) leads to (y, b'), say, along a path in W close to c.

I conjecture that to forbid such chaotic behavior it is necessary that the game exhibit a half-openness condition similar to the one found to be required for equilibrium in voting games. That is at any state (x, b), let $F(x, b)$ be the set of rational actions and beliefs that are possible from (x, b). If for every (x, b) there is some half space $H(x, b)$ such that $F(x, b)$ belongs to $H(x, b)$, then there is an equilibrium in action and beliefs. To provide some justification for this conjecture, Page and Wooders[50] have recently shown that in financial markets if there exist no exchange cycles (so the above half-open condition is satisfied) then a "belief" equilibrium does exist.

What about chaos in the Arrow-Condorcet research programs? It is obvious enough that voters use both their preferences and beliefs in determining how to behave. Where preferences predominate, the theory suggests that Madison's fear of factional instability (or "coalitional chaos") would be justified. However where beliefs about the true nature of the world predominate, then we may concur with Condorcet's optimism about communication and debate leading to agreement. It is more likely, in my view, that both economic and political markets can oscillate between chaotic and equilibrating modes. Recent events in Russia, Lebanon, Northern Ireland, and the Balkans should alert us to the possibility that apparently stable political economies can suddenly collapse into chaos. On the other hand it is possible for peace to break out (witness Northern Ireland in 1995). Recent work by Huberman and Glance, Bikhchandani *et al.*, and Karklins and Petersen[51] all discuss the theoretical and empirical possibilities of sudden transformations in collective behavior in many different contexts.

While none of these models imply that chaos is *necessary* in collective action situations, they do indicate that where choices are bifurcated (say into cooperation as against defection) then actual social behavior will strongly depend on the initial beliefs of the agents.

Conclusion

The models that we have considered in these four research programs all assume, in one way or another, that individuals are algorithmic in attempting to optimize in the context of a set of institutional rules (whether of the market or of the polity). The form of this optimization depends on the nature of the agents' beliefs about the optimization strategies, and thus the beliefs, of others. However it is unclear whether rationality can be algorithmic. To see what I mean, consider the simple game of paper, stone, scissors. Paper beats stone beats scissors beats paper. If each of the two agents playing this game wants to win, then the Nash (mixed) equilibrium strategy is to play each of the three options with equal probability. However, real people do not randomize in this way. It is more likely that i, say, looks for patterns in j's behavior (in the iterated game), and then realizes that j's play is a consequence of j's attempt to model i's own behavior. After a few moves, both players are deep into calculations of the kind "I think j thinks that I think ..." and the game usually ends with both laughing at the "reductio ad absurdum" intrinsic to the situation. Computations of this kind face Turing's "Entscheidungsproblem" or halting problem.[52] Penrose[53] has argued, on the basis of this problem, that rationality is non-algorithmic. For the same reason Nachbar's analysis of rational behavior in game situations suggests that it is impossible to construct a fully consistent or algorithmic model of choice involving both preferences and beliefs.

I infer that, even in rule-governed situations, individuals and collectivities will make choices that are surprising to an observer even where all the details of the situation are known. When chaos does break out, it can lead to entirely new possibilities, suggesting that social evolution is fundamentally path dependent.[54] It is plausible, then, to infer that the global social system is almost structurally stable, but that chaotic occurrences can, perhaps, shift it onto a different developmental path. One of the further possibilities that should be at the back of our minds is that our socio-political system is increasingly "coupled" to the global ecosystem. It is not implausible that human behavior (particularly with regard to pollution, etc.) may induce chaotic or even catastrophic changes in the global ecology.[55]

These observations do not diminish the deep insights of Adam Smith, Condorcet, and the Founding Fathers that essentially underpin the four research programs discussed in this essay. Just as the insights of Newton and Laplace on the physical universe had to be complemented by Poincaré's topological analysis, so do we need a qualitative theory of social mathematics that will combine these four different perspectives on preference and belief aggregation. In some sense the difficulty that we face in integrating these programs is as difficult as the task facing mathematical physicists in developing a unified theory of gravitation, electromagnetism, and the weak and strong nuclear forces.

Notes

Earlier versions of this chapter were presented at the Law and Policy Workshop, School of Law, McGill University, at the Roundtable on Formal Political Theory, Annual Meeting of the American Political Science Association 1994, at the International Meeting of the Society for Social Choice and Welfare 1994, and the European Public Choice Meeting, 1995. The ideas expressed here were developed while pursuing research supported by NSF Grant SBR-94-22548.

1. I. Peterson, *Newton's Clock: Chaos in the Solar System* (New York: Freeman, 1993).

2. S. Smale, "Structurally Stable Systems Are Not Dense," *American Journal of Mathematics*, Vol. 88, 1966, pp. 491–496.

3. M. Peixoto, "Structural Stability on Two-Dimensional Manifolds," *Topology*, Vol. 1, 1962, p. 101–120.

4. S. Kauffman, *The Origins of Order* (Oxford: Oxford University Press, 1993).

5. R. Thom, *Structural Stability and Morphogenesis*, D. H. Fowler, tr. (Reading, Ma.: Benjamin, 1972, 1975); G. Nicolis and I. Prigogine, *Exploring Complexity* (New York: Freeman, 1989); M. Waldrop, *Complexity: The Emerging Science at the Edge of Order and Chaos* (New York: Simon and Schuster, 1992).

6. W. H. Calvin, *The Ascent of Mind* (New York: Boston, 1990).

7. N. Eldridge and S. J. Gould, "Punctuated Equilibria: An Alternative to Phyletic Gradualism," in T.J.M. Schopf, ed., *Models in Paleobiology* (San Francisco: Freeman Press, 1972); S. J. Gould, *Wonderful Life* (New York: Norton, 1989).

8. P.W. Anderson, J. J. Arrow, and D. Pines, eds., *The Economy as an Evolving Complex System* (Redwood City, CA.: Addison-Wesley, 1988).

9. A. Smith, *The Theory of Moral Sentiments* (Oxford: Oxford University Press, 1759, 1976); A. Smith, *An Inquiry into the Nature and Cause of the Wealth of Nations* (Oxford: Oxford University Press, 1776, 1976).

10. Condorcet, M.J.A.N. Caritat, Marquis de, *Essai sur l'application de l'analyse à la probabilité des voix* (New York: Chelsea, 1972) and (orig. Paris: Imprimerie Royale, 1785).

11. B. Bailyn, ed., *The Debate on the Constitution: Federalist and Antifederalist Speeches, Articles and Letters.* 2 volumes (New York: Viking, 1993).

12. K. J. Arrow and G. Debreu, "Existence of an Equilibrium for a Competitive Economy," *Econometrica,* Vol. 22, 1954, pp. 265–290; L. McKenzie, "On the Existence of a General Equilibrium for a Competitive Economy," *Econometrica,* Vol. 27, 1959, pp. 54–71.

13. R. J. Aumann, "Agreeing to Disagree," *Annals of Statistics,* Vol. 4, 1976, pp. 1236–1239; R. D. McKelvey and T. Page, "Common Knowledge, Consensus, and Aggregate Information," *Econometrica,* Vol. 54, 1986, pp. 109–127.

14. K. J. Arrow, "Rationality of Self and Others in an Economic System," *Journal of Business,* Vol. 59, 1986, pp. 5385–5399.

15. F. Hayek, *Individualism and Economic Order* (London: Routledge and Kegal Paul, 1976).

16. K. J. Arrow, *Social Choice and Individual Values* (New York: Wiley, 1951).

17. D. Black, *The Theory of Committees and Elections* (Cambridge: Cambridge University Press, 1958).

18. Black, *The Theory of Committees and Elections,* p. 139.

19. C. R. Plott, "A Notion of Equilibrium and its Possibility under Majority Rule," *American Economic Review,* Vol. 57, 1967, pp. 787–806; G. Kramer, "On a Class of Equilibrium Conditions for Majority Rule," *Econometrica,* Vol. 41, 1973, pp. 285–297; R. D. McKelvey, "Intransitivities in Multidimensional Voting Models and Some Implications for Agenda Control," *Journal of Economic Theory,* Vol. 12, 1976, pp. 472–482; N. Schofield, "Instability of Simple Dynamic Games," *Review of Economic Studies,* Vol. 45, 1978, pp. 475–494.

20. Here, "generically" refers to an open dense set of smooth preference profiles: Schofield, N. "The C^1-Topology on the Space of Preference Profiles and the Existence of a Continuous Preference Aggregator," (Mimeo: Washington University, 1995).

21. T. Li and J. Yorke, "Period Three Implies Chaos," *American Mathematical Monthly,* Vol. 82, 1976, pp. 985–992.

22. D. Richards, "Intransitivities in Multidimensional Spatial Voting: Period Three Implies Chaos," *Social Choice and Welfare,* Vol. 11, 1994, pp. 109–120.

23. I. McLean and F. Hewitt, *Condorcet: Foundations of Social Choice and Political Theory* (Adershot, England: Edward Elgar, 1994).

24. Black, *The Theory of Committees and Elections,* p. 163.

25. P. J. Boland, "Majority Systems and the Condorcet Jury Theorem," *The Statistician,* Vol. 38, 1989, pp. 187–189.

26. N. Schofield, "Is Majority Rule Special?" in R. Niemi and H. Weisberg, eds., *Probability Models of Collective Decision Making* (Columbus, Ohio: Merrill, 1972).

27. The book by McLean and Hewitt, 1994, gives an excellent account of Condorcet's life and work.

28. W. S. Randall, *Thomas Jefferson: A Life* (New York: Holt, 1993).

29. I. McLean and A. Urken, "Did Jefferson or Madison Understand Condorcet's Theory of Social Choice?" *Public Choice,* Vol. 73, 1992, pp. 445–457.

30. D. McGrath, *James Madison and Social Choice Theory* (Unpublished doctoral dissertation: University of Maryland, College Park, Md., 1983).

31. T. H. Hammond and G. Miller, "The Core of the Constitution," *American Political Science Review,* Vol. 81, 1987, pp. 1155–1174.

32. Bailyn, *The Debate on the Constitution*, p. 405.

33. Bailyn, *The Debate on the Constitution*, p. 408.

34. Bailyn, *The Debate on the Constitution*, p. 410.

35. K. Ladha, "Condorcet's Jury Theorem, Free Speech and Correlated Votes," *American Journal of Political Science*, Vol. 36, 1992, pp. 617–634; K. Ladha, "Condorcet's Jury Theorem in the Light of de Finetti's Theorem: Majority Rule with Correlated Votes," *Social Choice and Welfare*, Vol. 10, 1993, pp. 69–86; K. Ladha and G. Miller, "Political Discourse, Factions, and the General Will: Correlated Voting and Condorcet's Jury Theorem," in Norman Schofield, ed., *Social Choice and Political Economy* (Boston: Kluwer, 1995).

36. In a sense a faction can only persist if the pairwise correlations in choice between its members are close to unity. In this case the faction should be treated like a single individual. If the faction is large then the probability that the society as a whole chooses the truth (namely p_j) is close to P_j (the average probability that a faction member chooses the truth). Clearly there is no reason for p_j to be close to unity even for a very large society. With heterogeneity, and low pairwise correlations, it is indeed possible for p_j to exceed P_j. More importantly, as Ladha and Miller, 1995, show by example, if the heterogeneity induces negative pairwise correlations, p_j can be higher than in a society whose individual choices are statistically independent.

37. J. Enelow and M. J. Hinich, *The Spatial Theory of Voting: An Introduction* (Cambridge: Cambridge University Press, 1984); P. J. Coughlin, *Probabilistic Voting Theory* (Cambridge: Cambridge University Press, 1992).

38. D. Saari, "On Oscillatory Motion in the Problem of Three Bodies," *Celestial Mechanics*, Vol. 1, 1970, pp. 343–346; D. Saari, "Expanding Gravitational Systems," *Transactions of the American Mathematical Society*, Vol. 156, 1971, pp. 219–240.

39. C. Sparrow, *The Lorenz Equations, Bifurcations, Chaos and Strange Attractors* (New York: Springer Verlag, 1982).

40. H. Scarf, "Some Examples of Global Instability of the Competitive Equilibrium," *International Economic Review*, Vol. 1, 1960, pp. 157–172.

41. H. Sonnenschein, "Market Excess Demand Functions," *Econometrica*, Vol. 40, 1972, pp. 345–354.

42. R. Mantel, "On the Characterization of Aggregate Excess Demand," *Journal of Economic Theory*, Vol. 7, p. 348.

43. G. Debreu, "Excess Demand Functions," *Journal of Mathematical Economics*, Vol. 1, 1974, pp. 15–23.

44. D. Saari, "Erratic Behavior in Economic Models," *Journal of Economic Behavior and Organization*, Vol. 16, 1991, pp. 3–35.

45. D. Saari, "A Chaotic Explanation of Aggregation Procedures," *Siam Review*, Vol. 37, 1995, pp. 1–22.

46. D. Fudenberg and E. Maskin, "The Folk Theorem in Repeated Games with Discounting and Incomplete Information," *Econometrica*, Vol. 54, 1986, pp. 533–554.

47. R. D. McKelvey and T. R. Palfrey, "Stationarity and Chaos in Infinitely Repeated Games of Incomplete Information" (Mimeo: California Institute of Technology, 1992).

48. J. Nachbar, *Prediction, Optimization, and Rational Learning in Games* (Washington University: Center in Political Economy, 1995); K. Gödel, "Uber Formal Unentscheidbare Sätze der Principia Mathematica und verwandter Systeme,"

Monatschefte für Mathematik und Physik, Vol. 38, 1931, pp. 173–198. Translated by B. Meltzer as *On Formally Undecidable Propositions in 'Principia Mathematica' and Related Systems* (New York: Basic Books, 1962).

49. Y. Nyarko, "Convergence in Economic Models with Bayesian Hierarchies of Beliefs." (Mimeo: New York University, 1992).

50. F. Page and M. Wooders, "Arbitrage with Price-Dependent Preferences and Unbounded Consumption Sets" (Mimeo: University of Alabama, 1995).

51. B. A. Huberman and N. S. Glance, "Beliefs and Cooperation," in A. Albert and P. Lemieux, eds., *Chaos and Society* (Amsterdam: IOS Press, 1995); S. D. Hirschleifer, Bikhchandani, and I. Welch, "A Theory of Fads, Fashion, Custom and Cultural Change as Information Crusades," *Journal of Political Economy,* Vol. 100, 1992, pp. 992–1026; R. Karklins and R. Petersen, "Decision Calculus of Protestors and Regimes: Eastern Europe 1989," *Journal of Politics,* Vol. 55, 1993, pp. 588–614.

52. A. M. Turing, "On Computable Numbers, with an Application to the Entscheidungsproblem," *Proceedings of the London Mathematical Society,* Vol. 42, 1937, pp. 230–265.

53. R. Penrose, *The Emperor's New Mind* (Oxford: Oxford University Press, 1989); R. Penrose, *Shadows of the Mind* (Oxford: Oxford University Press, 1994).

54. D. North, *Institutions, Institutional Change and Economic Performance* (Cambridge: Cambridge University Press, 1990); D. North, "Economic Performance through Time," *American Economic Review,* Vol. 84, 1994, pp. 359–368.

55. N. Schofield, "The Logic of Catastrophe," *Human Ecology,* Vol. 5, 1977, pp. 261–271.

Schematic Synthesis

Epilogue

By Way of Summary: A Schematic Synthesis of the Discussion at the Murphy Institute Conference

David Braybrooke

In conclusion, Braybrooke brings forward, as one more move to align and reconcile the diversity of points and perspectives carried forward from the Murphy Institute conference to the present book, the schematic synthesis of the discussion that he produced immediately after the conference.

The diversity of points and perspectives in the book is as great as was the diversity at the conference from which the book takes its origin. It is the same diversity. In the book, there have been a number of things done to give some order to this diversity, in the plan of the book, in the introduction, in the running commentary, and in several contributions that tie in explicitly with other contributions. It may still be helpful to conclude by reproducing the schematic synthesis of the discussion at the conference that I produced immediately after it was over.[1]

I began by making the point that our focus had been on settled social rules—not, for example, rules on their first promulgation, before one can tell whether they will "take" with the people subject to them; not with dead letter rules either, but with rules that people do actually, with some degree of intention, conform to.

Settled social rules belong to a class of phenomena in which conventions, various approximations to convention, and maxims for productive efficiency also figure [Sherry, Miller, Kornhauser]. Rules can be distinguished from these other things as being accompanied by provisions enforcing them with rewards or punishments[2]—whereas conventions as such, for example, may require no enforcement, given their mutual advantages and given no opportunity to seize these advantages by free riding. As it happens, both conventions and maxims commonly do transform into rules, since without provisions for enforcement people deviate too often out of carelessness or irrationality. Thus stopping for red lights, though clearly mutually advantageous, is not left to convention alone; penalties are brought in to give the convention more weight. Even in very sophisticated connections like the paradigms governing experimental procedure in science, rules tend to supplant mere conventions [Brown].

It remains true that not all social and historical phenomena fall happily within the embrace of the study of rules. Even phenomena intimately connected with settled social rules—for example, the goals that rules are set up to achieve—are perhaps best left outside rule-formulations. We could contrive to bring the goals into the picture by formulating rules of a higher order—i.e., rules about adopting rules to pursue certain ends rather than others. For example, the rule to change social arrangements always in the direction of promoting economic growth is one way of expressing the fact, if it is a fact, that economic growth is a major goal, perhaps the supreme one. To do so, however, might well underrate the flexibility and "gappiness" of goals [Miller]. There are a lot of other things that people want to make sure of besides economic growth; and some of them—personal health, limits on personal stress, safeguarding the environment—may on occasion win the day against economic growth, though it is unlikely that we could draw up once and for all an ordering that would enable us to predict the occasions exactly. Some attention needs to be given nevertheless to the interaction of rules with goals [Brown], in which we may see goals modified to accord with rules as often as we see rules adapted to the goals. Furthermore, we need to allow for the possibility that goals on occasion may be just the goals of having certain rules prevail [Schotch]—to reach, for example, the advanced stage of social and economic development in which Rawls's principles of justice can be applied in lexical order.

Rules themselves admit of many distinctions, not all of which we shall attend to. For example, in some connections it is important to distinguish between rules that treat the people subject to them as participants in collective actions and rules (more common in the Dalhousie team's examples and more common in the examples that come up in the present book) that treat the people subject to them as individual agents acting each on their own [Schofield]. The question of just what rules if any did medieval English manor courts follow in resolving disputes among villeins is perhaps a case in point [Bonfield]. Were the manor courts acting from a "sense of the meeting," shifting intuitively from case to case, to reach in every instance what seemed to them a fair and reasonable compromise of conflicting interests? This attention to compromise according to the sense of the meeting may be looked upon as a rule prescribed for the collective action of the manor courts. Or were the manor courts (as the historians that Bonfield criticizes incline to think) applying to the individual persons coming before them settled rules laying down the conditions in legitimate birth for individual persons to inherit property?

Here and elsewhere, the first thing for champions of a logic of rules to do is to persuade historians and social scientists that the logic does express rules in a sense that converges with the conception of rules that the historians and social scientists already hold [Behlmer]. The next thing to show is that in cases like the manor court one where the evidence is controversial and can be resolved only by delicate balancing [Bonfield], subtle differences in the formulation of the rules will play a part in determining the controversy one way or another. Bonfield's evidence suggests, for example, that the rules of inheritance (so far as there were such rules) may not have been fully aligned with the rules establishing marriage; betrothal (trothplight) may have sufficed to establish children's claims to an inheritance, while marriage itself was required for a woman's claim to dower-rights.

Already we have passed from treating rules as subject matter to treating them as ingredients of explanation [Sayre-McCord], e.g., of why the manor courts made the decisions that they did. (In this instance, Bonfield is inclined to argue, we may have passed too quickly, assuming the existence of rules that did not exist; but then the controversy is about whether parallels with other instances of explanation can be realized in this one.) The case for using a logic of rules is in important part a case for clarifying the ingredients and structures of such explanations. But such a logic has a great deal to contribute simply to the description of social and historical phenomena. It is well-nigh indispensable, for example, to sorting out issues where, because many rules are involved, perhaps at various levels of nested processes [Aminzade], the issues reach a certain level of complexity. To ascertain how one rule bears upon another we need to specify and compare the demographic scope of the two rules, the actions or sequences of actions (what the Dalhousie team calls "routines") prohibited by each, the conditions, possibly very complicated and subtle, under which the prohibitions of the one and the other operate.

With or without such complications to deal with, a suitable logic should be able to make clear in what circumstances a given set of rules combine consistently and in what circumstances conflicts appear within the set. One class of cases in which questions about consistency and inconsistency are crucial to understanding what was going on consists of cases in which the presence of certain rules helps explain why certain others come into being or fail to do so. The abolition of the British slave trade, a case studied in detail in the Dalhousie book, is a case in point, several times over: rules about respecting property rights—applied to plantations in the West Indies—for decades on end stood in the way of a rule abolishing the trade.

Thus we return to the use of rules (and of a logic of rules) in historical explanations. It is, to be sure, hardly likely that application of the logic will ever suffice to explain decisions [Behlmer]. The logic does not by itself suffice, for one thing, to explain the origin and variation of attachment to any given rules. Yet application of the logic will sharpen the focus of the explanations offered. It has in many quarters been too easily assumed that the Constitution of the United States obstructed the formation of national political parties. Focusing (as one chapter of the Dalhousie book focuses) on the question of just what party-forming routines, if any, are forbidden by the Constitution knocks out any attempt to invoke such obstruction as an explanation of failures in party-formation. The logic will knock out many other attempts at explanation as equally lacking in relevance. The logic will help identify gaps—which might otherwise go undetected—in the explanations that survive, and thus alert historians to the need to search for ingredients to fill the gaps. How was it, for example, that the plantation-owners' property rights did not in the end defeat the project of abolishing the slave-trade? In one otherwise careful account of the abolition (Porter's)[3] the rights just disappear from the scene.

Origin of Rules

It is not just change from one settled social rule to another that requires explanation. The coming into being of rules in the limiting case where before there were no rules, or no rules on the given topic, is a sort of change in rules that itself requires explanation as much as any other. It also demands attention for the light that it may throw upon other sorts of changes in rules.

The occasion for a rule's coming into being may often be looked upon as one in which costs (transaction costs, the costs of getting into a position to make an an exchange with someone else, on a very general view of the costs of getting anyone else to do what you want of him) either betoken the absence of social cooperation or stand in the way of extending it [North, Heiner]. Perfectly rational and knowledgeable agents would not need rules, because they would discern from moment to moment the maximum gains to themselves from cooperation [Heiner], though to say this we may have to build into them a level of rationality that transcends free-rider problems. Would such agents make sure of benefits to other people (where the benefits are not payments for productive reciprocation)? We could build into their preference-functions other-regarding values (most important, benevolence) and look upon rules as means to attaining these as well. We could thus follow the lead that David Hume gives with his "natural" virtues and think of such values as a source of motivation for moral conduct that operates so regularly with some people as to be a matter of rule.[4]

Suppose we say that the function of a rule is to reduce or eliminate costs whenever doing so increases the gains from social cooperation [North,

Heiner]. This supposition allows that rule-makers may deliberately incur costs of some kinds (e.g., costs of enforcement), if a net increase in the gains from cooperation ensues. It is also consistent with some costs rarely if ever ensuing in such increases (e.g., those of personal violence, family instability, and theft, within the given rule-adhering group). Not expecting gains from bearing such costs, we would not expect to find rules accepted that were recognized to have such costs.

A settled social rule exists if and only if there is a corresponding pattern of conformity and enforcement: It is a rule that people repay their debts. Typically, most people conform—they do pay up; and in at least a substantial number of instances, non-conformity gets punished. However, this pattern is hardly ever so perfect as not to be accompanied by unpunished violations [North]. Moreover, there is a great deal of variation in the time that passes before a rule can be counted (if it ever can be) as imperfectly, but sufficiently established to be called "settled." Sometimes, explicit legislation shortens the time required for establishment. On the other hand, the time taken to establish some rules, even ones that early in the process are explicitly legislated, extends over generations, even over centuries. One reason for this is that "promulgative" information is not optimized; not all lawsuits that might give decisive information are prosecuted to the end; judges do not publish full treatments of the issues involved even when decisions are reached [Silver].

Setting aside cases of oppressive imposition, widespread belief in the presence of net gains attributable to the rule in question will be a necessary condition for establishing the rule, though this belief will not by itself solve problems about free riders [Silver]. Moreover, there will be some tendency for this belief to survive only if it is well-founded on gains actually realized; evolutionary processes working in the law will tend to displace inefficient rules [Kornhauser].

It is worth remarking that these processes are in many respects subtle— too subtle to capture, we might think, without asking the questions that a logic of rules raises. To understand them we might have to compare the formulas by which the rules are commonly understood with formulas— which would be applicable if people thought of the rules this way—that made the gains more matters of immediate inference. Subtle, too, are some of the features of the rules once established. For example, enforcement of the rules that are associated with paradigms of scientific inquiry may take the form of simply not inviting deviants to join research teams [Brown].

Even when established, rules vary in the degree to which people subject to them are attached, and in that sense vary in force [North]. Philosophers and lawyers may incline to think of established rules as matters of rigid attachment, and furthermore, more plausibly, to treat them as matters recognized by the people subject to them as beyond their power as individual persons to change or defy [Kornhauser]. Economists, however, at the other extreme on these issues, incline to associate each rule with cost functions for the persons subject to them. The functions show in each case the prices that have to be paid for various amounts (frequency times extent) of violating the rules [North].

These views can be harmonized. On the one hand, rigidity of attachment, resulting from stamping in explicit rule-formulas, and persisting in the face of ordinary temptations in price-offers, is something to be sought as an aspect of the effectiveness of rules [Heiner]. On the other hand, as the opportunity costs of adhering to a given rule increase, attachment will begin to decay, first maybe for a few people, then for many [North]. Thus as the market came in to establish prices for labor, manor lords no longer found it advantageous to avoid in the customs of the manor haggling over prices; services in labor for the manor lords became commuted into rent payments.

It helps in this connection to think of everybody as equipped, relative to the existing rules, with multiple preference functions, which are brought into play by differences in the sets of alternatives [Baigent]. Thus, were the alternative presented to (say) James Madison to selling his mother into slavery or prostitution or simply foregoing a bundle of money or comforts for himself, his price for violation would (we might hope) be infinite. But should the alternative be a unique opportunity to save hundreds of millions of human lives, old and young, many people's attachment, normally, like Madison's, quite high, to the rule, "Honor thy father and thy mother," might turn out to be unreliable. Fortunately, such opportunities are not just rare, but imaginary. More common are cases in which the contrast is with having a set of alternatives that include one departing from an innocent status quo to start up a nefarious practice—there people would shun such a departure; if, in the present case, however, the nefarious alternative is one that continues an existing practice on which the livelihood of many depend (the tobacco industry), a different preference function applies. What, in ordinary cases, makes rules stable in respect to attachment is presumably that alternatives which meet for most people finite prices for violations rarely if ever figure in the sets of alternatives and in the preference functions that the people conforming to the rules respectively encounter and apply.

Changes in Rules

Rules do, of course, change, however far it may be from being the case that all social change consists of changes in rules.

Some will say, rules change because with changes in circumstances (including techniques of production) the relative prices affecting attachment change [North]. Attachment to the customs of the manor is one example; attachment to the rules protecting common property, another. Given the change in prices, there may be overt demands for "recontracting" in respect to given rules [North]. Or there may be such an increase in violations that enforcement cannot keep up with them; the rules lapse along with the pattern of conformity and enforcement [Kornhauser].

Some will say, rules change because social groups disfavored by the rules have acquired the power to overturn them [Miller]. Thus the French bourgeoisie in the course of the Revolution abolished the privileges of the nobility with respect to not paying taxes.

Again, these are views that can be harmonized; they are both present, for example, in classical Marxist theory. The power newly acquired by a social group is power acquired in the presence of a given distribution of personal sets of preference functions and arises from the relation of these sets of functions to changes in circumstances and in relative prices.

Moreover, the harmonized views offer an important place for rules themselves as conditions favoring some changes in rules and blocking others. Some rules have internal features calling for changes in rules—for example, the rule governing the development of clinical medicine that called year by year for higher standards of correlation in diagnosis between overt symptoms and pathological conditions. Stage by stage, a rule with one specific standard gives way under the rule of development to a rule with a higher standard.[5]

The distribution of attachment to some rules sets limits to the modification of others. If the limits are narrow, the system of rules will be inflexible, perhaps disastrously so [North, Heiner]. In the Dalhousie logic of rules, a rule is a prohibition and what it prohibits (under, it may be, certain conditions only) is a routine—an action or sequence of actions. A rule, by forbidding every routine in which the routine that it specifically forbids is included, forbids infinitely many routines. It also, taken by itself, leaves infinitely many open. (It may be assumed that forbidding a routine **r** is pointless if it is inevitable that **r** occur, hence not feasible, to do **not-r**; new scope for rules opens up when there is a change in feasibility [Schofield].) Nevertheless, those left open may all be very costly; or very narrowly circumscribed relatively to the pursuit of life-plans (for example, for some given people in some circumstances, marriage or change of occupations may not be present in any of the life-plans open to them).

Rules and systems of rules that circumscribe liberty narrowly will leave people less liberty to experiment with life-plans, and hence to explore possible gains from social cooperation [Riley]. This limitation may combine with the inflexibility of attachment mentioned earlier to make the systems in question less adaptable to changes in circumstances.

The Dalhousie project has taken a special interest in changes of rules that pass through quandaries, where two or more rules to which attachment is approximately equal will combine to forbid at once all routines, both those including **r** and those including **not-r**. British MP's were for a time in such a quandary about abolishing the slave-trade: forbidden by Christian principles (as these had lately become understood) to connive at the trade's continuing; forbidden by the rules protecting property rights, in particular the rights of plantation-owners to keep their plantations in production, to abolish the trade. For a time, such a quandary may hold up changes in other rules; or hold up other sorts of changes. But it will also often drive people to find a resolution, which will involve a change of rules. Not everything that looks like a quandary at first sight will prove to be one in the canonical sense [Miller]; some, for example, will just be situations in which every alternative is rather costly. Yet understanding even situations that pull people in different directions without being quandaries is something that can be advanced by applying a suitable logic of rules. Standard deontic logics fail to deal adequately with quandaries proper; they are liable to paradoxical explosions, in which the rules appear at once to forbid, license, and require every routine. A suitable logic will avoid such explosions. It will also enable us to show how other rules may figure in the resolution of the quandaries when they do occur.

Notes

1. Several people are named in the schematic synthesis who took part in the conference but have not contributed to the book. Some have contributed something different to the book from what they contributed to the conference; it is the latter that is at issue in the schematic synthesis.

2. Readers of *Track* will note that this conception of rules has been superseded in my mind and the minds of other members of the Dalhousie team since the conference took place. If we were to distinguish rules as associated with sanctions, the present paragraph could stand without qualification. However, it is (we now think) best to say that rules by definition involve blockings (corrections); sanctions appear only when the people upholding the rule find that blockings (or warnings of impending blockings) do not suffice to obtain conformity.

3. Dale H. Porter, *The Abolition of the Slave Trade in England, 1784–1807* (Hamden, Conn.: Archon Books, 1970). See the discussion in *Track*, Chapter Ten.

4. Hume, *A Treatise of Human Nature*, ed. L. A. Selby-Bigge (Oxford: The Clarendon Press, 1988 [1739]), Part III, Section I, pp. 574–591.

5. See the discussion of Foucault's *La Naissance de la clinique* in *Track*, Chapter Eight.

APPENDICES

Appendix 1

Proofs Relating to Chapter 11

Lewis A. Kornhauser

Some Notation

There are n rules with rule i less efficient than rule j if and only if $i < j$. q_A is the vector of litigation rates for process A; that is $q_{i,A}$ is the probability that rule i will be litigated. Without loss of generality, one may assume that q_A is a probability vector. Q_A is the nxn matrix with $q_{i,A}$ on the diagonal and 0 elsewhere.

The judicial process for legal process A is described by an nxn matrix P_A in which p_{ij} represents the probability that the judge will change rule i to rule j. Since I seek conditions on q_A and q_B that insure that legal process A is more efficient than legal process B I shall hold the judicial process constant; that is in all examples $P_A = P_B = P$. The legal process A combines the rates of litigation Q_A and the judicial process P; it is defined by an nxn matrix

$$A = (I - Q_A) + Q_A P$$

$Q_A P$ represents the influence of the judicial process, appropriately discounted by the frequency with which it is invoked. $(I - Q_A)$ represents the "inertia" in the system created by the rates of litigation. A legal rule "persists" not only when the legal rule is announced in an adjudication, but also in periods after its announcement but prior to the next litigation.

I assume throughout that P is indecomposable and aperiodic. It is well-known that every indecomposable and aperiodic matrix B has an unique stationary vector y such that $yB = y$. The judicial process P has stationary vector z, i.e., $zP = z$. Then z_i represent the percentage of time that the judicial process P spends in state i. I shall assume that, for every i, $0 < q_{i,A} \leq 1$. Consequently, A too is indecomposable and aperiodic with unique stationary vector x_A ($x_A A = x_A$). $x_{i,A}$ represents the percentage of time that the process A spends in state i. Because the stationary vector of a process is unique, we may identify the process A with its stationary vector x_A.

To compare the relative efficiencies of process A and process B, one must compare their stationary vectors. One says that process A is more efficient than process B or $x_A R x_B$ if and only if for every $t = 1, 2, ..., n$

$$\sum_1^t x_{i,\,A} \le \sum_1^t x_{i,\,B}$$

Since x_A and x_B are probability vectors the relation R is the relation of first-order stochastic dominance.

Results

As noted in the text, the claim that efficient rules are "naturally selected" because inefficient rules are litigated more often than efficient rules gives rise to two related conjectures which, given the notation, may be phrased as:

Conjecture 1:   Let P be any aperiodic and indecomposable judicial process with stationary vector z. Let the vector q_A of litigation rates be such that $q_{i,A} \ge q_{j,A}$ if and only if $i \le j$. Then, if x_A is the stationary vector of the process $A = (I - Q) + QP$ then $(x_A)Rz$ (or the process A is more efficient than process P).

Conjecture 2:   Let P be any aperiodic and indecomposable judicial process. Consider two vectors q_A and q_B of litigation rates with $(q_A)R(q_B)$; i.e., inefficient rules are litigated more frequently in process B than in process A. Then $(x_B)R(x_A)$ where x_A is the stationary vector of the process $A = (I - Q_A) + Q_A P$ and x_B the stationary vector of the process $B = (I - Q_B) + Q_B P$; that is, efficient rules persist longer in process B than in process A.

Conjecture 2 implies Conjecture 1 as the pure judicial process P has the same steady state as the process $N = (I - Q_N) + Q_N P$ where $q_{i,\,N} = 1/n$ for each i. Any litigation vector q in which inefficient rules are litigated more frequently than efficient rules must stochastically dominate q_N. Proposition 1 and its corollary show that both conjectures are true when there are only two rules.

Proposition 1:   Suppose $n = 2$. Let P be any 2×2 aperiodic, indecomposable matrix. Let z be the stationary vector of P and q any probability vector with $q_1, q_2 > 0$. Define

$$A = (I - Q) + QP,$$

with x the stationary vector of A. Then, xRz if and only if $q_1 \ge q_2$.

Proof: Consider an arbitrary 2×2 matrix B that is aperiodic and indecomposable. Then the stationary vector y of B is given by

$$y_1 = b_{21}/(b_{21} + b_{12}) \tag{1}$$

and

$$y_2 = b_{12}/(b_{21} + b_{12}). \tag{2}$$

Note that:

$$A = \begin{bmatrix} q_1 p_{11} + 1 - q_1 & q_1 p_{12} \\ q_2 p_{21} & q_2 p_{22} + 1 - q_2 \end{bmatrix}$$

We thus have:

$$z = (p_{21}/(p_{21} + p_{12}),\ p_{12}/(p_{21} + p_{12}))$$

and

$$x = (q_2 p_{21}/(q_2 p_{21} + q_1 p_{12}),\ q_1 p_{12}/(q_2 p_{21} + q_1 p_{12}))$$

Thus xRz if and only if

$$q_2 p_{21}/(q_2 p_{21} + q_1 p_{12}) \leq p_{21}/(p_{21} + p_{12})$$

which holds if and only

$$q_2 p_{21}(p_{21} + p_{12}) \leq p_{21}(q_2 p_{21} + q_1 p_{12})$$

if and only if

$$q_2 \leq q_1.$$

Q.E.D.

Corollary: Consider two 2×2 processes A and B that differ only in their rates of litigation q_A and q_B; i.e.,

$$A = (I - Q_A) + Q_A P$$

and

$$B = (I - Q_B) + Q_B P.$$

Then $x_A R x_B$ if and only if $q_B R q_A$.

Proof: Using equations (1) and (2) allows us to conclude that $x_A R x_B$ if and only if

$$q_{2,A} P_{21} / (q_{2,A} P_{21} + q_{1,A} P_{12}) \leq (q_{2,B} P_{21} / (q_{2,B} P_{21} + q_{1,B} P_{12})$$

which reduces to:

$$q_{2,A} q_{1,B} \leq q_{2,B} q_{1,A} \text{ or to}$$
$$(1 - q_{1,A}) q_{1,B} \leq (1 - q_{1,B}) q_{1,A}$$

from which we have immediately that $x_A R x_B$ if and only if $q_{1,B} \leq q_{1,A}$. Q.E.D.

The following counterexample proves that conjecture 2 is, in general, false.

Counterexample to Conjecture 2:

Judges may choose from three rules with rule 1 less efficient than rule 2 less efficient than rule 3. The pure judicial process P is given by:

$$P = \begin{bmatrix} .6 & .4 & 0 \\ .8 & .15 & .05 \\ .9 & 0 & .1 \end{bmatrix}$$

Suppose $q_A = (.625, .25, .125)$. We may calculate the movement A of the entire process from q and P with $A = (I - Q_A) + Q_A P$. This yields:

$$A = \begin{bmatrix} .75 & .25 & 0 \\ .2 & .7875 & .0125 \\ .1125 & 0 & .8875 \end{bmatrix}$$

A has stationary vector $x_A = (.4334, .5099, .0567)$.

Now consider a second legal process B that differs from A only in the rates at which varying rules are litigated. Specifically, let $q_B = (.5, .375, .125)$. We may write the process B as $B = (I - Q_B) + Q_B P$ or as :

$$B = \begin{bmatrix} .8 & .2 & 0 \\ .3 & .6813 & .0187 \\ .1125 & 0 & .8875 \end{bmatrix}$$

B has stationary vector $x_B = (.577, .362, .061)$.

Conjecture 2 states that, because q_B stochastically dominates q_A, i.e., that $(q_B)R(q_A)$, x_A should stochastically dominate x_B or $(x_A)R(x_B)$. Recalling the definition of the relation R, this requirement means that $x_{1,A} \leq x_{1,B}$ and that $x_{1,A} + x_{2,A} \leq x_{1,B} + x_{2,B}$. But a simple calculation shows conjecture 2 to be false because $x_{3,B} = .061 > .0567 = x_{3,A}$ which contradicts the second condition; alternatively, because process B spends more time in the most efficient state than process A.

I have neither a proof of conjecture 1 nor a counterexample. Proposition 2 establishes conjecture 1 for a broader class of processes than covered by theorem 4 in Cooter and Kornhauser. Proposition 2 may be said to generalize that theorem in that it assumes only differential litigation (i.e., that $q_i \geq q_j$ if and only if $i \leq j$) and an extended version of Cooter and Kornhauser's symmetry axiom A5(ii).

Proposition 2: Consider a judicial process $T = P + S$ where S is a diagonal matrix with s_i in the ith diagonal position and where $p_{ij} = p_i = (1 - s_i)/n$. Consider some q with $q_i \geq q_j$ if and only if $i \leq j$. Then $x_A R x_T$ where $A = (I - Q) + QT$.

Proof: First, calculate x_T and x_A. To do so, we recall that $\Sigma_i x_{i,T} = 1 = \Sigma_i x_{i,A}$ and that x_T and x_A are unique. It is easy to see that

$$x_{i,T} = \frac{\prod_{j \neq i} p_j}{\sum_i \left(\prod_{j \neq i} p_j \right)} = \frac{\frac{1}{p_i}}{\sum_i \left(\frac{1}{p_i} \right)}$$

and that

$$x_{i,A} = \frac{\prod_{j \neq i} q_j p_j}{\sum_i \left(\prod_{j \neq i} q_j p_j \right)} = \frac{\frac{1}{q_i p_i}}{\sum_i \left(\frac{1}{q_i p_i} \right)}.$$

Next define, for any n-vector r and any integer t in $\{1, ..., n\}$

$$m(r,t) = \Sigma_{k=1 \text{ to } t}(1/[r_k p_k]). \tag{3}$$

We may then write

$$\Sigma_{k=1 \text{ to } t} x_{k,A} = m(q, t)/m(q, n)$$

and

$$\Sigma_{k=1 \text{ to } t} x_{k,T} = m(1, t)/m(1, n).$$

Recall then that $x_A R x_T$ if and only if, for every t in $\{1, ..., n\}$

$$m(q, t)/m(q, n) \leq m(1, t)/m(1, n)$$

or, for every t,

$$m(q, t)m(1, t) \leq m(q, n)m(1, n). \tag{4}$$

To prove (4) we show that for every t in $\{1, ..., n-1\}$

$$m(q, t)/m(1, t) \leq m(q, t+1)/m(1, t+1)$$

which is true, if and only if

$$m(q, t)m(1, t+1) \leq m(q, t+1)m(1, t)$$

which may be rewritten as

$$m(q, t)[m(1, t) + 1/p_{t+1}] \leq [m(q, t) + 1/(q_{t+1}p_{t+1})]m(1, t)$$

and which reduces to

$$m(q, t) \leq [1/(q_{t+1})]m(1, t). \tag{5}$$

The inequality (5), however, follows directly from the assumption of differential litigation (that $q_{t+1} \leq q_i$ for $i \leq t$) as

$$\sum_{k=1 \text{ to } t} \left(\frac{1}{q_k p_k}\right) \leq \left(\frac{1}{q_{t+1}}\right)\left(\sum_{k=1 \text{ to } t} \left(\frac{1}{p_k}\right)\right)$$

Hence, for every t in $\{1, ..., n\}$,

$$m(q,t)/m(q,n) \leq m(1,t)/m(1,n)$$

or,

$$(x_A)R(x_T).$$

Q.E.D.

The process $T = P + S$ is quite simple. The diagonal matrix S gives the strength of stare decisis, which may vary depending on which rule prevails. The matrix P illustrates "blind justice" in that, other than a possible preference for affirming the prevailing rule, the judge is equally likely to announce any of the other possible rules.

Appendix 2

Deliberation and Rational Choice (Nicholas Baigent) and Comment (Lewis A. Kornhauser)

Two remaining contributions to the conference appear in this appendix, assigned here not because of any decision about their general merits, but because they did not fit easily into the plan now adopted for the book as a whole.

In their approach to rules economists and the philosophers who have followed their lead in decision theory have generally begun with an interest in identifying very general, comprehensive rules governing personal choices. In axiomatic models of personal choice economists have worked out the implications of adopting as axiomatic various rules divided, as Nick Baigent shows in this contribution, between revealed preference, single-objective, and all-things-considered preferences.

There is a second division, equally committed to axiomatic models, important in the literature, between rules suitable for certainty about outcomes, for risk, and for uncertainty.

Commonly, axioms expressing these rules are applied directly to preferences (conceived as whatever issues in choices) to produce some sort of preference function. Left in obscurity is the question how preferences are arrived at. Many economists are no doubt willing to have other people, like psychologists, deal with the question in its entirety. However, some economists (Lancaster,[1] Sen,[2] here Baigent) have taken another approach, moving back a stage to consider how preferences for market goods might emerge from deliberation about characteristics (goods of a higher order that can each be found in a variety of market goods) or from deliberation under metapreferences. On both approaches, a general rule like maximization of utility may be invoked, to which the particular rules, "Given an amount x of g_1, choose an amount no more than y of g_2," are subordinated. Or instead of maximization in this sense a general rule involving some sort of dominance relation between alternatives (as, again, in Baigent's treatment) may be brought forward.

Notes

1. Kelvin Lancaster, *Consumer Demand: A New Approach* (New York: Columbia University Press, 1971).
2. Amartya Sen, "Rational Fools: A Critique of the Behavioral Foundations of Economic Theory," *Philosophy and Public Affairs*, Vol. 6, 1977, pp. 317–344.

Deliberation and Rational Choice

Nicholas Baigent

Introduction

As Schelling says,[1] "Just how one decides whether one is in the mood for broiled salmon or roast duck isn't the concern of the decision sciences, *at least not unless the way it is done turns out to conflict in some fashion with the rest of the model of rational choice.*" The way it will be done in this paper is to give a central role to deliberation; and the conclusion is that in general, the choices of rational agents need not bear any particular relationship to a preference. Thus, inquiring how agents decide on their choices does indeed conflict with the rest of the model of rational choice.

The paper begins by distinguishing three variants of the model of rational choice which may be called the pure choice approach, the single objective approach, and the trade-offs and multiple objectives approach (TAMO). Within each of these variants choice is associated in an essential way with a preference. Then, the details of a deliberative procedure will be sketched and it will be shown that the resulting choices violate what is considered to be one of the main rules of rational choice in decision theory and economics. This rule is known as condition α. Since it is well known to be a necessary, but not sufficient, condition for choice to be based on a preference, it follows that rationally deliberated choice in general has little to do with preference. Thus, a central feature of the model of rational choice depends on the exclusion of deliberative considerations from the model.

It may be asked how deliberation can be explicitly accommodated in a model of rational choice. After all, agents are usually characterized so sparsely that there is nothing to deliberate non trivially about. For example, for agents characterized by a single preference that ranks all of the alternatives[2] and an objective of optimizing that preference, only the mechanical role of finding best available alternatives remains for deliberation. Therefore, the richer characterization used by Sen in his famous paper on Rational Fools[3] will be used in this paper. Accordingly, agents will be characterized by a set of preferences and a metapreference which ranks these preferences. It must be emphasized however that this characterization by itself is not inconsistent with preference-based choice. It is the way in which deliberation links choice and Sen's characterization of agents that is inconsistent with preference based choice.

The results on which the argument in this paper depends are either well known or require minor modifications of well known results.[4] Therefore, the argument will be presented without technicalities.

Non-Deliberative Rational Choice

Much of the literature in decision theory, economics and game theory focuses on the consistency of choices *in themselves*. Such an approach may be called the *pure choice* approach. One of the origins of this approach is the revealed preference analysis introduced by Samuelson (1938). The type of consistency involved is well illustrated by the Weak Axiom of revealed preference. It requires that if one alternative x, is chosen and another y, is rejected in one situation, then in any other situation y is never chosen if x is available. In such axioms, only the choices themselves play a role. If choices satisfy this axiom then it is known that they also satisfy the following axiom known as condition α. This condition requires that if an alternative x is chosen in one situation then it is also chosen in any other situation in which it is present but in which some previously present alternatives are no longer present. For example, if x is chosen from x, y, and z then it must also be chosen from x and y.

In this variant of the model of rational choice, preference plays no independent role. Even so, preference may be a useful descriptive device for cases in which choice happens to be consistent with a preference. But that is all it is. Preference has no prior status independent from choice. However, the consistency that is typically required in the form of the weak axiom of revealed preference or condition α, cannot provide sufficient conditions for the rationality of choices. For example, consider an agent who does subscribe to a single preference but whose choices are always the opposite of those that are induced by the preference. Such choices will not only satisfy both of the consistency axioms mentioned above but just about all other known consistency axioms as well.[5] Such choices are perfectly consistent but highly irrational. What this example shows is that rationality requires that choices bear some relation to something other than themselves. Simply requiring consistency between choices is not enough. It will be shown later that it is nothing at all, once choices are arrived at by an explicit deliberative process.

Another variant of the model of rational choice is the single objective approach. In this variant, agents are characterized by a single objective that takes the form of a preference over the alternatives, together with the goal of choosing so as to optimize according to this preference. In this case, preferences exist independently of choices. This approach may be very useful for the analysis of choices in some simple situations. For example, if the alternatives only differ in one way, say in the amount consumed of one desirable commodity, then choices induced by the optimization of a single preference may be reasonable. However, such a severe restriction on the scope of the theory of rational choice would greatly detract from its usefulness and interest.

The third variant is probably the most popular, at least in microeconomics, and it does not presume that agents have a single objective. Rather, it is usually assumed that the preference on which choice is based is arrived at by establishing trade-offs between different objectives. That is, agents may have multiple objectives that conflict, but any such conflict is resolved by the agent's trade-offs into a single *all things considered preference* (ATC preference). It is presumed that the deliberation of a rational agent will result in an ATC preference, but that the particular trade-offs with which the agent resolves conflicting objectives into an ATC preference is not a legitimate concern of the theory of rational choice. Thus, the ATC preference is taken as the appropriate starting point for the characterization of agents in the theory of rational choice.

The ATC preference is therefore a great divide. On one side lies deliberation and on the other lies the modern theory of rational choice. In fact, it often seems as if there is a taboo on crossing the great divide separating the theory of rational choice from deliberation.

One of the reasons for the reluctance of rational choice theory to embrace deliberation is that establishing trade-offs between different objectives is something that is distinct from considerations of rationality. Consider the problem of trying to establish trade-offs between any pair of conflicting objectives. Is there anything in the content of the concept of rationality that rules out particular trade-offs being established? There may be a question of the consistency of these trade-offs with those established between other pairs of alternatives.[6] Viewed in isolation however, there seems to be no reason why the trade-off between any particular objectives should take any particular value. Thus, the conventional view would be that trade-offs are whatever agents themselves claim they are. In other words, considerations of rationality should place no restriction on the value of trade-offs.

For some purposes, there are probably stronger objections to considerations of rationality "interfering" with the establishing of trade-offs. Consider one of the major purposes for which the theory of rational choice has been used, that of providing part of the foundations for the measurement of individual welfare. There is a justifiable concern here with the "autonomy" of the individual. That is, the measurement of individual well-being should not be sullied by the hands of the rational choice theorist. Furthermore, if, as is often the case, the measurement of individual well-being is itself to be used as the basis for collective judgements of group well-being, then it would be considered quite wrong if the measurement of individual well-being were tainted with values that were not the individual's own values. The appeal of this view is immediate and widespread. It is however, completely irrelevant for the issues being addressed in this paper. The issue of whether or not there is something about rationality that requires trade-offs is obviously prior to the issue of whether trade-offs are restricted by the requirements of rationality. It is the former issue that is central in this chapter.

What reasons are there for insisting that rationality requires that trade-offs be established between conflicting objectives leading to choice based on an ATC preference? It is difficult to find an explicit argument in the literature. However, the following view is probably widespread among economists. For most of the purposes for which the theory of rational choice is used, there is no possibility of not choosing. Opting for the status quo or "doing nothing" is itself an alternative. Since some choice has to be made, it may be thought that, whatever the choice is, it necessarily reveals a trade-off between objectives. It is as though the formation of trade-offs is forced upon the rational agent by the fact that some choice has to be made. Stated more formally, if some choice has to be made then trade-offs must be established. But, in fact, it is certainly not the case that trade-offs are logically required by choice. That choice implies preference is a non sequitur can be established by the following simple counter example.

Consider an agent with several objectives whose choices are determined by the Narrow Borda Score. This method of choosing uses only the part of the rankings induced by the objectives of the alternatives in the particular subset from which a current choice has to be made. Points are assigned to alternatives according to their position in the rankings in such a way that more points are awarded for higher positions in the rankings. The choice then consists of all the alternatives with the highest scores. It is well known that this method of choice is not generally consistent with a preference. Therefore, and this is strictly a matter of logic, no trade-offs could be revealed by such choices. Many more examples could be given of ways of choosing in the presence of conflicting objectives that would be inconsistent with *any* system of trade-off. Therefore, the proposition that choice implies trade-offs is false.

Apart from logical necessity, is there any other general argument that can be given to justify an insistence on resolving conflicts between different objectives into a single ATC preference by means of trade-offs between objectives? The following argument does just the opposite in that it establishes that there cannot be trade-offs between some objectives.

Agents may well care about the distributional consequences of their choices together with other sorts of consequences. This is obviously the case for individuals holding egalitarian values having to choose between candidates in an election where the policies of the candidates have different distributional consequences. It will also be the case in choosing between employment opportunities in different locations if the other family members have different preferences regarding the places in which they would like to live and the agent making the choice wishes to take into account the preferences of other family members. In such cases, it may not be possible to form trade-offs between an egalitarian objective and other objectives. The reason is that objectives have to be measurable in a certain sort of way for trade-offs to be possible between them. In general, distributions may not be completely ordered. If the Lorenz curves of two distributions do not intersect then one distribution is objectively more equal than another. However, if there are intersections in the Lorenz curves then it will not be possible to rank the two distributions according to their degrees of equality. Two objectives cannot be resolved by trade-offs into a single preference if one of the objectives takes the form of a strictly partial ordering.

In such cases, why not find some way to complete the partial orders? It may be possible to do this in some special cases but it is difficult to regard this as a general solution. Indeed, the way in which the partial ordering of distributions according to Lorenz domination has been extended to a complete ordering in the literature on economic inequality[7] fails in the present context. It is instructive to see why this is the case. Consider a social welfare function that assigns a level of social welfare to any distribution and which respects the ordering induced by Lorenz domination. Then, if x is any distribution, let x* denote the perfectly equal distribution that gives the same level of social welfare according to the given social welfare function. (x* may be called the equally distributed equivalent of x relative to the given social welfare function.) Now consider two distributions, x and y. These two distributions may still be ranked even if their Lorenz curves intersect by comparing their equally distributed equivalents, x* and y*, as follows. Distribution x may be considered at least as good as distribution y if and only if the level of income in x* is at least as high as the level of income in y*. This procedure will certainly complete the partial ordering of distributions induced by Lorenz domination. It is important to stress however that the completion is performed by the use of values embodied in the social welfare function. Therefore, the complete ranking of distributions does not only reflect objective inequality.

In the context of a single agent attempting to form trade-offs between objectives some of which take the form of strictly partial orderings of the alternatives, what is it that corresponds to the social welfare function? It would have to be some function that took account of all the objectives of the agent. But this would then be an ATC preference that aggregated the multiple objectives of the agent and this cannot be assumed to exist from the outset when the very purpose of the analysis is to see whether trade-offs can generally establish an ATC preference in the presence of objectives that take the form of strictly partial orderings. To do so would be to assume the solution of the problem!

This is not to say that there may be some contexts in which conflicts between different objectives may be resolved by establishing an ATC preference by means of trade-offs between objectives. However, there remains an important class of cases in which objectives take the form of strictly incomplete orderings of the alternatives. In these cases, trade-offs cannot result from deliberation for strictly logical reasons.

In concluding this section the main points will be briefly recapitulated. Three variants of the model of rational choice were distinguished. In the pure choice variant, it was argued that the rationality of choices requires something other than the consistency conditions that are usually imposed. It remains to be seen whether deliberation can play this role. The single objective variant is so limited in its scope that it cannot be taken seriously as general theory. As for the TAMO variant, it was argued that there are some objectives that take the form of preferences that are not complete and are not completable by the usual means. In such cases, which arise quite naturally, conflict between objectives cannot be resolved by establishing trade-offs between objectives. Finally, it therefore follows that in such cases, rational choice cannot be based on an ATC preference.

Agent Characterization

In situations in which deliberation cannot establish trade-offs between conflicting objectives, what role can it play? This issue is the subject of this section and the next.

Consider then an agent having to make choices for which many concerns are relevant, and between which trade-offs cannot be established. Each concern induces a preference, some of which may be incomplete. The impossibility of trade-offs between objectives does not mean that some other sort of weighing up of the priorities may not be possible. Indeed, whatever the reasons for trying to establish trade-offs where possible, those same reasons presumably suggest that some less demanding judgements between concerns should be attempted in situations in which the formation of trade-offs is not possible.

Of course, it may be that in some cases the concerns may be so overbearing that the agent will simply not be able to say that one concern is more compelling than another. These are the hard choices. However, agents would be able to make a judgement that one concern is more compelling than another for some types of choices. Consider the choice between jobs in different locations referred to earlier and assume a family consisting of both adults and some children. Abstracting from bargaining and other strategic considerations, the adult facing the choice may consider that adult preferences are more compelling for such choices than the preferences of young children.[8] Thus the agent may rank any of the adult preferences above any of the childrens' preferences. Furthermore, the agent may not be able to rank two adult preferences for reasons that were discussed in the previous section. If pairs of concerns can be ranked then surely such rankings of concerns are relevant in determining a rational choice.

Thus, it makes sense to characterize agents by a set of preferences and a metapreference where the latter ranks some pairs of preferences. The set of preferences consists of a preference for each concern that the agent considers relevant for the choice in hand and some of these preferences may be incomplete. The metapreference is a ranking of the preferences; and it, too, may be incomplete. Notice that this rich characterization includes the usual characterization in terms of a single preference as a special case.

Characterizing agents in this way was first proposed by Sen (1977). He considers several interpretations that differ from the one that is relevant here. Indeed, one of Sen's main purposes was to set out a framework that would be rich enough to be useful for a variety of problems. In the present context it is natural to extend Sen's concept of metapreference so that subsets of preferences are ranked as well as pairs of preferences. After all, in comparing two alternatives, x and y, what matters is whether all the concerns that favor x over y are more compelling than all the concerns that favour y over x. Therefore, in what follows agents will be characterized by a set of preferences and a metapreference that ranks pairs of subsets of the agent's preferences. However, the metapreference does not have to rank every possible pair of subsets of preferences.[9]

This still leaves the question of how agents characterized in this way can make rational choices. One approach that is briefly discussed by Sen is to determine choices as maximal alternatives. However, there are several different ways of defining maximality in the present context. One way is to use the following dominance relation. Alternative x dominates alternative y if and only if the metapreference ranks any preference for which x is strictly preferred to y higher than any preference for which y is strictly preferred to x. The set of chosen alternatives then consists of all that are undominated. There are obvious strengthenings and weakening of the dominance relation that could be used in the same way. These will not be pursued here because the purpose of this paper is to focus on deliberation and its role in rational choice. Of course, the consistency of choices based on dominance relations of the kind just described, with choices determined by explicitly modelling the steps of a rational deliberation, remains as an important question for future work.

Deliberation

In this section a sequential deliberative procedure will be described. It should be stressed however that there is no reason to expect that a single procedure for deliberation can be distinguished as *the uniquely rational procedure*. Rather, there may be several procedures none of which is more rational than any of the others. All that should be expected from such a "thin" theory of rationality is that alternatives for which there are good reasons for rejection should not be chosen.

There is something else that it is important to emphasize before getting into details. An explicit account of the steps of a rational deliberation may be called an *extensive* theory of rational choice to distinguish it from the usual *axiomtic* theory.[10] Axiomatic approaches simply postulate rules of rational choice such as condition α. No justification beyond the immediate appeal of these rules is thought necessary. Thus, in the axiomatic approach *rules* of rational choice are taken to be self-evident and are imposed by the theory at the outset. In the extensive theory of rational choice on the other hand, no rules of rationality are imposed by the theory from the outset. The extensive approach to the theory of rational choice offers a stylized but explicit account of the way choices are decided.[11] It may be possible to distinguish features of choice which occur frequently or under a wide variety of ways in which choice may be decided. However, in this case, rules of rational choice are not imposed by the theory. Rather, they emerge as implications of the account of the way choices are decided. The nature and role of rules is therefore quite different in the two approaches to the theory of rational choice and it is possible that no rules of choice at all may emerge from an extensive theory.

Given the characterization of agents described in the previous section, the following dominance relation seems crucial. Let alternative x dominate alternative y if and only if the subset of preferences for which x is strictly preferred to y is at least as compelling as the subset of preferences for which y is strictly preferred to x according to the metapreference. Given that indifference is possible in the metapreference it is possible for there to be "indifference" in the dominance relation. Thus the terminology "strictly dominates" will be used if x dominates y but y does not dominate x.

The deliberative procedure that will be described is sequential in that all of the alternatives are listed and then considered in the order in which they are listed. Suppose then, that the alternatives are listed in an arbitrary order. (Ignore the arbitrariness of the order of the listing for the moment—it will be dealt with later.) Designate the first alternative as a *tentative choice*. Now move to the second alternative. Loosely speaking, what has to be considered is whether there are reasons that are good enough to justify replacing the first alternative by the second as the tentative choice. There would certainly be a good reason if the second alternative strictly dominated the first according to the dominance relation defined above. Consider now the situation after several alternatives have been considered in this way so that the process is somewhere in the middle of the list. At any such point in the deliberation there is a tentative choice. It is also the case that in reaching this point in the deliberation, some alternatives that have already been considered have been tentative choices and some have not. This partition of all alternatives that have been considered at any point in the deliberation into those that have been tentative choices and those which have not will be important in what follows.

The next step involves applying criteria for whether the current tentative choice should be replaced by the next alternative in the list and become the new tentative choice. Several such criteria are possible, each giving rise to a different deliberative procedure. The one used here certainly seems reasonable. It requires that the next alternative replace the current tentative choice if and only if two conditions are met. The first condition is that it strictly dominate the current tentative choice. The second condition is that it weakly dominate all the alternatives that have been tentative choices up to that point in the deliberation. Thus, at any point in the deliberation the alternatives that have been considered up to that point are partitioned into those that have, at some point, been tentative choices and those that have not. For the next alternative to replace the current tentative choice it should stand in a Pareto-like relationship to the subset of alternatives that have been tentative choices. Finally, the alternative that is the tentative choice after the list is exhausted is a final tentative choice.[12]

Of course, a different alternative could well have been a final tentative choice if the alternatives had been listed in a different order. Since the order is arbitrary, it makes sense to consider all possible ways in which the alternatives may be listed. Therefore, the set of rational choices should consist of *any alternative that is a final tentative choice for some possible listing of the alternatives.*

Consider the following example. Suppose an agent has a set of preferences and a metapreference that induces a dominance relation in which y dominates x and x dominates z but in which there is no dominance between y and z. In this case the dominance relation is incomplete over y and z. Take the alternatives listed in the order zxy. Alternative z begins as a tentative choice but it is immediately replaced by x since x dominates z. However y does not then replace x because, although y strictly dominates x it does not dominate z. Therefore x is a rational choice since it is a final tentative choice for some listing of the alternatives. If the alternatives are listed in the order xyz then y is a final choice. However, z can never be a final choice however the alternatives are listed. Therefore, the subset consisting of x and y constitutes a rational choice in this case. Now suppose that z turns out to be unavailable. In this case a choice has to be made from x and y. Since only two alternatives are available and y dominates x, only y can be a final tentative choice. This violates condition α. In fact, it seems easy to come up with examples that violate many of the consistency conditions that are used in axiomatic approaches to rational choice.

Of course, different criteria may be used for replacing a current tentative choice by a new one. However, it is fairly clear that consistency axioms may well be violated. This leads to the main conclusion of the paper. Once deliberative procedures are explicitly included in a model of rational choice, consistency axioms that provide the foundations for the usual models of rational choice lack justification. In particular, condition α is a necessary condition for choices to be consistent with a preference. It therefore follows that rationally deliberated choices need bear no relation to any particular preference.

The conclusion therefore is that conditions on choices such as condition α should not be viewed as rules of rational choice. Furthermore, it seems most unlikely that any conditions of the type that focus purely on the consistency of choices with each other can survive the treatment given to condition α in this paper. This does not mean that there are no rules of rational choice. Rather, it means that they should be sought differently in the processes of choosing and in the consistency of choices with these processes, rather than in the consistency of choices in themselves.

Notes

1. Schelling (1985).
2. In economics this preference ranks commodity bundles and is oftern portrayed by indifference curves.
3. Sen (1977).
4. All of the results can be found in Sen (1986) or Suzumura (1983).
5. See Sen (1985).
6. This type of inconsistency would allow a sort of intrapersonal arbitrage.
7. Atkinson (1970).
8. This is not to say that adults ignore the interests of young children.
9. Thus, the characterization used here differs from that used by Sen in two details. The set of preferences may contain preferences that are incomplete and the metapreference is a binary relation on the power set of preferences rather than the set of preferences.
10. This terminology is deliberately chosen to reflect a similar distinction in game theory.
11. That is, the extensive approach focuses on exactly that which Schelling says is no concern of the theory of rational choice, in the quotation which opened this paper.

12. For an extended discussion of this procedure and some others in the context of social choice, see Banks and Bordes (1988). The dominance relations they deal with are complete. However, incompleteness does not seem to introduce any real difficulties.

References

Atkinson, A. B. 1970. "On the Measurement of Inequality," *Journal of Economic Theory*, 2: 244–263.

Banks, J. S. & G. A. Bordes. 1988. "Voting Games, Indifference, and Consistent Sequential Choice Rules," *Social Choice and Welfare*, 5(1): 31–44.

Schelling, T. 1985. "The Mind as a Consuming Organ," in Elster, Jon, ed., *The Multiple Self.* Cambridge & Oslo: CUP & Universitetsforlaget AS.

Sen, A. K. 1977. "Rational Fools: A Critique of the Behavioral Foundations of Economic Theory," *Philosophy and Public Affairs*, 6: 317–344.

Sen, A. K. 1986. "Social Choice Theory," in Arrow, K. J. & M. Intriligator, *Handbook of Mathematical Economics, Vol. 3.* Amsterdam: North Holland.

Suzumura, K. 1983. *Rational Choice, Collective Decisions and Social Welfare.* Cambridge, Mass.: Cambridge University Press.

Comment

Lewis A. Kornhauser

In a provocative essay, Professor Baigent criticizes the "bare" or "stark" conception of practical reason embodied in the formal models of decision theorists, economic theorists, and game theorists because it precludes the analysis of "deliberation." Moreover, Professor Baigent argues that acknowledgement of deliberative aspects of practical rationality leads one to reject a fundamental premise of the standard theory. I agree with the criticism of rational choice theory but I think that Professor Baigent's argument neither succeeds fully nor goes sufficiently far to provide a basis for the formal modelling of deliberation.

In the theory of rational choice, each agent has an extremely simple "psychology" or "motivation." To decide, an agent consults her preference ordering (variously over outcomes, lotteries, or actions) and her beliefs.[1] As Professor Baigent notes, no interpretation of the formal theory admits a plausible account of deliberation. Often, the analyst interprets this preference ordering as "desires" on which the agent acts directly. The ordering might as easily be interpreted as an "all-things-considered" set of judgments. This second interpretation apparently admits a more complex weighing of reasons but the ordering resolves whatever conflicts the agent may face among her desires and other reasons for action such as morality. Thus, all deliberation precedes the invocation of rational choice theory. That the resolution of these conflicts results in a complete and transitive ordering may appear to be an heroic assumption and it is that assumption that Professor Baigent attacks.[2]

The formal models exclude completely a second form of deliberation as well. In the models, the ordering by which the agent evaluates her options in light of her beliefs is "fixed," or a datum of the problem. The models thus exclude the possibility that agent's evaluative norms develop from (or within) choice situations themselves. Both these theoretical simplifications contrast sharply with Aristotelian views of practical reason.[3] Specifically, practical reason, under the Aristotelian view, is characterized precisely by conflicts among incommensurable values and by the need to articulate clearly the values that the agent holds.

Professor Baigent offers a framework in which non-prudential concerns may not only influence an agent's choices through their incorporation in an all-things-considered ranking but one in which non-prudential concerns might be said to conflict with or override prudential ones. To accomplish this end, Professor Baigent substantially modifies the standard decision-theoretic model. Most fundamentally, he assumes that each agent has a set of (first-order) preferences over alternatives and then he introduces a set of metapreferences over subsets of first-order preferences.

As both first-order and metapreferences are "given" in Professor Baigent's model, as it stands, it offers no means to consider "value formation." Under the Aristotelian conception of practical reason, one may criticize an agent's action not merely on the grounds of the inconsistency of the agent's means with the agent's ends, but also on the grounds of the illegitimacy or inappropriateness of the ends themselves.

Baigent's model does permit some examination of deliberation among already formed values. Deliberation, for Professor Baigent, consists in the construction of a single all-things-considered judgment in a choice situation through application of the metapreferences to the underlying set of first-order preferences. He constructs the all-things-considered judgment through a process of iterated dominance of the sets of preferences that prefer a given alternative to other available alternatives. Not surprisingly, this dominance relation may violate the minimial consistency criteria we impose upon choice. Thus, in Baigent's model, even though actions x and y are both available to me in two distinct choice circumstances A and B, I may consistently choose x in situation A and y in situation B. Somewhat oddly, then, Professor Baigent's formalism places less stringent restrictions on decisions than the standard decision theoretic model even though it aspires to incorporate a broader class of grounds on which one might criticize a decision.

One might more readily accept this weakened consistency condition if some consistency condition were imposed upon the metapreferences. But, in the current version of the paper, no consistency conditions are imposed at all. In the version of the paper presented at the conference, Professor Baigent considered a richer model which included not only the metapreferences but also a function that identified a set of "concerns," i.e., a subset of the first-order preferences, relevant to the choice situation. Even this formulation, however, placed insufficient constraints on the deliberative process. The weight concern K carries in situation A bears no relation to the weight it carries in situation B. Two assumptions about information accounted for the weakness of the consistency requirements. First, and less important, Professor Baigent allows only ordinal metapreferences (and preferences). Thus, the metapreferences themselves carry little information. More importantly, any consistency condition on the metapreferences that operates across choice situations will require some notion of *similarity* between choice circumstances. For a belief that a given concern K should carry roughly equivalent force in situation B as in situation A rests on some notion that A is similar to B (in terms of K).

The addition of such similarity relations would introduce one method of objecting substantively to an agent's deliberation, objections not possible in Professor Baigent's formulation either in the current paper or in the version presented at the conference. One may criticize an agent's choice not only because it violates some plausible consistency requirement but also because one believes that the preference (or meta-preference) is inappropriate, unacceptable, or wrong. In Baigent's terms, one can state this only as a claim that the function R, which picks out relevant concerns for situations, identifies the wrong set R(A) of concerns. Professor Baigent offers no criteria for making such a claim but nothing in his discussion prevents the introduction of such criteria.

Most philosophical discussions of Aristotelian practical reason emphasize its fluidity. They seem to suggest that our process of practical reason cannot be captured in any mathematical formalism. Professor Baigent's discussion gives us reason to believe that this pessimism is unfounded. Formal models can capture and illuminate aspects of Aristotelian practical reason. Further work might, I have argued, address two major problems. First, one must articulate plausible similarity criteria for sets of alternatives. Second, these criteria must be sufficiently stringent to impose some constraints on the possible choices an individual might make in a given choice situation.

Notes

Copyright 1991 by Lewis A. Kornhauser.

These comments were prepared for the Murphy Institute Conference on the Logic of Social Change in April 1988. Though I have revised the comments slightly to conform a bit more closely to the text of the paper appearing in this volume, the published version of Professor Baigent's paper raises a different set of issues that have not received the attention they deserve.

1. I am using the term "belief" in the restrictive sense of "factual belief" or "belief about the state of the world." On some accounts, moral obligations might reduce to some mental state akin to "belief" in some broader sense or some emotional state perhaps akin to a desire. The text does not attempt to identify the appropriate "psychology" of actors; it rather points out the starkness of the psychology embedded in the game theoretic conception of rationality.

2. Actually, Professor Baigent attacks the assumption of contraction consistency which is weaker than transitivity. It implies acyclicity of the base ordering of a choice function and is "close" to equivalent to path independence. Sen (1982).

3. An excellent illustration of an Aristotelian view is D. Wiggins (1975, 1978).

References

A. K. Sen. 1982. "Social Choice Theory: A Re-examination," in *Choice, Welfare and Measurement*. Cambridge, Mass.: MIT Press.

David Wiggins. 1975–1976. "Deliberation and Practical Reason," *Proceedings of the Aristotelian Society* 76 (n.s.): 29–51.

David Wiggins. 1978–1979. "Weakness of the Will, Commensurability and the Objects of Deliberation and Desire," *Proceedings of the Aristotelian Society* 79 (n.s.): 251–77.

About the Book

This collection is a pioneering effort to bring together in fruitful interaction the two dominant perspectives on social rules. One, shared by philosophers, lawyers, anthropologists, and sociologists, directly invites formalization by a logic of rules. The other, originating with economists, emphasizes cost considerations and invites mathematical treatment, often in game-theoretical models for problems of coordination—models that some philosophers have taken up as well.

Each perspective is represented by new and recent work that moves this important topic toward increased conceptual precision and deeper insight. As a whole, the collection strikes a balance between historical illustrations and theoretical argument, offering in both a rich body of suggestions for further work.

Index

9 780813 391038